DAVID BLEWETT is a member of the Department of English at McMaster University.

In the light of recent critical emphasis on the language, imagery, and structure of fiction, *Defoe's Art of Fiction* re-examines Defoe's four most important novels. David Blewett rejects any notion that Defoe was merely a forerunner of what was later to become the English novel. He emphasizes Defoe's growing artistic self-consciousness and argues that the novels reveal a greater unity of theme and structure, a more effective use of language and imagery, and a greater degree of concern with craft than has previously been recognized. Close readings of *Robinson Crusoe, Moll Flanders, Colonel Jack*, and *Roxana* are set against the background of Defoe's life, the period in which he wrote, and his increasing preoccupation with social issues.

Defoe's achievement in the history of the English novel is considerable. He not only drew fiction away from romance and allegory and towards realism, but he focused upon a universal human problem: the clash between personal needs and desires and the social forces which demand compromise and accommodation. Fiction after Defoe, in ways often more subtle and complex than his, explored and developed the complicated interplay of social and personal relations: the tension between public respectability and private corruption and despair fascinated Richardson and Fielding, Dickens, George Eliot, and James, as it did Defoe. Professor Blewett demonstrates that Defoe stands within, not apart from, this tradition. In his work we can see the ways in which his moral vision of man was transmuted into the art of his novels.

University of Toronto Press / Toronto Buffalo London

Defoe's Art of Fiction

Robinson Crusoe
Moll Flanders
Colonel Jack &
Roxana

DAVID BLEWETT

© University of Toronto Press 1979
Toronto Buffalo London
Printed in Canada

_191909_

Library of Congress Cataloging in Publication Data

Blewett, David, 1940–
    Defoe's art of fiction—Robinson Crusoe, Moll
Flanders, Colonel Jack & Roxana.

    Includes bibliographical references and index.
    1. Defoe, Daniel, 1661?–1731—Fictional works.
    I. Title.
    PR3408.F5B5   823'.5   79-12827
    ISBN 0-8020-5447-1

For my father and mother

Contents

Preface / ix

1   The Artist's Vision and the Art of the Novel / 3

2   The Island and the World / 28

3   Moll as Whore and Thief / 55

4   Jacobite and Gentleman / 93

5   Roxana's Secret Hell Within / 116

6   Epilogue: Defoe's Artistry and the Tradition of the Novel / 146

Notes / 153

Index / 171

Preface

Daniel Defoe is not always readily accorded a window in the House of Fiction, that marvellous façade pierced by countless windows from which the narrators of fiction observe and record the human scene. Or, rather, if he has a window, it is 'slitlike and low-browed,' and not 'broad or balconied.' In Henry James's famous architectural metaphor[1] the window stands for 'literary form'; it is the frame through which the consciousness of the artist absorbs, defines, and describes his choice of subject. As artist, Defoe has been thought to be unconscious of his role. In the shadowless world of his novels the narrator describes a washed-out landscape, without significant detail, without appropriate form.

Or so the old argument went. However, this position has been challenged by a critical reassessment of Defoe so that two views of his fiction, an old and a new, can now be said to exist side by side. The older view, enshrined in the literary histories, and in that sense 'established,' holds that Defoe accidently stumbled into fiction, wrote as always hastily and casually, and remained largely unaware of the narrative and structural possibilities of the literary form he had discovered. Consequently we need not look for or expect to find much evidence of overall planning; the power of Defoe's fiction is the power of the single, brilliantly actualized episode. This view gained a renewed respectability in the late 1950s with the publication of Ian Watt's impressive and influential book *The Rise of the Novel*,[2] a work that sees Defoe's novels as a response to the demands of a small but rising middle class for novels that purported to be actual accounts of the lives of real individuals. Defoe is an exponent of 'formal realism,'[3] that is, the form of his novels realistically copies life; art is subordinate to authenticity.

Of Defoe's narrative method Watt says that he 'merely allowed his narrative order to flow spontaneously from his own sense of what his protagonist might plausibly do next. In so doing Defoe initiated an important new tendency in fiction: his total subordination of the plot to the pattern of the autobiographical memoir is as defiant an assertion of the primacy of individual experience in the novel as Descartes's *cogito ergo sum* was in philosophy.'[4] Though Watt finds a philosophical justification for Defoe's clearly limited method (as he sees it), yet his explanation of Defoe's narrative art recalls Arthur W. Secord's much earlier conclusion, after examining the 'sources' of Defoe's fiction, that *Robinson Crusoe* 'imitates life in its very shapelessness.'[5] James Sutherland in an introduction to *Moll Flanders* draws attention to Watt's book which, he says, 'helps to account for our feeling that when Defoe has given us so much it is a pity he hasn't given us the little more that would have transformed his prose narratives into genuine novels.'[6] Jonathan Bishop is able to take the position that Defoe 'imposed on his heap of empirical situations a simple moral pattern,' and he speaks of 'whatever structure his novels possess.'[7] And Mark Schorer, in a famous article, says that Defoe 'had no adequate resources of technique to separate himself from his method' and that we discover the meaning of *Moll Flanders* 'in spite of Defoe, not because of him.'[8] Secord's opinion, reinforced by the more impressive scholarship of Ian Watt, has become a settled tradition, and Defoe is still for many readers the novelist *malgré lui*.

The foundation for a new approach to Defoe was laid down by the publication of Maximillian Novak's two books, *Economics and the Fiction of Daniel Defoe* (1962) and *Defoe and the Nature of Man* (1963).[9] Through investigations of Defoe's economic and moral concepts Novak shows that not merely incidents but ideas, however unsystematic and unoriginal, lay behind the creation of Defoe's fiction. The respect for Defoe's artistry which Novak's two works exhibit and encourage is reflected in a number of essays that appeared about this time,[10] and then in two fine independent studies of the relationship between late seventeenth-century Puritan spiritual writing, particularly autobiography, and the form of Defoe's fiction. G.A. Starr[11] and Paul Hunter[12] provide a useful sifting of Puritan spiritual writing, clearly a formative influence in early fiction, and offer valuable insights into the thematic and structural coherence of *Robinson Crusoe*. This new regard for Defoe's artistic seriousness is again strongly evident in two more recent books which attempt to account for the essential coherence we feel within the multiplicity of situations and conflicting information that Defoe's novels provide. John Richetti[13] sees in the self-assertion of the protagonists a central coherence which, he argues persuasively, liberates them from the confines of ordinary experience. Essentially, however, Richetti, like Watt, understands Defoe as a writer seized by the 'dynamics' of the genre he unself-consciously employed; the deepest level of coherence is thus well below the surface of authorial intention. Everett Zimmerman[14] is equally concerned with the centrality of character, but, like Novak, he emphasizes Defoe's long career as a manipulator of men and ideas and sees Defoe as an experienced writer who was largely aware of what he was doing. Such an awareness, Zimmerman suggests, facilitated Defoe's development of fictional techniques in the course of writing his novels.

My study grew out of the belief that, in the words of Barbara Hardy, 'form is essentially the expression of the artist's vision.'[15] The new respect for the mind and the artistry of Defoe demonstrated by Novak, Starr, Hunter, and others has suggested that Defoe's art of fiction, like that of any other novelist, is to be found in the means by which vision achieves form. By an examination of Defoe's social and moral views as they are expressed in his extensive writings, especially in his letters and in his works on social behaviour and values, I attempt in the first chapter to draw the outlines of Defoe's vision of the human experience. Both here and later I indicate the historical contexts of Defoe's fiction, particularly his preoccupation with social issues which grew as the novels advanced. In the four chapters on the major novels I suggest the ways in which this vision informs his fiction as a whole. In this connection I trace the evolution of Defoe's attitude to fiction from Puritan dislike to a more open acceptance of what he is really doing. His developing artistic self-consciousness, observable in the changes from *Robinson Crusoe* to *Roxana*, holds important implications for the direction of the novel after Defoe.

In chapters 2 to 5 I am concerned first of all with the analysis of Defoe's fictional techniques, for its is through the techniques of narration that the artist's vision of life becomes the art of the novel. In arguing that Defoe's novels, at least the best of them, *Robinson Crusoe*, *Moll Flanders*, *Colonel Jack*, and *Roxana*, reveal a unity of theme and structure, an effective use of imagery and of language, a depth of concern with craft, I hope to demonstrate both the development and the achievement of Defoe's art of fiction. Though some of the finer strokes of artistic creation may spring unbidden from the subconscious mind, works of art do not simply happen. If we recognize the power of Defoe, we must attempt to explain it.

This book would not have been written without the early help and encouragement of Margaret Stobie, who first taught me how to read Defoe. I am grateful for the advice of John Carroll, who supervised the doctoral thesis upon which the book is based, and to Donald Greene, who encouraged the project from its beginning. I should like to express particular thanks to the following, who read the book in draft and made suggestions and criticisms: Robert Hume, Paul Hunter, and Arthur Sheps. I owe much to those friends who offered encouragement and aid: Brian Abel-Smith, Bentley Bridgewater, Joan Coldwell, Brian Fothergill, Lois Reimer, and Rupert Schieder. My thanks are due too to Audrey Alexander, who patiently typed and retyped the various drafts. And I deeply appreciate the editorial skill of Joan Bulger of University of Toronto Press.

I would like to record my thanks to McMaster University for a Summer Research Stipend, to the Canada Council for a Research Grant, and to the staff of the following institutions: The British Library, the Bodleian Library, the University of London Library, the Institute of Historical Research (London), the library of the Reform Club, the Robarts Library, the Thomas Fisher Rare Book Library, University of Toronto, Mills Library, McMaster University. Parts of this book appeared in slightly different versions in *English Studies in Canada* and in *The Modern Language Review* and are here reproduced with the kind permission of their editors.

This book has been published with the help of a grant from the Canadian Federation for the Humanities, using funds provided by the Social Sciences and Humanities Research Council of Canada, and a grant to University of Toronto Press from the Andrew W. Mellon Foundation.

DB *McMaster University*

Defoe's Art of Fiction

1 The Artist's Vision and the Art of the Novel

All Defoe's novels were written in the first person, clearly in order to enhance authenticity, but the device was congenial to Defoe for another and possibly more important reason. It permitted him to imagine himself in the position of the protagonist and, since his novels were presented as works of fact, not fiction, to pass himself off as a series of other people – a middle-class prodigal son of Yorkshire, the illegitimate female child of a whore and thief transported from Newgate, an orphan left to the mercy of the world, a pirate and soldier of fortune, an ordinary woman who became a famous courtesan. Moreover, the novels share certain common elements: a sudden blow of fortune, following upon some years (usually those of childhood) of relative calm, throws the protagonist into a new mode of life in which because of his (or her) natural qualities of leadership or some other ability he (or she) rises after many years[1] to a position of importance attained generally by means of concealment or disguise, a fact that naturally makes life during the time of writing somewhat precarious. The emphasis given to this pattern in each novel varies, but repeatedly the rhythm of disaster and slow recovery informs the fictional structure.

When we turn to Defoe's own life we discover a pattern of experience that was later to shape his novels, and a vision of the human condition that was to provide some of their most powerful themes. Defoe (1660–1731) did not write his first novel, *Robinson Crusoe*, until he was 59 years old, after a life in which he suffered a variety of fortunes almost as great as those of his protagonists. Raised in a dissenting family and educated in dissenting schools, Defoe intended to enter the Presbyterian ministry. For reasons never wholly explained he renounced that intention in 1681 and two years later set himself up as a merchant adventurer dealing in many kinds of goods and travelling widely on the Continent. His business acumen was adversely affected by his recklessness in overextending himself, and nine years later he was declared bankrupt for the very large sum of £17,000. His career as a political writer (later to lead to his becoming a government spy) began at the same time as his trading career, and it would be difficult to say which of these two occupations brought him into greater difficulties. Possibly the three most significant turning-points in his life of almost constant political danger and near financial disaster are his first bankruptcy in 1692, the publication of *The Shortest Way with the Dissenters* in 1702 (which led to his imprisonment in Newgate and the pillory), and the fall of his benefactor, Robert Harley, Earl of Oxford and Lord Treasurer, in 1714. The collapse of his fortune in 1692 must have emphasized to Defoe the uncertainty of life, a view that would have been confirmed by his second bankruptcy in 1703 and his arrest for debt again in 1713. From February 1704 to June 1713 Defoe was the editor (that is, the writer) of a government news journal, the *Review*, and there he printed some verses which present a point of view that he was to expound throughout his writings, particularly in the novels:

> Man's a short-sighted Hair-brain's Wretch, that knows
> Little of what he does, less where he goes,
> In vain our own Prescriptions we apply,
> We split upon the very Rocks we fly.

These lines are part of Defoe's paraphrase of some Latin verses which had been troubling a reader who had written to the *Review* for advice. To that anonymous reader Defoe writes: 'If the Gentleman will please accept of this hasty Paraphrase, we shall be oblidg'd to him, if they do not agree with his Case, the Author tells him they do with his Own.'[2]

The sequence of events that followed upon the publication of *The Shortest Way with the Dissenters* appears to have been traumatic for Defoe. Having recovered from his financial disgrace of 1692, he had rapidly made his way in the world until he became an adviser to William III, a man whom he always afterwards spoke of with admiration. Then, suddenly, in the midst of apparent prosperity, he found himself in the hell of Newgate, later described in *Moll Flanders*; his pamphlet, intended ironically but widely taken at face value, had infuriated the high Tories, particularly the Earl of Nottingham,[3] and embarrassed the government. In a letter to his friend William Paterson Defoe admits that 'Jayls, Pillorys and Such like with which I have been So Much Threatn'd have Convinc't me I want Passive Courage, and I Shall Never for the Future Think my Self Injur'd if I am Call'd a Coward,'[4] rare language for Defoe who is more often to be found, sometimes rather boastfully, justifying his actions. And in his first letter to Harley, who got him out of Newgate, Defoe compares himself to the 'One Gratefull wretch' among the ten Lepers healed by Christ, who alone returned to express his gratitude. In the same letter he refers to his delivery from Newgate as a 'Miracle.'[5]

Defoe's experience of Newgate appears to have been shattering, and his unexpected rescue left him with a heavy debt of gratitude to Harley, who for the next twelve years took advantage of it. Defoe went to work for Harley as a political writer and spy, roles that clearly suited his temperament and abilities, but for which he was never adequately recognized or rewarded. One of the first pieces of advice that Defoe offered to Harley was, characteristically, 'a scheme of an Office For Secret Intelligence at Home and Abroad,'[6] and Harley wisely entrusted Defoe with the job of setting up a secret service network throughout England and Scotland. The purpose of such a service, as Defoe explained in a long letter to Harley, was to give the government information about the views of important men and the mood of the country so that it could make itself more secure in office. The lines of communication were organized through dissenting clergymen, who were disposed to be friendly towards Defoe since he too had suffered for his religious and political views. One of the most valuable tasks this service carried out was in Scotland at the time of the Union. Defoe went himself to Scotland to assess for Harley the reaction to the proposals for Union and to spread oil on troubled waters whenever possible. In spite of considerable personal danger, for had he been discovered as a spy 'the Mob of Edin. [burgh] had pulled him to pieces,'[7] Defoe clearly enjoyed, and was extremely clever in, his Proteus-like existence. On 26 November 1706 he wrote to Harley:

I have Compass't my First and Main step happily Enough, in That I am Perfectly Unsuspected as Corresponding with anybody in England. I Converse with Presbyterian, Episcopall-Dissenter, papist and Non Juror, and I hope with Equall Circumspection. I flatter my Self you will have no Complaints of my Conduct. I have faithfull Emissaries in Every Company And I Talk to Everybody in Their Own way. To the Merchants I am about to Settle here in Trade, Building ships &c. With the Lawyers I Want to purchase a House and Land to bring my family & live Upon it (God knows where the Money is to pay for it). To day I am Goeing into Partnership with a Membr of parliamt in a Glass house, to morrow with Another in a Salt work. With the Glasgow Mutineers I am to be a fish Merchant, with the Aberdeen Men a woollen and with the Perth and western men a Linen Manufacturer, and still at the End of all Discourse the Union is the Essentiall and I am all to Every one that I may Gain some.[8]

As G.H. Healey, the editor of Defoe's letters, rightly remarks in a note on Robert Harley, 'Both [Defoe and Harley] rather enjoyed secrecy and mystification.'[9] Certainly Defoe enjoyed a reputation for dissimulation in his own time,[10] and disguise and deception fill the pages of his novels. All his protagonists, from Crusoe to Roxana, are masters of the arts of disguise, of passing themselves off as someone else, and it is this ability that accounts for their survival and their success and, to a great extent, for the shape of the novels.

Defoe's work in Scotland may well have been one of the few jobs undertaken for Harley that he wholeheartedly entered into. Though Harley and he had many things in common, such as their dissenting backgrounds[11] and love of intrigue, yet they were of different temperaments and of different political persuasions. Harley was lazy, moderate, a Tory. Defoe was energetic, inclined to extremes though he learned moderation, and a Whig.[12] But however often Defoe must have sold his political beliefs, he had one principle to which he adhered, a belief in the revolutionary settlement of 1689.[13] He believed that to secure for England a Protestant succession in perpetuity, and thus political and economic stability, it was necessary to control Scotland by making it part of a united kingdom run from Westminster.

With the fall of Harley in 1714 the period of Defoe's most intense political involvement was over and, although he still continued in the pay of the government, toning down the stronger anti-government articles in *Mist's Weekly-Journal*,[14] he never again earned his living solely as a political journalist. In the years 1716, 1717, and 1718 Defoe published a flood of tracts dealing with the leading political and religious issues of the day, but from this time until the end of his life he became increasingly concerned with larger questions of social order and family responsibility. In 1715 he published *The Family Instructor, In Three Parts*, the first of his long didactic works. This book, which proved to be one of the most popular moral treatises of the century, was followed by a second volume, *The Family Instructor, In Two Parts* (1718), and by *Religious Courtship* (1722), *The Great Law of Subordination Consider'd* (1724), *Conjugal Lewdness* (1727), and *A New Family Instructor* (1727). Defoe's treatises on social and family order are particularly important in an examination of the themes of the novels since they were written in the same years and in many cases at the same time as the novels.

The three *Family Instructors* deal with the duties and responsibilities within the family, above all those of parents and children. These works tirelessly enforce Defoe's view that family relationships (including those with household servants and apprentices) rest upon a system of mutual obligations. Defoe clearly felt very strongly about the need for proper family government, for he believed that upon the foundation of the family lie the whole order and stability of society. It is in the family that national moral disorder begins for, as a neighbour points out to the Father, 'of all the kinds [of disputes] family passions are the worst, they generally are in their beginnings more extravagant, rise to the greatest height, are acted with the greatest violence, and attended with the worst consequences,'[15] a remark that foreshadows not only *Moll Flanders* and *Roxana*, but *Clarissa* as well.

Defoe's other didactic works grew out of areas of family concern touched on in *The Family Instructor*. *Religious Courtship* compares the contrasting marriages of two sisters (one happy, the other unhappy) and draws the conclusion that marriage partners must be of the same religious persuasion if they are to be happy. *Conjugal Lewdness: Or, Matrimonial Whoredom* considers the question of forced marriages and makes the point that children must not be forced by their parents into a marriage that is against their conscience: 'The Limits of a Parent's Authority, in this Case of Matrimony, either with Son or Daughter, I think, stands thus: The Negative, I think, is theirs, especially with a Daughter; but, I think, the Positive is the Childrens.'[16] Defoe's argument, which in many respects follows Milton's,[17] is that a marriage in which there is no love is little better than a 'matrimonial whoredom' and the partners in it 'little more than legal Prostitutes' (*Conjugal Lewdness*, pp 102–3).

The Great Law of Subordination Consider'd, like the third part of *Religious Courtship*, which deals with the difficulties of employing irreligious servants, enquires into 'The Insolence and Unsufferable Behaviour of Servants in *England*' and urges 'House-keepers and Heads of Families in *Great-Britain*' to use their 'utmost Interest (especially at this Junction) to obtain sufficient Laws for the effectual Regulation of the Manners and Behaviour of their Servants.' Defoe often complained that it was becoming difficult to distinguish maidservants from their mistresses in matters of dress,[18] a situation that upsets the great law of subordination, the normal arrangement of the social structure in degrees. Amy, Roxana's servant, often dresses as well as her mistress and more than once passes for her, a fact that reflects the moral and social disorder in the world of that novel. Moll Flanders, too, is guilty of the same sin. She began life little better than a servant but passes often as a great lady. Clearly there is a link between the social criticism of Defoe's didactic works and the punishment meted out to some of his characters in the novels.

Defoe's growing preoccupation with social and moral questions from 1715 onward reflects his conviction that England was moving into an age of widespread moral degeneration, a conviction that did not abate as the reign of George I advanced. For Defoe the obvious and deeply disturbing parallel was with the age of Charles II, when immorality at court encouraged, he believed, a decline in the morals of society as a whole.[19] Hence, of course, part of the reason for his admiration of William III: 'Let them view the Example of the late Royal Pair King *William* and Queen *Mary*, how Vice learn'd to blush, and being banish'd from the Court by the Royal Example, Virtue and good manners became the Mode there.'[20] Defoe believed that morally the age of George I was turning back to the age of Charles II, so that it is significant that three of his fictional works, *Moll Flanders*, the *Journal of the Plague Year*, and *Roxana*, are set in the reign of Charles II. These works illustrate the consequences of not following the precepts to be found in Defoe's social criticism. His claim to be giving instruction in the novels should be taken seriously: the readers of the 1720s were meant to see the parallels between the world of the novels and their own age.

Defoe's vision of man and the human lot was traditional and pessimistic, and whenever he speaks of the nature of man he emphasizes either man's ignorance of his own best interests, as in the verses from the *Review* quoted above, or our natural degeneration and the need for the control of reason and religion, as in this representative passage from the second *Family Instructor*: 'Nature is vitiated and tainted with variety of infirmities ... there are powerful inclinations to do evil in everyone, and where these are not governed by the power of our reason or sense of religion, they become our governors and push us upon unavoidable folly.'[21] In *Conjugal Lewdness* Defoe accuses man of failing to live by either the rule of decency or the law of nature, which would make him superior to the beasts, and of giving way to lust and 'conjugal Lewdness':

But Man! ungoverned Man! neither influenced by the Laws of GOD, or of Nature, gives himself a loose to his corrupted Desires, and subjects Nature, Reason, and even Religion it self, to his Appetite, a furious outrageous Gust, his Will governs his Understanding, and his Vice governs his Will; the brutal Part tyrannizes over the Man, and his Reason is over-ruled by his Sense.   (P 295)

Man is not of course at all times such a slave to his passions, and this passage is extreme even for Defoe. Even so, his most generous view was that man is at best a short-sighted creature, knowing little of his own nature or the events that lie ahead of him and subject therefore to all sorts of cheats, tricks, and shams.[22]

The *Review* gives us a good idea of the degree to which Defoe saw fraud and guile in day-to-day affairs in, for example, politics, religion, marriage, and trade. It is not surprising, given eighteenth-century election practices, that he was disgusted by the 'infinite Briberies, Forgeries, Perjuries, and all manner of Debauchings of the Principles and Manners of the Electors' (*Review*, preface to vol. II, 1705), though this sort of language is also typical of his descriptions of other human affairs. The 'pretence of Religion,' he pointed out, is often simply a cover for ruthless political ambition: 'Religion's made the Foot-ball of Princes, to be kick'd about the World as it suits their occasions, to gloss over the worst of Treasons, Sanctify the horridest Villanies, and be a Cloak to all the Tyrannies in the World' (*Review*, 29 July 1704). Very early in the life of the *Review* Defoe introduced his 'Scandal. Society,' an imaginary committee formed to consider scandalous matters submitted by readers and to offer 'Advice from the Scandal. Club.' As we might expect, many of the letters run upon the subject of deception in marriage, and from them we may quickly gather that the relations of the sexes are coloured by the same deceits and pretences as other human relations. Similarly, when the Scandal. Society launches out into the 'great Oceans of Trade,' its members soon 'discover so many Gulphs of Villany, so many hidden Rocks of Trick, Cheat, and abominable Frauds, in and upon which, Innocent Families Suffer Shipwreck, split, and are undone, that they cannot pass them over in Silence.' Defoe's advice for 'a Sharping Tricking Generation' is plainly put: 'Gentlemen, in Trade there are Rogues, Thieves, and Pickpockets, every Day upon *Change*, have a care who you Trust' (*Review*, 24 February 1705).

Defoe's sense of the radical infection of human affairs with deceptions of all sorts finds expression, and explanation, in his account of the machinations of the devil. In *The Political History of the Devil* (1726) he considers the operation of the devil in both ancient (that is, biblical) and modern history and points out endlessly that the devil never works by 'Fury and Violence' but always 'with Strategem and Cunning,' with conspicuous success of course in his first great triumph, the fall of man:

He may tempt, and he does prevail; but it is all legerdemain, it is all craft and artifice, he is still Διαβολή, the calumniator and deceiver, that is, the misrepresenter; he misrepresents man to God, and misrepresents God to man; also he misrepresents things; he puts false colours, and then manages the eye to see them with an imperfect view, raising clouds and fogs to intercept our sight; in short, he deceives all our senses, and imposes upon us in things which otherwise would be the easiest to discern and judge of.[23]

The story of the fall of man, as Defoe presents it in this work, is not so much a tale of disobedience as of deception. And human experience ever since has been the history of artifice and deceit.

In the war between good and evil, which Paul Hunter has seen as one of the symbolic oppositions in the structure of *Robinson Crusoe*, it is, finally, not the devil but God who triumphs.[24] Human history for Defoe is providential, and providence he defines as 'the administration of heaven's government in the world.'[25] The devil succeeds only in the short run. On the other hand, man suffers from a severely restricted vision of future events and is therefore constantly subject to sudden reversals of fortune which the devil, acting in disguises, contrives to bring about. Paradoxically, part of the mercifulness of providence is that we are not able to see before us in the world, for man is surrounded by such dangers that, as Robinson Crusoe observes, 'the Sight of which, if discover'd to him, would distract his Mind, and sink his Spirits.'[26] Defoe's vision of the life of man can be seen in the image of the labyrinth, an image he occasionally uses, in which man moves along and, bewildered by the choices and turns, often stumbles into traps, blind passages, and hidden dangers. In his slow journey forward he is helped from time to time by providential intervention, often in the form of 'hints' and impulses which come from 'an invisible world of spirits'[27] intermediate between angels and men, limited from interfering in the affairs of men by positive action, yet capable of giving men warnings of dangers. With their aid he may succeed, at least for a time, in extricating himself.

It is not surprising that Defoe gained a reputation in his own day for craftiness and duplicity. He first became widely known when the authorship of *The Shortest Way with the Dissenters* was discovered; the tract had suddenly became a hoax. His skill in posing as a fanatical high-churchman and his subterfuge in the 'Brief Explanation' attached to a second edition raised a cloud of pamphlets[28] attacking him as a dissembler, a 'fox,' a hatcher of 'hellish designs.' One such pamphlet, which refers only to the 'Author and his Party,' says in exasperation, 'some think him a Papist, some a Nonjurant Parson, and others think him a Dissenter. I don't much concern myself which of these he belongs to, or what his Design may be, or if he acts in Disguise, for be that how it will, he is certainly one of the worst of men.'[29] Defoe's arrest again in 1713 was another occasion for his enemies to point out his time-serving and deceitfulness. In the anonymous *Judas discuver'd, and catch'd at last: Or, Daniel de Foe in Lobs Pound* (1713), the author speaks of Defoe in the language and images that are increasingly to be used of him: 'An *Animal* who shifts his Shape oftner than *Proteus*, and goes backwards and forwards like a Hunted *Hare*; a thorough-pac'd, true-bred *Hypocrite*, an *High-Church Man* one Day, and a *Rank Whig* the next' (p 3). Charles Gildon in 1719 wrote what is undoubtedly the best-known contemporary tract against Defoe, entitled (after the full title of *Robinson Crusoe*) *The Life and Strange Surprising Adventures of Mr. D----- De F--, of London, Hosier*. In the preface to this attack on *Robinson Crusoe* Gildon also emphasizes Defoe's Proteus-like abilities at dissembling:

The Fabulous *Proteus* of the Ancient Mythologist was but a very faint Type of our Hero, whose Changes are much more numerous, and he far more difficult to be constrain'd to his own Shape ... The *Dissenters* first would claim him as theirs, the *Whigs* in general as theirs, the *Tories* as theirs, the *Non-jurors* as theirs, the *Papists* as theirs, the *Atheists* as theirs, and so on to what Subdivisions there may be among us.

In the letter written from Scotland to Harley (quoted above, pp 5–6) Defoe, some thirteen years earlier, had proudly said much the same thing about himself. It is clear that Defoe had acquired a reputation for being able to take any side in an argument, indeed, for appearing to either side to be supporting it, and for changing sides at will. In this connection Leslie Stephen, the author of the article on Defoe in the *Dictionary of National Biography*, draws our attention to an interesting quarrel between two leading journalists, Mist and Read:

He [Mist] flatly denied in answer to contemporary attacks in 'Read's Journal' that Defoe was employed by him, and a separation took place. Read observed that Defoe's share was sufficiently proved by the 'agreeableness of the Style and

Manner; the little Art he is truly master of, of forging a Story and imposing it on the World for Truth,' a remark that shows Defoe's reputation just before the appearance of 'Robinson Crusoe.'[30]

Defoe clearly had a name for fictionalizing some time before he began to write his major works of fiction.

THE ART OF THE NOVELS

When at the age of nearly sixty Defoe came to write his first novel, the use of disguise and deception for literary purposes had become a habit of mind. For years he had survived as a political agent and thrived as a writer because he was so readily able to assume other identities. A large number of his existing letters to Harley, quite apart from those signed with a secret symbol and those written in a disguised hand, pretend to be from someone else and are signed by the pseudonyms of Alexander Goldsmith and Claude Guilot. One of the more remarkable features of Defoe's many tracts and books is the variety of literary poses he assumes:[31] an extreme high-churchman, a pirate, an explorer and adventurer, Angli-Poloski of Lithuania, one Church of England clergyman writing to another, an important French plenipotentiary, a captive in Madagascar, a Freemason, a public-spirited citizen called Andrew Moreton, and so forth. What is more, Defoe clearly enjoyed the sense of passing for someone else; he delighted in role-playing, and it is this preoccupation which passes into the novels and helps to explain the motivation of many of the characters.[32] It is perhaps surprising then, in the light of Defoe's propensity for role-playing in his other writing, that he should have worried about the untruthfulness of his novels. Yet when we come to examine Defoe's attitude towards fiction,[33] it becomes apparent that he shared the concern of many of his contemporaries who had Puritan backgrounds about lying in print.

In the preface to *The Storm* (1704), which he signs as 'The Ages Humble Servant,' Defoe is greatly taken up with his position as historian: 'Tis the Duty of an Historian to set everything in its own Light, and to convey matter of fact upon its legitimate Authority, and no other.' His purpose in telling of the storm is, however, not impartial; he intends to point the moral, to 'act the Divine, and draw necessary practical Inferences,' and he is aware that he may be accused not only of telling a falsehood but, worse, of telling it in order to reform the reader, and, in this way, be committing a 'crime' greater than the one he is attempting to cure: 'endeavouring by a Lye to correct the Reader's

Vices, and sin against Truth to bring the Reader off from sinning against Sence.'[34] Defoe, here and throughout the preface, protests too much. His professed abhorrence of falsehood is designed to enhance the accuracy of his report. At the same time Defoe inherited from the sixteenth and seventeenth centuries a respect amounting almost to awe for the immortality, and therefore for the power and influence, of printed books, which he contrasts with the spoken word that, even in a sermon, 'extends no farther than the strength of Memory can convey it': 'but if a Book Printed obtrudes a Falsehood, if a Man tells a Lye in Print, he abuses Mankind, and imposes upon the whole World, he causes our Children to tell Lyes after us, and their Children after them, to the End of the World.' Defoe's view of the almost sacred duty of the historian allows him to dismiss as 'meer Romance' a great deal of imaginative literature before him from 'the Histories and Original of *Saturn Jupiter*, and the rest of the Celestial Rabble' down to 'the Stories of St. *George* and the *Dragon*, *Guy* Earl of *Warwick*, *Bevis* of *Southampton*, and the like.'

Defoe's movement towards fiction from the preface of *The Storm* is conditioned by his recognition of the value of the fable in conveying the moral. In a letter to Harley probably written only a month or two after *The Storm* Defoe expresses a different attitude towards dissimulation. Urging Harley to court 'Popular Esteem,' he gives advice which, though no doubt politically astute, might well have surprised readers of *The Storm*:

as a Lye Does Not Consist in the Indirect Position of words, but in the Design by False Speaking, to Deciev and Injure my Neighbour, So Dissembling does Not Consist in Putting a Different Face Upon our Actions, but in the further Applying That Concealment to the Prejudice of the Person; for Example, I Come into a persons Chamber, who on a Surprize is Apt to Fall into Dangerous Convulsions. I Come in Smileing, and Pleasant, and ask the person to Rise and Go abroad, or any Other Such question, and Press him to it Till I Prevail, whereas the Truth is I have Discovred the house to be On Fire, and I Act thus for fear of frighting him. Will any Man Tax me with Hypocrisye and Dissimulation?

In your Perticular Post Sir you may so Govern as That Every Party Shall believ you Their Own.[35]

In this form of deception the end is justified by the means. Though I do not think that Defoe's position in public as presented in the preface to *The Storm* will quite square with his attitude expressed in the privacy of the letter to Harley, it is none the less true that Defoe makes a justifiable distinction between two kinds of lying that accounts for the seeming contradiction of these two positions. The difference resides in the *intention* of the lie, as Defoe explains in the *Serious Reflections of Robinson Crusoe*. One kind of lying has as its end 'to deceive, to injure, betray, rob, destroy and the like':

Lying in this sense, is the concealing of all other crimes; it is the sheep's clothing hung upon the wolf's back, it is the Pharisee's prayer, the whore's blush, the hypocrite's paint, the murderer's smile, the thief's cloak; 'tis Joab's embrace and Judas's kiss; in a word, it is mankind's darling sin and the devil's distinguishing character. (P 97)

The other king of lying is not really lying at all but a parable, or a story told for the purpose of the moral to be taken from it. As he remarks in the preface to the *Serious Reflections*: 'The Fable is always made for the moral, not the moral for the fable.' Hence tales which are sheer invention and lack didactic import are a 'scandalous crime' (p 99), and Defoe is anxious to disassociate his own work in fiction from this kind of thing:

The telling or writing a parable, or an allusive allegoric history, is quite a different case, and is always distinguished from this other jesting with truth, that it is designed and effectually turned for instructive and upright ends, and has its moral justly applied. Such are the historical parables in the Holy Scripture, such 'The Pilgrim's Progress,' and such, in a word, the adventures of your fugitive friend, 'Robinson Crusoe.' (P 101)

Defoe's attitude to contemporary writers of fiction such as Aphra Behn, Mrs Manley, and Mrs Haywood, the authors of the kinds of 'Novels and Romances' that the Mother in *The Family Instructor* forbids her children to read, seems to have been governed by the fact that there was no moral justification for their invented tales. Although Defoe's novels, particularly after *Robinson Crusoe*, share some characteristics of the novels of intrigue (such as the use of disguise and dissimulation to advance the plot, or to reveal character), until *Roxana* at least his novels never share the two chief distinguishing elements of most of those works, the aristocratic setting at court or in great houses, and a plot revolving around love intrigues. In *Mist's Journal* he attacked 'the feigned Stories, the Romances, the Secret Histories, and the Accounts given of Kings' Courts and Persons, in which we have been made to take the Characters and Histories of Persons of the best Quality from the *Inventions of Men*, nay, and sometimes of Women too.'[36] It is curious, then, that Defoe's final novel is about a courtesan and was published under a title, *The Fortunate Mistress*,[37] which is typical of the romances and easily taken for one by contemporary readers. In fact *Roxana* is quite unlike those salacious and unrealistic stories. Defoe's ostensible reason for telling the story is at odds with his real purpose, which is didactic.

In the opening pages of the first *Family Instructor* Defoe, with apparent reluctance, justifies his use of dialogues, which he calls 'historical discourses,' in order to put across the moral point. Although the method is, he claims, 'entirely new,' readers who find it odd must 'blame their own more irregular tempers, that must have everything turned into new models; must be touched with novelty, and have their fancies humoured with the dress of a thing' (p 2). Here, then, not only the fable, but the style, is justified by the moral. But the petulant tone of Defoe's remarks reveals a reluctance to accept instruction *and* delight as the ends of imaginative art. Better, clearly, to swallow the bitter pill of instruction unsugared; but better to take it sugared than not at all: 'anything, or any method, if we may but bring the main end to pass' (p 4).

When we come to the prefaces to the novels themselves two changes are discernible in Defoe's theory of fiction. First, he is increasingly willing to recognize the delightfulness of fiction in itself. Secondly, he is increasingly willing to admit that he is writing fiction and even that there is a distinction between the protagonist and the author. Although the prefaces insist on an absolute fidelity to facts, yet the 'agreeable manner of the performance' now begins to command almost equal attention. There is no hint that the stories have been dressed up by a reluctant author merely to satisfy the demands of modern readers for novelty, as in *The Family Instructor*. Rather, *Robinson Crusoe*, for example, is recommended 'as well to the Diversion, as to the Instruction of the Reader.' In the preface to *Colonel Jack*,[38] written three years later, the quality of delight and instruction is more emphatically stated. The editor refers both to 'the useful and instructive Part' and to 'the pleasant and delightful Part' which, he says, 'speaks for it self.' In *Roxana*[39] the editor recommends both the improving and the diverting elements of the tale and suggests that for the 'Virtuous Reader' the story may 'be read both with Profit and Delight.'

One of the curious changes from the preface of the first part of *Robinson Crusoe* to that of *Roxana* is the shift in emphasis from the authenticity of the tale, which makes *Robinson Crusoe* 'worth making

Publick,' to the 'Performance,' the 'dressing up the Story,' the 'Words' which are used to puff Roxana's story. The editor of *Robinson Crusoe* tells us that he 'believes the thing to be a just History of Fact; neither is there any Appearance of Fiction in it' and that the 'Story is told with Modesty, with Seriousness, and with a religious Application of Events.' In the preface to the *Father Adventures of Robinson Crusoe*,[40] however, there is a significant shift in the direction of *performance*. For the first time in a preface to one of the novels that important word in Defoe's critical vocabulary 'invention' (i.e., fiction) makes its appearance: 'The just Application of every Incident, the religious and useful Inferences drawn from every Part, are so many Testimonies to the good Design of making it publick, and must legitimate all the Part that *may be call'd Invention, or Parable in the story*' (my italics). He complains of pirated editions which abridge the work by leaving out the 'reflections' and thus 'leave the Work naked of its brightest Ornaments.' And then in a curious piece of double-talk he half admits that the story is a fiction: 'if they would, at the same Time pretend, that the Author has supply'd the Story out of his Invention, they take from it the Improvements, which alone recommends that Invention to wise and good Men.' The editor here seems to want both to deny and to justify his 'Invention.' The third part of *Robinson Crusoe*, the *Serious Reflections during the Life and Surprizing Adventures of Robinson Crusoe*, carries this ambiguity further. After speaking of the first two volumes as 'fable' he then says:

I have heard that the envious and ill-disposed part of the world have raised some objections against the two first volumes, on pretence, for want of a better reason, that (as they say) the story is feigned, that the names are borrowed, and that all is a romance; that there never were any such man or place, or circumstances in any man's life; that it is all formed and embellished by invention to impose upon the world.

Here, rather than an 'editor,' Robinson Crusoe speaks of his own work, revealing himself as the slippery character Gildon had suggested: 'I, Robinson Crusoe ... do hereby declare their objection is an invention scandalous in design, and false in fact ... the story, though allegorical, is also historical.' Crusoe is clearly determined to have it both ways.

In the preface to *Moll Flanders*[41] Defoe is content to assert the genuineness of the story, realizing perhaps that the less said the better: 'The World is so taken up of late with Novels and Romances, that it will be hard for a private History to be taken for Genuine, where the Names and other Circumstances of the Person are concealed, and on this

Account we must be content to leave the Reader to pass his own Opinion upon the ensuing Sheets, and take it just as he pleases.' Instead he devotes a great deal of space to the problem of his role as editor. The editor plays a much larger role in *Moll Flanders* than in *Robinson Crusoe* since 'To give the History of a wicked Life repented of, necessarily requires that the wicked Part should be made as wicked, as the real History of it will bear,' and he admits that he 'has had no little difficulty to put it into a Dress fit to be seen.' There is a wider gap here than in *Robinson Crusoe* between the 'real History' and the one presented to the public. What is particularly interesting here is that the part of the story the editor 'makes' is spoken of in the imagery of clothing – the 'new dressing up this Story.' Fiction is appearance and to some extent disguise.

The editor of *Colonel Jack* naturally recommends his book in the hope that 'Every wicked Reader will here be encouraged to a Change,' but here the editor is less concerned with the truthfulness of the story: 'neither is it of the least Moment to enquire whether the Colonel hath told his own Story true or not; If he has made it a *History* or a *Parable*, it will be equally useful, and capable of doing Good; and in that it recommends it self without any other *Introduction*.'

In *Roxana* the distinction between the 'real History' and the story introduced by the editor is advanced another stage. *Robinson Crusoe* had had an 'editor' who was really little more than a publisher. The intervening novels had 'editors' who openly admit that certain changes have been found necessary before the 'real History' can be given to the world and that the work may be a 'parable,' not a history. Instead of an editor *Roxana* has a 'Relator' who, like any author, takes the faults of the work on his own shoulders.

If it is not as Beautiful as the Lady herself is reported to be; if it is not as diverting as the Reader can desire, and much more than he can reasonably expect; and if all the most diverting Parts of it are not adapted to the Instruction and Improvement of the Reader, the *Relator* says, it must be from the Defect of his Performance; dressing up the Story in worse Cloaths than the *Lady*, whose Words he speaks, prepar'd it for the World.

Here the clothing image is more complicated than in *Moll Flanders*. The editor's job in the earlier novel was to dress up Moll's story in words fit to be printed. The language of the novel was the 'outside' supplied by an editor. But Roxana's own story is itself dressed up when she prepares it for the world, and the 'Relator' in turn clothes that story in his words. Like Plato's cave-dwellers we have only the image of an image.

Although Defoe insists that 'the Foundation of this is laid in Truth of Fact' and that it has moral utility, we are clearly a long way from his horror of forging a story and imposing it on the world which we found in the preface to *The Storm*. His attitude to fiction is not one of straightforward and unrelieved verisimilitude. Rather it is a reasonably sophisticated, if only partially formulated, concept involving creativeness and, above all, art (the 'clothing' he speaks of in two of his prefaces) which is controlled by a moral end. However faltering he may have been in his approach to the idea of fiction, Defoe saw to some degree that the works of fiction he was writing used words and images to transmute the raw lump of experience into the art of the novel.

Before we come to the novels themselves it will be useful to examine briefly Defoe's semi-fictional works, such as the *Memoirs of a Cavalier* or *The King of the Pirates*, and his criminal biographies, the lives of men like Sheppard, Gow, and Wild, for in these works there are elements characteristic of Defoe's narrative techniques, although the works themselves can scarcely be called novels. Maximillian Novak draws our attention to the importance of the semi-fictional memoirs in his article on 'Defoe's Theory of Fiction' where he points out that, 'For all their pretence to truth, these works frequently occupied a middle ground between history and fiction.'[42] Like historical works they appear to be written by historically identifiable people, but like fictional works they are created on a basis of fact by Defoe. His main purpose in writing such spurious memoirs seems generally to have been for propaganda of one sort or another. For example, his *Memoirs of John, Duke of Melfort, Being an Account of the Secret Intrigues of The Chevalier de S. George, Particularly relating to the Present Times* (1714) was written in support of Harley, while his *Memoirs of Majr. Alexander Ramkins* (1718) exposes the self-delusions of the Jacobites. It was only a step, in the words of Arthur Secord, to move 'from fictitious propaganda to fiction in which propaganda is incidental to the narrative.'[43] Although I think that in the novels propaganda is almost always integral rather than incidental, Secord was correct in stressing the link between Defoe's semi-fictional works and his fiction.

The memoirs differ from the novels in ways that help to make clear the particular achievement of Defoe's fiction. Although written in the first person, the memoirs are not complete autobiographies; only the adult life is touched upon and then only in relation to certain kinds of events, such as military exploits or geographical exploration. Typically, we learn virtually nothing of family affairs. As a result no pattern of life comparable to that found in the novels emerges from the procession of similar though generally unrelated episodes. When a little adventure has gone on long enough Defoe simply arranges for a new episode to set the story moving in another direction. The narrator of the memoir, moreover, is subservient to the propaganda or to the history of his times. He (and it is significant that there are no memoirs of women) exists not so much to tell us about himself as to recount episodes involving other people and places. From *The Memoirs of a Cavalier* we may derive some notion of what it must have been like to have been a soldier on the Continent and in England between 1632 and 1648, of the confusion of issues, the ease with which a man could change loyalties, the need for cunning and stratagem to survive, the hardship of a soldier's life, the pretences and delusions of princes and commanders, but we do not ever learn the soldier's name. There is no pattern of themes or images, such as we will find in the novels, that strengthens the biographical form and shapes the work. Robinson Crusoe and Moll Flanders and Colonel Jack, by giving us some account of their childhood disobedience or aspirations, offer an explanation for the events that follow and establish themes that recur and give unity to their histories.

On the other hand, in the memoirs and similar works such as *The King of the Pirates*, *The Four Years Voyages of Capt. George Roberts*, and *A New Voyage Round the World* Defoe employs techniques that he uses as well in the novels. His ability to imagine himself in the position of someone else, which seems to have come naturally to him, but which was fostered by his years of political espionage and pamphleteering, accounts in large measure for what literary merit these works possess. There is always a lively sense of a narrator, even if we do not always know his name or very much about him, who by his energy and cunning and power of observation lives an eventful life and gives us a vivid account of it. The narrative method of these semi-fictional forms relies to a remarkable extent on the use of disguise and pretence, a technique that passes into the novels where, linked with a stronger biographical pattern, it is able to give shape and meaning to the form of the novels.

In *The King of the Pirates*, for example, Defoe's fictitious 'memoir' supposed to have been written by Captain Avery, the 'Mock King of Madagascar,' Avery and his gang operate as pirates by pretending to be respectable traders or at least privateers. They pass, so disguised 'as to be taken for Spaniards,'[44] or as traders loading logwood 'under the pretence of selling' (p 40), or by dressing themselves up 'like merchant strangers' (p 65) and, finally, in 'Vests and long gowns' as 'Armenian merchants' (p 85).[45] And Avery ends his life, as he had lived it, by disguise and evasion. He announces that he will go to France, 'from where I intend to go and live in some inland town, where, as they have perhaps no notion of the sea, so they will not be inquisitive after us' (p 90). Defoe takes a particular delight in creating a situation in which the persons being spoken to are unaware of the identity of the speaker, a device of irony that he often uses in the novels: 'I told them jestingly, we were good, honest Christian pirates, and belonged to Captain Avery (not at all letting them know I was Avery himself)' (p 69). And of course Avery rarely misses an opportunity to strengthen his position by taking advantage of this kind of situation: '"But," said I, "you in England greatly wrong Captain Avery, our general (so I called myself, to advance our credit)"' (p 72). Defoe's own experiences in Scotland, where he appeared in various professional guises to argue the cause of the Union, clearly lies behind his account of Avery's success. The overwhelming impression to be gathered from Defoe's various memoirs and first-person accounts of pirates and explorers is that life for the narrators is a series of cheats, providing for the wary and the clever an opportunity of advancement by cunning, trickery, disguise, and pretence.

The various lives of notorious criminals to which Defoe turned after he had written his last novel display much the same attitude to life and employ, consequently, a similar narrative method, although the protagonists are not ultimately successful and the accounts are not generally written in the first person. What fascinated Defoe about these criminals was their extraordinary skill in deceiving the people they robbed and sometimes killed. In his *A Narrative of the Proceedings in France, for discovering ... the murderers of the English gentlemen* (1724) (sometimes called 'An Account of the Cartoucheans in France') Defoe makes a distinction between Cartouche who was 'admirably dextrous, subtle, and wary' and his accomplice Bizeau who 'had no cunning.'[46] The success of the Cartoucheans rested on their ability *to act*, to pass as servants, or merchants, or officers as need and design required. Defoe was very little interested in thieves who simply broke into houses at night or who robbed by force, but he was fascinated by 'artful rogues' who 'delude the most vigilant eyes in some contrived cases where the ignorant party has no thought or guess at the design' (p 116). He takes a particular delight in a man's sense of playing a role. His account of the methods of Jonathan Wild, the original of Gay's Peachum, who received stolen goods from criminals and boldly returned them to their owners for a fee betrays Defoe's admiration for a man who knew how to act a part:

He openly kept his counting-house, or office, like a man of business, and had his books to enter everything in with the utmost exactness and regularity. When you first came to him to give an account of anything lost, it was hinted to you that you must first deposit a crown; this was the retaining fee. Then you were asked some needful questions – that is to say, needful, not for his information, but for your amusement – as where you lived, where the goods were lost, whether out of your house or out of your pocket, or whether on the highway, and the like; and your answers to them all were all minuted down, as if in order to make a proper search and inquiry; whereas, perhaps, the very thing you came to inquire after was in the very room where you were, or not far off. After all the grimace was at an end, you were desired to call again or send in a day or two, and then you should know whether he was able to do you any service or no, and so you were dismissed.[47]

A passage such as this tells us a great deal about Defoe's narrative art. Here we have not merely the invention of realistic detail, but also Defoe's enjoyment of Wild's contriving mind, above all, of Wild's ingenious method of establishing a reputation for honesty by a fussy pretence at legitimate book-keeping. To call this verisimilitude – if by that we mean that Defoe was concerned primarily with getting the physical details of place right – is to miss half the point. When, to take another example, Moll Flanders gives us a list of the actual streets in London which she took as an escape route after a theft, what Defoe is drawing our attention is to her *deviousness*, not her accuracy of memory or his own knowledge of London's streets. Many of Defoe's contemporary readers, familiar with the intricate maze of London streets, would have realized at once just how clever Moll or Colonel Jack had been in taking a particular tortuous route. Defoe's art lies in putting himself in the place of the person he is describing (hence of course his fondness for the first person) and imagining the situation at hand. The truth to reality springs from imagination, not merely from observation.

What we also find in this passage from *Jonathan Wild* which is central to Defoe's narrative art is his development of situational irony. Jonathan Wild, like any good actor, is responding to an audience. It is his knowledge that 'the very thing you came to inquire after was in the very room' which enlivens our sense of the scene. In this way it corresponds to Moll's idea of herself as the 'greatest Artist' of her time, or to Roxana's deception of the fashionable world in St James, or to Crusoe's pleasure in calling himself the 'Governour' of his island. If we place this passage against one from the novels, we can see the same sense of the irony of situation:

When I shew'd my self to the two Hostages, it was with the Captain, who told them, I was the Person the Governour had order'd to look after them, and that it was the Governour's Pleasure they should not stir any where, but by my Direction; that if they did, they should be fetch'd into the Castle, and be lay'd in Irons; so that as we never suffered them to see me as Governour, so I now appear'd as another Person, and spoke of the Governour, the Garrison, the Castle, and the like, upon all Occasions.   (P 271)

Here Crusoe is attempting to enhance his prestige as 'Governour' by speaking of 'the Governour, the Garrison, the Castle, and the like.' At the same time, like Wild, he takes an obvious pleasure in the irony that he knows more than he reveals and is, in fact, the very person he is speaking of.

Although they employ many of the same techniques, neither the lives of actual criminals nor the semi-fictional memoirs and histories are novels. Defoe himself points out the limited scope of the criminal lives: 'Nor is it their lives, or the history of their lives, as men, that is the subject of this tract, but their history as rogues, their lives as streetrobbers, housebreakers, thieves and murderers.'[48] Similarly the memoirs and histories, although generally longer and closer to fiction, concentrate on limited aspects of the lives they present and lack the shape of a whole life. It is only when Defoe's vision of the uncertain human lot, expressed through his techniques of disguise and deception, is united with an account of a man or woman's whole life that a novel is created. His deep sense of the awful individuality of every man's life made him a novelist and dictated the form of his novels. His knowledge that 'no Simile, no Allusion, no Comparison' can capture the unique quality of a man's life taught him that ''Tis even the whole Work of Life to describe Life.'[49] In the novels, as distinguished from the fictional biographies, Defoe attempts 'to describe Life,' that is, to write of men as men, and not merely as rogues, housebreakers, thieves, and murderers. 'Every single Man's History,' Defoe believed, 'were it to be written down, would be a History of odd Incidents, new, surprizing, and particular to itself.'[50] In this sense perhaps the most important statement that Defoe ever made about his fiction is to be found in the revolutionary manifesto of the first line of the preface to *Robinson Crusoe*: 'IF ever the Story of any private Man's Adventures in the World were worth making

Publick, and were acceptable when Publish'd, the Editor of this Account thinks this will be so.'

The pattern of development we have observed in the prefaces to the novels from *Robinson Crusoe* to *Roxana* is reflected in other ways in the novels themselves. This pattern, in which an increasing acknowledgment of the works as fiction is accompanied by the gradual, though never complete, distinction between the protagonist and the relator, is mirrored in the names of the heroes and heroines which provide the titles of the novels, the ever more restricted geography, and the darkening vision of the novelist.

All of Defoe's eponymous protagonists, with the possible exception of Robinson Crusoe, bear names that are meant to suggest their characters and careers. That Defoe should have selected names such as Moll Flanders, Colonel Jack, and Roxana is very much in accordance with the common eighteenth-century practice in both fiction and drama of naming characters suggestively, even, as is sometimes the case, by outrageous puns (e.g., Peachum, Thwackum). This is not at all the same thing, it should be added, as using type names (such as Mr Worldly Wiseman) to denote particular qualities. Rather, the significant break that the early eighteenth-century novelists made with tradition was to name characters, as Ian Watt has pointed out, 'in such a way as to suggest that they were to be regarded as particular individuals in the contemporary social environment.'[51] Certainly names such as Robinson Crusoe, Pamela Andrews, or Tom Jones would have been credible in ordinary life. None the less, there is often a sense in the name, however authentic it sounds, that is appropriate to the character; Watt cites the cases of Richardson's Mrs *Sin*clair and Sir Charles *Grand*ison. But I believe Watt is wrong when he maintains that 'Defoe's use of proper names is casual and sometimes contradictory ... and most of the main characters such as Robinson Crusoe or Moll Flanders have complete and realistic names and aliases.'[52] Defoe certainly seems to have selected Robinson Crusoe's name for a realistic purpose since his paramount concern is that the reader should take Crusoe for an actual person.[53] But in the succeeding novels he moved steadily away from this practice, as the increasing insubstantiality of the names indicates. 'Moll Flanders' is an assumed name; 'Colonel Jack' is a facetious nickname; and 'Roxana' is a name bestowed on her at a party and known to very few of the other characters in that novel. Roxana is less a name than first a compliment and afterwards an accusation, and in much of the novel, particularly in the dark final portions, she is in great fear of being recognized as the courtesan once called 'Roxana.' While strongly maintaining the appearance of actuality in his stories, Defoe relied less and less on the protagonist's name to perform this authenticating function and was, as we have seen in the changing tone of the prefaces, slightly more prepared as he went on, to admit, and therefore to justify, the fact that he was writing fiction.

The shift of tone from *Robinson Crusoe* to *Roxana*, reflected in the prefaces and names, underlines the growing darkness of Defoe's vision. *Robinson Crusoe* is in many ways the most optimistic of Defoe's novels. It is shaped by the curve of comedy, like the story of the Prodigal Son to which it has an affinity. Crusoe's fortune sinks in the first part of the novel, but through God's providence and his own repentance and reform it rises again in the second half until he becomes 'King' and 'Governour' of his now populated island. Here one sees enterprise, caution, and cleverness leading to ultimate success. In the middle novels, *Captain Singleton*, *Moll Flanders*, and *Colonel Jack*, Defoe turned to the underworld of pirates, prostitutes, and thieves that he explored in some of the memoirs and later in the criminal lives. Here the pattern of sin and redemption is complicated by the existence of an unjust fate and an unjust society; Singleton, Moll, and Jack are abandoned children and orphans. The protagonists of these novels are as much sinned against as sinning. The shape of their stories is still comic, but that shape is less distinct. Although they rise from rags to riches, exposure threatens their prosperity even at the end. They live by their wits, that is, in disguises and through deception. Finally, in *Roxana* we have Defoe's only tragic novel. Like Crusoe, Roxana is a middle-class heroine. But unlike Crusoe, after an initial setback her material fortune rises steadily until she becomes not only vastly wealthy, but, so it is hinted, the King's mistress. The novel ends, however, darkly, after the reappearance of one of her abandoned children, Amy's murder of the child, and an unspecified but 'dreadful Course of Calamities.'

The gloom that settles over the final pages of *Roxana* thickens through the five-year span of Defoe's novels. We have already observed how Defoe's fictional works are related to his moral and social tracts, such as *The Family Instructor*, and that the tone of those tracts becomes more shrill as the decade of the 1720s advanced. One of the themes of the social tracts is the special relationship between parents and children, and Defoe's preoccupation with this theme can be traced through the novels where it becomes increasingly more sinister. The motif of the Prodigal Son in *Robinson Crusoe*, Crusoe's disobedience and the punishment that follows, is reinforced first by contrast with Friday's affectionate relations with Crusoe ('like those of a Child to a Father') and then by Friday's ecstatic rapture when, with Crusoe's aid, he recovers his own father. The protagonists of the middle novels are the victims of an unjust social system (which Defoe was anxious to reform) and of rather casual parents. The sort of lives they lead, though this is only partially true of Moll Flanders, is conditioned by the absence of adequate 'publick Schools and Charities ... to prevent the Destruction of so many unhappy Children.'[54] In Moll's case, although she was well looked after as a child, her ignorance of her mother's identity and her brother's existence leads to an incestuous marriage and a child by her own brother. And Moll herself falls into the habit of abandoning her own children, a practice that Defoe deplores in his other writings, and for which Moll is punished. In *Roxana* we have a Prodigal Mother story. Roxana is the unfaithful parent who abandons her own children, one of whom, Susan, later becomes her servant and then claims her as mother. Because Roxana sees Susan as an avenging fury Amy murders her and Roxana is guilty of complicity in the murder of her own daughter.

The geography of the novels, which is increasingly restrictive, emphasizes a similar pattern. Although Crusoe is for many years a captive on his island, he is also something of a globe-trotter. He is a slave for two years in Sallee (a Moroccan seaport), he works for a while in Brazil, his island is situated in the mouth of the Orinoko, he returns to England via Spain, the Pyrenees, and France, and in the second volume of his travels he crosses Asia from China to Archangel. Singleton, similarly, is a great traveller who crosses the continent of Africa, much of which was then virtually unknown.[55] In *Moll Flanders* and *Colonel Jack*, however, London is for the first time the geographical centre of the novels. Both Moll and Jack go to America, but their rehabilitation there serves as a means of returning to England. Colonel Jack, in particular, speaks of being 'Buried alive' in the New World, and Moll on her second visit is, of course, a transported criminal. Roxana, although she spends some time on the Continent, never leaves Europe and, in fact, the central scenes of her story take place in the very heart of a corrupt London, her 'apartments in the *Pall-Mall*.' In the final section of the novel she struggles to escape from England but is prevented more than once by her daughter. In short, in each successive novel there is a tendency for the movement of the protagonist to be more restricted. He or she is more trapped by circumstances and his or her own fate. The increasingly restricted geography, like the increasingly sinister theme of unhealthy relations between parents and children, reflects Defoe's darkening vision of the corruption of society and family responsibilities in the third decade of the eighteenth century.

Although disguise and deception were practised by Defoe throughout his life, they are none the less associated by him with the devil, grow in importance through the novels, and give further emphasis to the pattern we have been examining. Crusoe's use of deception is largely in the form of traps: he lays snares for animals and he traps, or tricks, the cannibals as well as some of the Europeans who visit his island. But in making his table and chair or growing his corn Crusoe is simply an honest and tireless worker. The protagonists of the middle novels live by deception; they are, of course, thieves. Even Jack, who is not entirely averse to doing an honest day's work, lives a life pretending to be someone other than he really is. Finally, in *Roxana* disguise, in the form of a masquerade and Roxana's famous Turkish costume, becomes central both to the plot and to the moral commentary of the novel.

Although it was the particular achievement of Defoe in the history of fiction to sense the importance of shaping his vision of 'any private Man's Adventures in the World' in the form of an autobiography, it is the extreme egocentricity that his sort of autobiographical method imposes upon the narrator's point of view that explains Defoe's limitations as a novelist. There is very little feeling in Defoe, such as we find in the great nineteenth-century novelists like George Eliot or Dickens, of the vast interconnected, interwoven pattern of life, of characters, destiny, events moving inexorably, but seen in a wide perspective, towards an end. As readers we do not stand back from the action with the narrator and watch the protagonist in the midst of the great moving pattern of his or her life. Rather, we see everything through the eyes of the protagonist. We focus upon one scene, one person, one event, at a time, and when that examination is complete, we move to another. That is why, once other characters have crossed the path of the protagonists, they simply disappear. There is a world outside the narrow focus of the narrator that we never see. We never learned what becomes of Xury, of Moll's Governess, of Amy, of any number of husbands, wives, and lovers. Even when a character, such as Moll's Lancashire husband, reappears we are given only a sentence or two to fill in the story of what he has been doing in the interval. As Moll so accurately remarks on this occasion: 'this is my own Story, not his' (p 301).

The autobiographical form need not of course be so restrictive, but in Defoe's case the intense focus on the immediate scene is a reflection of his view that man is at best a short-sighted creature who sees but a little way before him. In the world of Defoe's novels pitfalls may open up or disasters strike at any moment. Hence of course the importance of the large external events – storms, the plague, floods. But not only can man not reckon on the smooth operation of natural forces, he cannot trust his fellow creatures, a point that Defoe makes frequently in his non-fiction and which is amply illustrated in the novels. The intense loneliness of all Defoe's leading characters reflects his own sense of the essential isolation of human beings in a world where they can see little and trust few. There is some perspective in the novels, created by distance in time (the narrator looks back over his life) or by irony (the narrator sees himself from a changed point of view), but these devices are not extensively used. Moreover, there is no analysis of, or even very little sensitivity to, emotional subtleties. The universal passions – love, hate, envy, above all fear – motivate the characters. These are Defoe's limitations, easily noted by anyone who cares to place him beside the greatest novelists, but his limited range, his intensity of focus within the narration, is also part of his strength. In as much as the concentration on the immediate scene is an expression of Defoe's conception of the life and nature of man, technique and vision come together.

2 The Island and the World

In *Robinson Crusoe* (1719)[1] Defoe's vision of humanity found its first appropriate form in fiction. Ideas about the nature and life of man that he expressed in his political and social non-fiction are transmuted into the themes of the novel, and in the deft and complex interweaving of these themes the structural pattern of the novel takes shape. The overriding themes of all the novels, such as man's short-sightedness and providence's 'chequer work,' demand a form that is resilient rather than climactic, accumulative rather than contained. The special shape of *Robinson Crusoe*, formed within these demands, arises from the rhythm of imprisonment and deliverance which can be felt throughout the novel and which establishes the basic alternation of the world and the island. From this contrast of two modes of existence Crusoe's double tale of passions and temptations and, conversely, of a new life totally isolated from worldly evil derives its full significance. This pattern is reinforced by the theme of reason and fancy, which calls attention to the difference between the island and the world, and is complicated by patterns within the pattern formulated by these themes. In addition, the patterns, large and small, are expressed and supported by the repetition of phrases and images which may make a casual first appearance but which accumulate and form patterns of their own. In these ways the interweaving themes are developed and controlled and changed as the novel advances.

Defoe's techniques of organization, his interlinked themes and ironic anticipations, his repetitions of events and phrases, and his understated use of images are embedded in the narrative surface of the novel where they may easily be passed over unnoticed. There is no intrusive narrator to exhume them for us, nor a backdrop of familiar myth onto which the characters are projected and their modern diminished stature ironically exposed as, for example, Bloom, standing pathetically in the shadow of Ulysses, reveals an ironical parallel. The references to biblical parallels are casual and diffuse; they lack the consistency and concentration necessary for a sustained authorial comment and point to a habit of mind rather than a structural principle. They serve, rather, to dramatize aspects of Crusoe's tribulations emblematically.[2] Outwardly, the story gives the appearance of an astonishing but straightforward tale told without artifice, or even very much design. Defoe's consummate skill, after all, lay in passing his fiction off as fact and as memoir.

Robinson Crusoe's powerful hold upon the imagination of readers from the first, however, points to a controlling vision behind the episodic casualness. Throughout the novel causal relationships are established – crimes are punished, dreams fulfilled, prayers answered – which, suspended over large sections of the novel, produce tension and suggest the working of divine providence. Moreover, Crusoe's insistence upon the value of 'secret Hints' and warnings, his developing sense of the nexus of crime and punishment, and his demonstration of coincidences such as the curious 'Concurrence of Days' (p 133) strengthen and extend a vision of the life of man, distilled in a key passage towards the end of the novel:

So little do we see before us in the World, and so much reason have we to depend chearfully upon the great Maker of the World, that he does not leave his Creatures so absolutely destitute, but that in the worst Circumstances they have always something to be thankful for, and sometimes are nearer their Deliverance than they imagine; nay, are even brought to their Deliverance by the Means by which they seem to be brought to their Destruction.   (P 252)

Here is the central paradox of human existence as the novel presents it. Man's blindness, the cause of his continual disasters, prevents him from seeing the means of God's deliverance.

What this means, in narrative terms, is that Defoe does not merely seek, as Ian Watt has suggested, what might plausibly happen next. Though there are loose ends and inconsistencies – as in life itself – there is also a shaping vision which finds what might *most effectively* happen next within the demands of the fictional form. Defoe's narrative method is not just the episodic, but the episodic accumulative. It is the method of art, not chance.

Modern readers and commentators are especially indebted to

studies of *Robinson Crusoe* which have demonstrated the presence of an important spiritual pattern in the novel. In 1951, in an article on the 'Symbolic Elements in *Robinson Crusoe*,'[3] Edwin Benjamin emphasized what ought never to have been forgotten, namely, that *Robinson Crusoe* is 'a conversion story,' and he saw several of the details of the novels as symbolic components of an interlocking system of biblical parallels that comes very close to allegory. Later Maximillian Novak,[4] in replying to Ian Watt's argument that Robinson Crusoe is the embodiment of economic man, pointed out that the novel cannot be understood unless we recognize the relationship between Crusoe's punishment on the island and his original sin in disobeying his parents. In 1964 William Halewood[5] imaginatively suggested that the 'unceasing' religious reflections really constitute a history of Crusoe's 'imperfect' religious life, a 'Puritan drama of the soul,' marked by shortcomings and lapses, but certainly the 'deliberate achievement of a novelist who knew what he was about.' Articles such as these have helped to make possible the longer critical analyses of G.A. Starr[6] and Paul Hunter[7] which have deepened our understanding of the spiritual context of *Robinson Crusoe* by revealing the novel's formal similarity to Puritan confessional literature. Many Puritans saw their lives as repetitions of a pattern of sin, repentance, conversion, and deliverance, and wrote accounts of their spiritual progress.[8]

The fact that *Robinson Crusoe* bears a strong formal resemblance to spiritual autobiography accounts for our sense that at times we are reading a religious allegory. When Crusoe, totally alone on his island, cries out from the depth of his despair, or when near the end he experiences something like Moses's sight from Mount Pisgah of a promised land, he becomes if only for a moment the embodiment of human suffering or of human hope, and his story is raised to the level of myth. The echoes of a universal condition give the novel its resonance, but it is probably safe to say that if *Robinson Crusoe* were simply an imaginary spiritual autobiography it would have disappeared long ago.

Like all enduring fictional structures *Robinson Crusoe* is shaped by a complex of techniques which may reinforce, qualify, or go beyond the formal imitation of another genre. Here the metaphor of spiritual pilgrimage towards salvation, which informs the novel, is modified and made more complex in fictional terms by the techniques Defoe uses. An examination of the recurrence of motifs, the repetition and variation of certain key words and concepts, the development of clusters of images, and the accumulation of successive disasters and deliverances into a pattern reveals Defoe's major structural devices. In seeking Defoe's art we are compelled to pay attention to those techniques by which patterns are built up and, through repetition and contrast and symmetry, give shape and meaning to the novel, thus rendering Defoe's vision of the human lot.

I

The main structural divisions of *Robinson Crusoe* are established by Crusoe's unique experience of a quarter-century of total isolation on an uninhabited island in the mouth of the Orinoko River. The line of action of the novel is the hero's movement towards his island, his imprisonment on it, and his eventual deliverance, spiritual and physical, from it. However, Crusoe's life in the world before and after the island episode frames the central section of the tale, giving it a depth and meaning that alone it would never possess. The dramatic opposition of his two modes of life – isolated from worldly evil on the island, and, by contrast, in the midst of human struggle and worldly desire – provides an appropriate arrangement for the presentation of Defoe's major themes. In this scheme the island expresses the central paradox of the novel. There Crusoe is both imprisoned and set free, and in ways more complex than he at first grasps. The complexity arises from the fact that, as Crusoe discovers, 'imprisonment' and 'deliverance' may have both a physical and a spiritual meaning.

The pattern of disasters and deliverances which marks the stages of Crusoe's spiritual enlightenment begins before the island episode and does not end, as we might expect, with his deliverance (in either sense) from it. In the course of the novel Crusoe is delivered from storms and shipwreck (three times), from slavery, from wild animals and savages, from starvation, from a small boat at sea (twice), from sickness, from his own blindness about God's providence, from cannibals, from blood-guiltiness, from his base passions (partially), from the island, and, finally, from the wolves. In addition, he is responsible for the deliverance of Friday, Friday's father, and the Spaniard, the victims of the mutiny on the ship which eventually rescues him, and, in intention at least, all the Spaniard's companions on the mainland. This long series of adventures, in which the special deliverance of the island is set, gives the novel its characteristic rhythm and emphasizes the puzzling repetitiousness of human endeavour.

In the opening section of the novel Defoe follows the pattern of spiritual autobiography fairly closely. Crusoe utterly fails to recognize the spiritual significance of his repeated misadventures. He cannot conquer his 'wandring Inclination.' Instead, he experiences a 'hardening'[9] into sin. He ignores the promptings of reason and the warnings which his escapes or deliverances should convey. In a word, he is a man increasingly estranged from God.

At the same time by the use of ironic anticipation and the accumulation of closely related events Defoe carefully prepares Crusoe, and his readers, for his miraculous deliverance and separation from the world. A succession of motifs runs throughout the episodes of the opening movement of the novel, linking them with one another and reinforcing the major theme of deliverance. These episodes – apparently random and dissimilar, but in fact ordered and linked – form a mounting series of disasters and establish a rhythm of danger (or imprisonment) and deliverance which will continue throughout the novel.

This pattern begins as the consequence of Crusoe's filial disobedience in running away from home. As a result of this act Crusoe undergoes two storms at sea and two corresponding 'Deliverances.' The storm scenes form part of an accumulating pattern of natural disasters and also dramatize Crusoe's mental state. There is an accompanying 'storm'[10] in Crusoe's mind, a continual struggle between reason and passion, in which his good intentions are repeatedly overpowered by an irrational wilfulness. In the terror of each storm Crusoe rationally resolves to return home, but in the calm that follows he entirely forgets 'the Vows and Promises that I made in my Distress' (p 9). As his reason is enthralled by his base passions, Crusoe, despite the 'loud Calls' of his 'more composed Judgment to go home,' finds that he is unable to do so. The largely figurative statement that 'he had no power' (p 14) to go home becomes literally true when Crusoe is made a slave and a prisoner in North Africa. In this sense Crusoe's failure to see his rescue from storm and from shipwreck as providential 'deliverances' leads directly to his physical confinement. Moreover, the appearance of the motif of slavery in the Sallee episode stirs an important undercurrent in the novel. The motif of slavery is part of the larger theme of imprisonment, later to develop into one of the chief sources of imagery in the island section; it links Crusoe's enslavement in Sallee, his escape with the slave boy Xury (who foreshadows Friday), his need for slaves in Brazil, and the subsequent African slaving trip on which he is shipwrecked for the last time. Together these forms of slavery lend ironic emphasis to Crusoe's bondage in sin and his eventual imprisonment on the island.

Crusoe's deliverance from this bondage, unlike his two earlier deliverances which required little exertion on his own behalf, is more difficult, demanding courage, cunning, and time, and it serves as a preparation for the greater trial of the island. Just as he will later be on the island, Crusoe is at first inactive; he hopes only to 'be set at Liberty' by being retaken by 'a *Spanish* or *Portugal* Man of War' (p 19). But after two years of meditating 'nothing but' his escape, he is finally able to achieve his 'Deliverance' by making for open sea in a small boat, not quite alone, but with only Xury to help him.

By this action he precipitates himself into a situation as difficult and infinitely more terrifying than the one from which he has just escaped. The African coast, where he must land from time to time for water, is infested with 'vast great Creatures,' wild beasts whose 'hideous Howlings and Yellings' (pp 24–5) terrify him. When he is rescued from this perilous state by a passing Portuguese ship, Crusoe realizes that once again he has been 'deliver'd ... from ... a miserable end and almost hopeless Condition' (p 33), but he fails to understand that not merely his immediate physical situation but the whole tenor of his aimless existence might be described in these terms. And when he expresses himself anxious to make some return to the Captain 'for my Deliverance' Crusoe of course has his physical deliverance in mind; only later on the island will he realize the spiritual significance of each of his many deliverances' and recognize them as 'visible Instructions' (p 14) sent by a divine providence.

Of course Crusoe displays the resourcefulness of the Defoe protagonist for adapting himself to the situation at hand, and he turns planter. Hard work and loneliness are the burdens of his new life, a reminder of his father's warnings and an ironic foreshadowing of his future existence: 'I used to say, I liv'd just like a Man cast away upon some desolate Island, that had no body there but himself' (p 35). His four years in Brazil appear as fortuitous to Crusoe as any of the other incidents in his life, but they are actually a last and lost opportunity for Crusoe to break the disastrous rhythm of his existence. Instead, as Defoe insists, Crusoe blindly repeats all his old mistakes. His sins, particularly his desire of rising faster in the world 'than the Nature of the Thing admitted' (p 38), are compounded when the opportunity arises of indulging his 'foolish inclination of wandring abroad' (p 38). Human wilfulness and short-sightedness, Defoe believes, impel us forward to our own destruction, indeed make us 'the Instruments of our Destruction' (p 14). Crusoe's career is a notable illustration of this vision, and Defoe nowhere makes this clearer than in his hero's attempt to return to Africa for slaves. Crusoe is as little able to restrain his 'rambling Designs' as when he first left home, and once again has to confess that he 'obey'd blindly the Dictates of my Fancy rather than my Reason' (p 40). Even the inauspicious day that he chooses to go on board ship – 'the same Day eight Year that I went from my Father and Mother at *Hull*' (p 40) – fails to impress a man so wholly oblivious to the warnings of earlier storms, imprisonments, and deliverances. The coincidence of time and event underlines the doubling of Crusoe's sin as he throws away this final chance.

Crusoe's separation from the world is brought about by a series of storms which wrecks the slaving expedition and deposits the exhausted Crusoe alone on the shores of the island. Defoe's description of the violent storms and Crusoe's miraculous escape from the shipwreck that takes the lives of all his companions is cast in two powerful metaphors which help make emphatic the break between life in the world and life on the island. The 'Fury of the Sea' is likened to some vast and monstrous 'Enemy which I had no Means or Strength to contend with,' which 'came rowling a-stern of us, and plainly bad us expect the *Coup de Grace*,' and then 'swallowed [us] up in a Moment' (p 44). His deliverance he describes in the equally forceful metaphor of 'Men going to Execution' (p 43). Deliverance this time is like a last-minute reprieve brought to a man at the very moment that he is 'tyed up, and just going to be turn'd off' (p 46). The violence of his deliverance, as in Donne's famous sonnet, is part of a divine paradox. Crusoe, whose reason has proved weak or untrue, must be forcibly divorced from the world, imprisoned on the island in order that he may be set free. The meaning of all this is something Crusoe only begins to comprehend as he stands, a lonely figure on the seashore, 'wrapt up in the Contemplation of my Deliverance' (p 46).

This deliverance gathers up and completes the motifs of deliverance in Crusoe's life up to this point – the dreadful storms, deliverance from the sea, from slavery, and from the wild beasts of Africa, and his condition in Brazil after his rescue 'like a Man cast away upon some desolate Island.' The weight of these earlier episodes bears heavily on his initial impression of the island which he realizes, and will realize more fully later, is a place both of deliverance and imprisonment. The island is, above all, an education, an experience shaped by the repetition of deliverance which reveals the blindness of man and the working of providence. From the rhythm of deliverance emerges the important contrast between the world, in which Crusoe is surrounded by powerful temptations, and the island to which he is inexorably driven and where, for a time, he lives a life cut off from worldly passions.

The island section of Crusoe's history is shaped by the series of deliverances which obsesses Crusoe's thoughts and motivates his actions. His arrival and his departure twenty-eight years later are both called deliverances, as well as many of the adventures in between these two events. 'Have I not been deliver'd, and wonderfully too, from Sickness? from the most distress'd Condition that could be, and that was so frightful to me' (p 95), he asks himself after his recovery. And he adds, since 'I had not own'd and been thankful for that as a Deliverance, ... how cou'd I expect greater Deliverance?' (p 96). These thoughts lead naturally to his sense of his own past wickedness and, in the conviction of it, to a sense of 'Deliverance from Sin' (p 97). In reviewing his life in the world he sees, with a new sight, the many deliverances he has already been granted: 'such as my Escape from *Sallee*; my being taken up by the *Portuguese* Master of the Ship; my being planted so well in the *Brazils*; my receiving the Cargo from *England*, and the like' (p 131). He compares his life on the island to the 'feeding [of] *Elijah* by Ravens' (p 132) and calls it 'a long Series of Miracles.' Later on he tells us with respect to the cannibals that religion joined with prudence in convincing him that he ought not to slaughter those 'innocent Creatures,' and he adds 'I gave most humble Thanks on my Knees to God, that had thus deliver'd me from Blood-Guiltiness' (p 173).

But while the rhythm of danger and deliverance continues to inform the life of Crusoe on the island, his religious awakening wholly alters his perception of the nature of his imprisonment and the deliverance he seeks. Just after his sickness and fever Crusoe's notion of deliverance begins to change as he realizes that he 'was merely thoughtless of a God, or a Providence; [and] acted like a meer Brute from the Principles of Nature' (p 88). In this clearer vision he can distinguish between his old illusion of deliverance, which was from storms and prison, and the reality of his imprisonment in sin which demands a more important kind of deliverance:

Now I look'd back upon my past Life with such Horrour, and my Sins appear'd so dreadful, that my Soul sought nothing of God, but Deliverance from the Load of Guilt that bore down all my Comfort: As for my solitary Life it was nothing; I did not so much as pray to be deliver'd from it, or think of it; It was all of no Consideration in Comparison to this: And I add this Part here, to hint to whoever shall read it, that whenever they come to a true Sense of things, they will find Deliverance from Sin a much greater Blessing, than Deliverance from Affliction. (P 97)

He finally understands how, through imprisonment, he has gained a true deliverance, a 'different Sense' of deliverance indeed from his former notion of 'being deliver'd from the Captivity I was in' (p 96).

One result of his spiritual deliverance is that he becomes more or less reconciled to his island life and is able to give up the world: 'I look'd now upon the World as a Thing remote, which I had nothing to do with, no Expectation from, and indeed no Desires about ... as a Place I had liv'd in, but was come out of' (p 128). The division between the world and the island now appears as wide as the *'great Gulph fix'd'* between Abraham and Dives. For a while at least the island becomes a sort of paradise, a partially renewed Eden,[11] and Crusoe leads a spiritually improved existence if only because, as he points out, he has none of his old temptations. One of the lessons the island teaches, however, is that deliverance is never final. At the moment of his greatest confidence and composure, when he seems to have escaped from the rhythm of disaster and deliverance, his illusion is abruptly shattered by a human footprint in the sand, and the movement of Crusoe from the island back to the world begins.

Defoe's treatment of the process of Crusoe's return to the world is of considerable interest and complexity and will be the subject of the next section of this chapter. But we must first take note of the continuation of the theme of deliverance, and the slight but important shift in emphasis in the presentation of that theme in the latter half of the book. Crusoe's various deliverances by providence 'from so many un-seen Dangers' (p 175) begin to give way, about half-way through his account of his life in the island, to a pattern of deliverances performed by Crusoe on behalf of others. Crusoe first rescues Friday and then Old Friday and a Spaniard, all prisoners of cannibals. The people who come to the island as prisoners and are rescued by Crusoe are poten-tially agents of his deliverance, though Crusoe is wary about employing them. The Spaniard has companions on the mainland with whose help it might be possible for Crusoe to leave the island, but he is worried lest he should be betrayed: 'I told him it would be very hard, that I should be the Instrument of their Deliverance, and that they should after-wards make me their Prisoner in *New Spain*' (p 244).

Eventually Crusoe's deliverance from the island is brought about by the captain of the English ship, which arrives at the island in a state of mutiny. But first Crusoe has to rescue the captain and two other victims of the mutiny. As a deliverer Crusoe appears to the English captain to be divine or, at least, angelic. 'The poor Man with Tears running down his Face, and trembling, looking like one astonish'd, return'd, *Am I talking to God, or Man! Is it a real Man, or an Angel!'* Crusoe quickly assures him that he is not an angel but 'an *English-man*' (p 254). However, deliverers appear as angels because they are agents of providence, a point of view that Crusoe later adopts when, embracing the captain 'as my Deliverer,' he looks upon him 'as a Man sent from Heaven to deliver me' (p 273). Thus Crusoe's physical deliverance from the island (as well as his spiritual deliverance on it) is seen as an act of providence.

With Crusoe's return to the world at last, after more than twenty-eight years on the island, the pattern of deliverances seems to be complete. Yet Crusoe has one more grave danger to go through and yet one more deliverance granted to him. This section of the novel, Crusoe's journey across the Pyrenees, is sometimes thought of as an anticlimax, something added as an afterthought.[12] In fact it is by means of the ending that the island section acquires a depth and meaning from the contrast with the world outside it. Crusoe's encounter with the wolves, like his much earlier encounter with the lions and tigers along the African coast, dramatically emphasizes the dangers that beset man in the world. Crusoe draws our attention to the similarity of these two events when he remarks: 'except the Noise I once heard on the Shore of *Africa*, of which I have said something already, I never heard any thing that filled me with so much Horrour' (p 297). Spiritually, however, Crusoe is now stronger and better able to resist the evils of the world, aptly symbolized by the ferocious animals. The playful episode with the bear and the stout resistance offered to the wolves contrast with his earlier terror (and spiritual ignorance) in Africa, but the point is that such evils are a constant and manifest danger. The novel does not end with Crusoe's conversion, or even with his deliverance from the island, because the meaning of the continuing series of deliverances springs from a complex vision of the life of man which Crusoe calls a strange 'Chequer Work of Providence' (p 156). Or, as he puts it later on: 'How frequently in the Course of our Lives, the Evil which in it self we seek most to shun, and which when we are fallen into it, is the most dreadful to us, is oftentimes the very Means or Door of our Deliverance' (p 181). Here then in the theme of imprisonment and deliverance, exemplified in the life of Robinson Crusoe in solitude and in society, may be found a vision of the human condition that gives the novel its appropriate and distinctive structure.

II

The central shaping theme of deliverance in which Defoe's vision of the human predicament is rendered is supported by a related theme, that of reason and passion (or 'Fancy'), which helps to define the difference between Crusoe's life in the world and his life on the island. In his pre-island days Crusoe always loses the internal struggle to conquer his passions; his ruinous wandering thoughts predominate over his reason as he slides further and further into sin. On the island, however, Crusoe is forcibly released from his ruling passion and, even before his religious conversion, his existence grows more settled and rationally ordered, as the narrative of his developing skills at housekeeping and husbandry makes clear. Giving way to despair is probably his greatest danger, but, as he observes in counting up the relative evil and good that he has experienced, 'my Reason began now to master my Despondency' (p 65). The exercise of his reason provides Crusoe with the necessities of life – shelter, a table and chair, a small herd of goats, and eventually even bread. Not without a touch of pride he tells us of his discovery that, 'as Reason is the Substance and Original of the Mathematicks, so by stating and squaring everything by Reason, and by making the most rational Judgment of things, every Man may be in time Master of every mechanick Art' (p 68). Then, in the dramatic experience of personal conversion to religious belief that comes to Crusoe during his illness, faith in revelation is added to reason. Two years later, reflecting on this remarkable change, Crusoe compares his life on the island to his life in the world and observes 'how much more happy this Life I now led was, with all its miserable Circumstances, than the wicked, cursed, abominable Life I led all the past Part of my Days' (p 112). With a new perception of things he discovers that 'my very Desires alter'd, my Affection chang'd their Gusts, and my Delights were perfectly new' (pp 112–13).

Crusoe had been providentially separated from the world because nothing less could accomplish his salvation, and for several years after his conversion Crusoe's religious faith and self-control are tested only in solitude. Religious awakening does not of course free him from desires and temptations even though in solitude they are less frequent. Despite his newly found control Crusoe is occasionally overwhelmed by the desperate loneliness of his solitary imprisonment: 'In the midst of the greatest Composures of my Mind, this [thought] would break out upon me like a Storm, and make me wring my Hands, and weep like a Child' (p 113). Moreover, Crusoe is quite capable of failing to follow reason and of being led along by his 'Fancy.' When, for example, he builds a boat that is too heavy to move to the water he explains that 'This was a most preposterous Method; but the Eagerness of my Fancy prevail'd' (p 126). More serious still, he is even on one occasion subject to his old wandering inclination. In his 'rash' attempt to sail around the island he is almost driven by the current 'a thousand Leagues' into the ocean, and sees then 'how easy it [is] for the Providence of God to make the most miserable Condition Mankind could be in *worse*.' In his panic he looks back to his 'desolate solitary Island, as the most pleasant Place in the World.' 'O happy Desart,' he laments, 'I shall never see thee more' (p 139). We are reminded by incidents such as these that Crusoe, although converted, still of course shares with all men the attributes of our fallen nature.

The island without other human creatures is, however, a demi-paradise, providing only a partial test of the strength of Crusoe's religious faith. The importance of the dramatic appearance of 'the Print of a Man's naked Foot on the Shore' (p 153) is not simply that it is unexpected and surprisingly sudden but that it shatters Crusoe's tranquil existence and opens the movement of the second half of the novel, the story of Crusoe's return to the world. From this point onward Crusoe is severely tried as the world begins to intrude upon his calm island life. The second half of the novel is the history of Crusoe's ultimately successful, but often nearly disastrous, readjustment to the demands and temptations of the world. The optimism that some commentators[13] have found in the providential interpretation of *Robinson Crusoe* is qualified by the frequency and seriousness of Crusoe's backsliding. Crusoe comes very close indeed into falling back irretrievably into his old passionate, headstrong, irreligious existence. Defoe develops with considerable skill the theme of reason and passion, showing us the nature of Crusoe's travail and the intricate relationship between the world and the island.

Of the various episodes in the latter half of the novel which illustrate Crusoe's internal struggles none is more important or more complex than his reaction to the knowledge that the island may be inhabited. In a few pages Crusoe rapidly alternates between temporary loss of faith, a renewed sense of the unforeseeable but 'infinitely wise and good Providence of God' (pp 156–7), and then a relapse into terror so great that he determines to destroy all evidence of his life on the island. Defoe's vision of the 'uneven State of human Life' (p 156) suggests that reason and even 'religious Hope' are eternally threatened by the force of the passions. 'O what ridiculous Resolution Men take,' Crusoe later reflects, 'when possess'd with Fear! It deprives them of the Use of those Means which Reason offers for their Relief' (p 159).

The threat to Crusoe's rational control as well as to the 'calm, sedate Way of Living' (p 167) to which he manages to return is renewed when he comes across the remains of a cannibal feast. His imagination runs wild with ingenious schemes for massacring the cannibals. But once again he manages to pull back from his 'outrageous' plans for killing the savages 'for an Offence which I had not at all entred into a Discussion of in my Thoughts' (p 170). Eventually 'cooler and calmer Thoughts' prevail and Crusoe is able to 'give most humble Thanks on my Knees to God, that had thus deliver'd me from Blood-Guiltiness' (p 173).

One of the lessons that Crusoe must learn, however, is that reason, although necessary to subdue his unruly passions, is in itself insufficient as a guide for all human activity. In the course of reflecting on the fact that he might easily have fallen into the hands of the cannibals, Crusoe comes to realize how often he has been delivered from unforeseen and unforeseeable dangers. This thought leads him to reflect that frequently he has been spared, sometimes from death, by a 'secret Hint' or 'strange Impression upon the Mind' (p 175) that has told him what to do and even overruled his rational inclination to do otherwise. In the course of his extraordinary life there are 'many Examples' of the value of obeying such non-rational dictates, especially, he argues, 'in the latter Part of my inhabiting this unhappy Island' (p 175) when he has learned to acknowledge such 'secret Intimations of Providence' (p 176). Episode after episode in the second half of Crusoe's story acts as an example of, and comment upon, the shortsightedness of man, his inability to see beyond the immediate appearance of things.

With the coming of other men, first the savages, later the Europeans, the distinction between the world and the island slowly breaks down, and as it does Crusoe learns to bear the strain of a renewed encounter with society. The long process of Crusoe's return to the world is as carefully planned and even more gradual than his journey to the island. At each stage of this movement towards physical deliverance from the island, his spiritual deliverance is threatened and tested by the worldly passions that enter the island.

The European world begins to intrude upon his solitude even before his rescue of Friday when a Spanish ship is wrecked offshore. Crusoe is deeply moved by the sight of the shipwreck and distressed that there are no survivors. This event naturally stirs in Crusoe's mind partially suppressed thoughts of escape and, in spite of the 'dear bought Experience of Time' (p 195), he confesses that, 'if I had had the Boat that I went from *Sallee* in, I should have ventur'd to Sea, bound any where, I knew not whither' (p 194). Crusoe recognizes that this plan of escape is a 'foolish Scheme' (p 195) and 'the fruit of a disturb'd Mind' (p 198), but he argues that the emotions he felt were beyond rational control: 'All the Calm of Mind in my Resignation to Providence, and waiting the Issue of the Dispositions of Heaven, seem'd to be suspended; and I had, as it were, no Power to turn my Thoughts to any thing, but to the Project of a Voyage to the Main, which came upon me with such Force, and such an Impetuosity of Desire, that it was not to be resisted' (p 198). Now once more 'the eager prevailing Desire of Deliverance' (p 200) overcomes his self-control and religious trust. It is only when events lead to his rescue of Friday that Crusoe, in instructing the poor savage in Christian doctrine, discovers that, 'in laying Things open to him, I really inform'd and instructed my self in many Things, that either I did not know, or had not fully consider'd before' (p 220). In short, Crusoe's slow return to the world and to the society of men is part of his long religious education. And the process of spiritual testing is not complete even when Crusoe eventually leaves the island. In the final section of the novel Defoe will return Crusoe to a world that is as difficult and as threatening as the one that had defeated him twenty-eight years earlier. Through the theme of reason and passion Defoe thus makes clear to us the nature of Crusoe's failures and the extent of his achievement.

Throughout the latter half of the novel Crusoe repeatedly draws our attention to the difference between the 'happy Posture of my Affairs, in the first Years of my Habitation' on the island 'compar'd to the Life of Anxiety, Fear and Care, which I had liv'd ever since I had seen the Print of a Foot in the Sand' (p 196). That event marks one of the pivotal moments in the novel for it not only initiates Crusoe's return from solitude to society, the action and the theme of half the novel, but shifts the centre of gravity of the novel from spiritual autobiography to the larger, though related, subject of the struggle of individuals in society. Crusoe's spiritual state continues to be of considerable importance, but its importance is assessed in relation to the nature of man as seen in society. Thus *Robinson Crusoe* resembles a spiritual autobiography but goes beyond it.

Despite the saving goodness of some individuals the picture of human nature in general that the latter part of the novel presents is not an optimistic one. Crusoe's first sight of other men is of the savages whose unregenerate nature horrifies him. He believes that their cannibalism is the result of their 'abominable and vitiated Passions' and their 'hellish Degeneracy' (p 170), but he then reasons that they 'were not Murtherers ... any more than those Christians were Murtherers, who often put to Death the Prisoners taken in Battle; or more frequently, upon many Occasions, put whole Troops of Men to the Sword, without giving Quarter, though they threw down their Arms and submitted' (p 171). And he justifies not attacking them, in spite of their 'brutish and inhuman' practice, on the grounds that to do so would be a justification of the 'Conduct of the *Spaniards* in all their Barbarities practis'd in *America* ... where they destroy'd Millions of these People' (p 171). Thus the cannibals are really spared not because they now appear any the less degenerate, but because they share their murderous instincts with Europeans.

It is significant that the English ship which finally delivers Crusoe from his long confinement on the island arrives in a state of mutiny. The captain, his mate, and a passenger are about to be marooned on the island, and a struggle between Crusoe's party and the mutinous crew is necessary before Crusoe is finally able to leave. The struggle, it is worth noting, is between two forces radically different in temperament; the mutineers are impulsive and wayward while the captain and his companions (after they recover from their initial, and justified, despair) along with Crusoe act coolly and carefully. In this way the internal conflict, the struggle between reason and fancy within Crusoe, is enlarged and placed in a social setting.

The world to which Crusoe returns, and which comes to him, is much like the world he left twenty-eight years earlier, though he is better able to cope with it than he had been before his island experience. With the entry of other men into the island, 'all the Wickedness of the World' (p 128) seems to enter with them. The island acquires its first prison, a man's corpse is strung up as a warning to others, elaborate disguises and stratagems have to be adopted. In a word, the peace and harmony that Crusoe had known in solitude are forever destroyed; Crusoe's spiritual strength does not remain a fugitive and cloistered virtue. The purpose of his slow and often difficult re-entry into the world of men is to equip him spiritually to face that world. The closing episode of the novel, Crusoe's dangerous journey across the Pyrenees, completes the theme and the symmetrical structure of the book. His successful battle with the wolves in the Pyrenees is the final and appropriate demonstration of Crusoe's control in the face of the terrors and dangers of the world.

III

The tidal flux of *Robinson Crusoe*, Crusoe's movement towards and then away from the island, which gives a symmetrical shape to the book, is reflected in various supporting motifs. Crusoe is frequently at pains to tell us about the state of his clothing, for example, and his gradual loss and then recovery of European clothing stresses the rhythm of his imprisonment and deliverance. When he arrived on the shores of the island he 'had no Clothes to shift me' (p 47); while the only sign of his drowned companions were 'three of their Hats, one Cap, and two Shoes that were not Fellows' (p 46). Later, 'rummaging for Clothes' (p 50) on the wreck, he took away 'all the Mens Cloths that I could find' (p 54). At this stage Crusoe still expects to be rescued, and his preservation of the clothes is just sensible stockpiling. Later, however, he comes to accept his isolation and with it the fact that the 'Things which I had brought on Shore for my Help, were either quite gone, or very much wasted' (p 133). Among these things are his rapidly deteriorating clothes which he replaces at first by cutting down 'the great Watch-Coats' in order to make jackets and then by stitching together new clothes from 'the Skins of all the Creatures that I kill'd' (p 134). With the loss of the last traces of the world from which he is separated Crusoe becomes a creature of the island, dressed in 'a suit of Cloaths [made] wholly of these Skins' (p 135). Crusoe is more than a little aware of the slightly ludicrous figure he now makes as he offers us a 'Scetch of my Figure,' commenting: 'had any one in *England* been to meet such a Man as I was, it must either have frighted them, or rais'd a great deal of Laughter' (p 149). Once the movement back to the world begins Crusoe gradually acquires European clothes which he lists in careful detail. The Spanish wreck brings him 'some very good Shirts ... and about a dozen and half of Linnen white Handkerchiefs, and colour'd Neckcloths' (pp 192–3) but, he complains, no proper *'English* Shoes and Stockings,' only some Spanish shoes, 'rather what we call Pumps.' However, the wreck provides Crusoe with some European clothing for Friday, whose rescue is the next event of importance in the story: 'I gave him a pair of Linnen Drawers ... which with a little Alteration fitted him very well.' The rest of Friday's new clothes have to be made by Crusoe: 'a Jerkin of Goat's-skin [and] a Cap, which I had made of a Hare-skin, very convenient, and fashionable enough.' And he adds this description of poor Friday's pleased but awkward first experience of clothing: 'and thus he was cloath'd for the present, tollerably well; and was mightly well pleas'd to see himself almost as well cloath'd as his Master; It is true, he went awkardly in these Things at first [but] at length he took to them very well' (p 208). Friday is only partly dressed as a European (though of course his having any clothes at all is clearly a step in the right direction in Crusoe's eyes), but Crusoe's description of the cap as 'fashionable enough' and of Friday's getting used to the clothes shows a returning European, that is worldly, consciousness. It is fitting, furthermore, that both master and man are dressed partly in salvaged clothes and partly in skins. Friday has not yet been converted to Christianity, and Crusoe's movement back to the world has only begun. When at last the English ship arrives, Crusoe appears in his outlandish costume before the startled captain who wonders whether Crusoe is *a real Man, or an Angel* (p 254). But he is assured that, 'if God had sent an Angel to relieve you, he would have come better Cloath'd.' Appropriately, when the captain rewards Crusoe for his assistance, his greatest gift, among 'Abundance of other things,' is clothing. Again Crusoe meticulously lists the clothes, adding 'In a Word, he cloathed me from Head to Foot' (p 274). The density of the description in Crusoe's regular and careful accounts of the changing state of his clothing helps to establish our sense of the various stages of his movement away from and then back to the world. When Crusoe finally resumes European dress he finds it 'unpleasant, awkward, and uneasy.' Detail of this sort is not only an example of Defoe's fine sense of Crusoe's likely reaction; it also aptly suggests the difficulties Crusoe inevitably faces on his return to the world after his long solitary life on the island.

The relationship between the island and the world is suggested subtly too by Crusoe's changing attitude towards money. Within his first fortnight on the island Crusoe discovers on a visit to the wreck 'about Thirty six Pounds value in Money, some *European* Coin, some *Brazil*, some Pieces of Eight, some Gold, some Silver' (p 57). He apostrophizes the money disdainfully, more like one who has just renounced the world than one who has been forcibly separated from it: 'I smil'd to my self at the Sight of this Money, O Drug! Said I aloud, what art thou good for ... I have no Manner of use for thee, e'en remain where thou art, and go to the Bottom as a creature whose Life is not worth saving' (p 57). 'However,' he continues in a famous afterthought, 'upon Second Thoughts, I took it away,' revealing in that action his hope of an early rescue.[14] Later in one of his reflections on his condition as a man cut off from the world, he echoes Locke's dictum that the 'Things of this World, are of no farther good to us, than they are for our Use' (p 129). Now he calls the thirty-six pounds 'nasty sorry useless Stuff' that he has 'not the least Advantage' from: 'but there it lay in a Drawer, and grew mouldy with the Damp of the Cave' (p 129). The Spanish shipwreck brings more money to the island. On the drowned boy Crusoe finds two pieces of eight and a tobacco-pipe, but his reaction is typical of his island mood: 'the last was to me of ten times more value than the first' (p 189). On the wreck itself he comes across 'three great Bags of Pieces of Eight, which held about eleven hundred Pieces in all; and in one of them, wrapt up in a Paper, six Doubloons of Gold, and some small Bars or Wedges of Gold,' all of course useless to Crusoe as he emphasizes once again: 'as to the Money, I had no manner of occasion for it: 'Twas to me as the Dirt under my Feet; and I would have given all for three or four pair of *English* Shoes and Stockings' (p 193).

None the less Crusoe, again as an afterthought, takes the money away: 'Well, however, I lugg'd this Money home to my Cave, and laid it up, as I had done that before, which I brought from our own Ship.' Crusoe's casual 'Well, however' takes us back to his first fortnight on the island. But the Spanish shipwreck, as we have already seen, is part of Crusoe's gradual return to the world, and the continuation of the sentence reflects Crusoe's reviving interest in money and the world: 'but it was great Pity as I said, that the other Part of this Ship had not come to my Share; for I am satisfy'd I might have loaded my *Canoe* several Times over with Money, which if I had ever escap'd to *England*, would have lain here safe enough, till I might have come again and fetch'd it' (p 193). Significantly, and in striking contrast to his earlier scorn for it, Crusoe is now not only concerned about securing the money, but is already thinking about his return to the world and the value of the money there. Clearly, the Spanish wreck has revived Crusoe's hope of rescue and escape from the island and, with his mind already running ahead to life in the world, he ceases to think of the money as 'nasty sorry useless Stuff.' The difference between the world and the island is skilfully caught in Crusoe's changing attitudes.

When he finally leaves the island (carefully recording that he 'forgot not to take the Money,' p 278), Crusoe enters a world busily concerned with looking after money and property. One of his earliest concerns is to inquire into the state of his plantation and he is delighted to find that his old friend the captain is able to give him an account and advice. Indeed, Defoe devotes several pages to a detailed summary of Crusoe's financial standing (now considerable) and plans. Crusoe's care in looking after his estate and his selfless kindness to trusted friends such as the widow makes clear the degree to which his long ordeal on the island has at last equipped him to live again in the world. As he aptly remarks of himself, 'the latter End of *Job* was better than the Beginning' (p 284).

On the other hand, there is a side of Crusoe that is able to look back, a little wistfully, to the simplicity of life on the island where there was neither need for money nor fear of theft. In the world, by contrast, 'I had ne'er a Cave now to hide my Money in, or a Place where it might lye without Lock or Key, 'till it grew mouldy and tarnish'd before any Body would meddle with it' (p 286). Crusoe's changing attitude towards money throughout the novel calls attention to the paradisal security of the island in the early days and the contrasting difficulty of life outside it. And Crusoe himself here explicitly makes the point that Defoe's subtle narrative device had earlier implied.

Crusoe's discovery of the footprint in the sand begins the succession of linked events which leads to the first visit of the savages, to the rescue of Friday and later of the Spaniard and Old Friday, and thus to the end of Crusoe's absolute isolation. Friday plays a crucial role in the crescendo of deliverance that fills the narrative of Crusoe's last few years on the island, in the gradual reintroduction of Crusoe into human society, and as a foil to Crusoe's filial disobedience which initiated the action of the novel. He extends the motif of deliverance not merely by being rescued by Crusoe, but also by his conversion and spiritual deliverance, which complements and completes Crusoe's own. Later, as Crusoe's trusted companion he is instrumental in the rescue of his father and the Spaniard, in the capture of the crew of the mutinous ship, and thus, ultimately, in the deliverance of Crusoe.

The reuniting of Friday with his father and Friday's deep affection and concern for the elderly savage contrast sharply with Crusoe's steady determination to leave home against his father's commands and his mother's 'Entreaties and Perswasions' (p 3). Friday, by contrast, when he found his father, 'kiss'd him, embrac'd him, hugg'd him, cry'd, laugh'd, hollow'd, jump'd about, danc'd, sung, then cry'd again, wrung his Hands, beat his own Face, and Head, and then sung, and jump'd about again, like a distracted Creature' (p 238). Crusoe is probably thinking of the shameful difference between his own heartlessness in leaving his parents and the excited demonstration of affection from the 'poor *Savage*' when he records 'how it mov'd me to see what Extasy and filial Affection had work'd in this poor *Savage*, at the Sight of his Father, and of his being deliver'd from Death' (p 238). The rebuke to Crusoe that the behaviour of Friday towards his father suggests is one of the lessons of the island.

Crusoe's final comment on his deliverance from the island is to note what he calls the 'strange Concurrence of Days' (p 133). His deliverance on 19 December from 'this second Captivity,' he points out, occurred on 'the same Day of the Month, that I first made my Escape in the *Barco-Longo*, from among the *Moors* of *Sallee*' (p 278). Crusoe has recorded similar concurrences earlier. In a long reflective passage about the events of his life he recalls that 'The same Day of the Year that I escaped out of the Wreck of that Ship in *Yarmouth* Rodes, that same Day-Year afterwards I made my escape from *Sallee* in the Boat' (p 133). 19 December, then, is by coincidence the day on which he makes three escapes. Similarly, if we put two passages together, we discover that 1 September is the day on which he begins to run into the difficulties from which he is later delivered on 19 December. Early in the novel Crusoe had noted that he began the slave-trading journey that led to his imprisonment on 1 September, 'being the same Day eight Year that I went from my Father and Mother at *Hull*' (p 40). Later, on the island, when he lists the concurrence of days, he adds that 'the same Day I broke away from my Father and my Friends, and run away to *Hull*, in order to go to Sea; the same Day afterwards I was taken by the *Sallee* Man of war, and made a Slave' (p 133). The double 'Concurrence of Days,' 1 September and 19 December, in which Crusoe thrice runs into difficulty and thrice escapes underlines the thematic rhythm of imprisonment and deliverance that we have examined in the novel's structure. The island episode is to be seen not as fortuitous, but as the culmination of a pattern of deepening misfortune brought about by Crusoe's obstinacy and blindness and resolved only by his total isolation from the society of other men.

A third example of the concurrence of days is an important part of Crusoe's providential interpretation of the events of his life. The '30th of *September*' is both Crusoe's birthday and the 'same Day, I had my Life so miraculously saved 26 Year after, when I was cast on Shore in this Island' (p 133). And so, Crusoe adds, 'my wicked Life, and my solitary Life begun both on a Day.' As Barbara Hardy has aptly observed, 'Crusoe anticipated the critic who wants to point out the archetypal rebirth pattern in the novel.'[15] The synchronicity of events reinforces the vital meaning of Crusoe's double life in the world and on the island.

IV

Two clusters of images help to control and concentrate the novel's main themes and motifs. First, there are the images of the prison, of which the chief is the 'Island of Despair' conceived as a prison. Secondly, there are the animal images, both the terrifying lions and tigers along the African coast and the wolves in the Pyrenees, and, in deliberate contrast, the benign animals that provide Crusoe with food, clothing, and 'subjects' in his island kingdom. These two groups of images often work together, reinforcing one another, since the ensnarement and enclosure of animals is part of the imprisoning motif, and because Crusoe's passions, symbolized by wild animals, are a prison from which he is, in part, delivered.

The theme of imprisonment is introduced when Crusoe becomes a prisoner and slave of the captain of the Turkish rover, an episode which anticipates his much longer imprisonment on the island. But the double image of the island as, paradoxically, a place both of deliverance and of imprisonment derives its initial force from Crusoe's metaphor of the stayed execution to which he compares his journey from the foundering ship to the beach. His 'Reprieve' from a watery death is in another sense 'a dreadful Deliverance,' for he is now exposed to cold, starvation, and the threat of wild animals and savages. This thought throws him 'into such terrible Agonies of Mind' that he loses all reason, becomes like a wild animal himself, and runs about 'like a Mad-man' (p 47).

Indeed, in one sense, far from being delivered or granted a reprieve, Crusoe is condemned to solitary confinement. The 'Island was certainly a Prison to me, and that in the worst Sense in the World' (pp 96–7), he reflects, 'and my very Heart would die within me, to think of the Woods, the Mountains, the Desarts I was in; and how I was a Prisoner lock'd up with the Eternal Bars and Bolts of the Ocean, in an uninhabited Wilderness, without Redemption' (p 113). In this mood he curses the horrid island of despair as a prison, a desert, a barren, uninhabited place, and calls it unhappy and desolate. References to prisoners are frequent in the novel and set up an undercurrent of imprisonment which makes Crusoe's ardent desire to be delivered more poignant. A great part of Crusoe's activity is fishing and hunting, making 'Enclosures' for his animals, and, indeed, securing his own 'Enclosure.' He devotes most of his time during one week to what he calls, somewhat facetiously, 'the weighty Affair of making a Cage for my Poll.' And then, he adds perhaps by the natural association of ideas, 'I began to think of the poor Kid, which I had penn'd in within my little Circle' (pp 111–12). Crusoe gives us, too, a fairly long description of the 'Art to trap and snare' goats (p 145), of which his most successful method is the 'Pit-Fall.' The vocabulary of ensnarement and imprisonment, which mirrors Crusoe's own thoughts and memories, pervades the heavy air of confinement by which Crusoe is surrounded and from which he longs to escape.

If much of the early part of the island section is concerned with the enclosure of Crusoe and his animals, the latter part is concerned with the prisoners of the savages and the imprisoning of the mutinous English crew. The footprint in the sand marks the transition, for once Crusoe has seen it he lives in perpetual fear of being captured by the cannibals. In fact, the reverse occurs; he rescues a cannibal as skilfully as he had captured his goats, and in this way obtains a servant, Friday, who at first fails to realize his good fortune and stands 'trembling, as if he had been taken Prisoner' (p 203). With Friday's help he is able to rescue 'a white Man who lay upon the Beach of the Sea, with his Hands and Feet ty'd, with Flags, or Things like Rushes' (p 233) and also 'another poor Creature ... bound Hand and Foot' (p 237) who is Friday's father. After the subsequent departure of the Spaniard and Old Friday to the mainland to assist the Spaniard's companions there, Crusoe and Friday are able to effect the deliverance of the commander, the mate, and a passenger of an English ship and eventually, through a stratagem that resembles that of Prospero and Ariel in another 'inchanted Island,'[16] to take all the mutinous crew prisoner. In order that these men may be effectively held Crusoe, dividing his prisoners, sends three with Friday 'to the Cave, as to a Prison; and it was indeed a dismal Place, especially to Men in their Condition' (p 269). The others he sends to his bower 'and as it was fenc'd in, and they pinion'd, the Place was secure enough.' When all has been successfully accomplished, Crusoe rather smugly admonishes his prisoners in a metaphor characteristic of the imagery of the novel: 'I told them, I had had a full Account of their villainous Behaviour ... but that Providence had ensnar'd them in their own Ways, and that they were fallen into the Pit which they had digged for others' (p 275).

But while the island is a prison, it is also, and at the same time, a place of deliverance, a 'Reprieve' for Crusoe himself as well as for those who arrive as prisoners and are set free by Crusoe, who acts, as he says with reference to the Spaniards, as the 'Instrument of their Deliverance' (p 244). In a still more profound way the island is a deliverance, for although, as Crusoe remarks, 'the Island was certainly a Prison to me ... I learn'd to take it in another Sense' (pp 96–7). The novel's constant play on physical and spiritual imprisonment and deliverance (and the paradoxical nature of Defoe's vision which it reflects) is reinforced by the graphic image of the island as prison, a prison which becomes the (divine) means of his deliverance.[17]

In the chastened mood following his spiritual deliverance Crusoe sees his unhappy solitary imprisonment in a new light: 'How mercifully can our great Creator treat his Creatures, even in those Conditions in which they seem'd to be overwhelm'd in Destruction. How can he sweeten the bitterest Providences, and give us Cause to praise him for Dungeons and Prisons' (p 148).[18] Entirely cut off from the world, Crusoe is also, as he has come to realize, cut off from 'all the Wickedness of the World' (p 128), and he refers to 'my Reign, or my Captivity, which you please' (p 137), emphasizing in this phrase the paradoxical nature of the island that the language and imagery of the novel establish and reinforce.

This paradox, analogous to, and indeed involved in, the Christian paradox of freedom in service, is rooted in two modes of perception within the novel: man's immediate and limited impression of things (sight) and a God-given vision of things as they really are (insight). 'Thus we never see the true State of our Condition, till it is illustrated to us by its Contraries' (p 139), laments Crusoe when he is almost drowned while attempting to circumnavigate his island. Because of man's natural short-sightedness – 'So little do we see before us in the World' (p 252) – the human condition is fraught with uncertainty, insecurity, unexpected changes and turns. Indeed, at the best of times man is surrounded by unseen dangers that, if he were to know of them, would drive him to the brink of madness. As Crusoe observes:

How infinitely Good that Providence is, which has provided in its Government of Mankind, such narrow bounds to his Sight and Knowledge of Things, and though he walks in the midst of so many thousand Dangers, the Sight of which, if discover'd to him, would distract his Mind, and sink his Spirits; he is kept serene, and calm, by having the Events of Things hid from his Eyes, and knowing nothing of the Dangers which surround him. (P 196)

It is part of the human condition for man, as the life of Crusoe illustrates, to suffer terrible and unexpected turns of fortune because of his limited sight, while at the same time his blindness preserves him from the unbearable vision of his true state. The double image of the island as deliverance and prison helps to express and concentrate this essential paradox.

A constant reference to animals, which impinge upon Crusoe's life at nearly every point, establishes a second major pattern of imagery that serves both to deepen the significance of the dual nature of man by recalling his kinship with the beasts, and to throw into relief those special properties which mark the difference between life on the island

and life in the world. Both before and after the central island section, as we have noticed, Crusoe is in considerable danger from ravenous wild creatures, but on the island, though at first he is terribly afraid of the possibility of ferocious beasts, in fact nearly all the animals are benign and useful.[19] Significantly, threats to Crusoe's life from other creatures come from outside the island, specifically in human form. On the island Crusoe is cut off from 'the Wickedness of the World'; the savages come to Crusoe's island as intruders.

His first encounter with animals is along the African coast just after he has escaped from Sallee in a small boat. When Crusoe is forced to put into shore for water, he is in considerable danger, 'for to have fallen into the Hands of any of the Savages, had been as bad as to have fallen into the *Hands* of Lyons and Tygers' (p 25; my italics). The slight personification here reflects Crusoe's feelings about the similar nature of beasts and men – at least of savage men – and anticipates his fears on the island from these two sources. Similarly at the end of the novel Crusoe and his companions are in danger from the wolves, which behave 'as regularly as an Army drawn up by experienc'd Officers' (p 298), and 'from a kind of two-legged Wolves, which we were told, we were in most Danger from, especially on the *French* side of the Mountains' (p 291). And at another point, in a metaphor that seems natural to Crusoe who often sees human behaviour in animal terms, he remarks, 'I had rather be deliver'd up to the *Savages*, and be devour'd alive, than fall into the merciless Claws of the Priests' (p 244). The language and metaphors which associate the conduct of Europeans with that of savages and wild beasts emphasize the brutal side of man's dual nature, and provide a context for the parallel theme of the struggle in Crusoe between his reason and his base passions, of which the latter betrays his kinship with the beasts.

Defoe uses animal imagery to suggest how 'irrational the common Temper of Mankind is' (p 15). Similarly he uses different kinds of animals to suggest the difference between Crusoe's life alone on the island and life among men in the world. From his experience of the monstrous and frightening wild creatures of the African coast Crusoe expected and feared wild beasts on the island. In fact, all the island animals prove harmless and generally useful to Crusoe for food, clothing, even companionship. The change is marked by the first animal that Crusoe encounters after his arrival.

I found no Sign of any Visitor, only there sat a Creature like a wild Cat upon one of the Chests, which when I came towards it, ran away a little Distance, and then stood still; she sat very compos'd, and unconcern'd ... I presented my Gun at her, but ... she was perfectly unconcern'd at it, nor did she offer to stir away; upon which I toss'd her a Bit of Bisket ... and she went to it, smell'd of it, and ate it, and look'd (as pleas'd) for more, but I thanked her, and could spare no more; so she march'd off.   (Pp 54–5)

Unlike the 'monstrous' wild cats outside the island, this cat seems to be part of Crusoe's new world, sharing the island with him on equal terms. His facetious remark to the cat indicates a new relationship with the animal kingdom, a foreshadowing of Crusoe's eventual rule over the island when 'like a King' he dined alone with 'two Cats, one on one Side the Table, and one on the other, expecting now and then a Bit from my Hand, as a Mark of special Favour' (p 148). The kingdom over which Crusoe reigns numbers among its subjects not only the cats, dog, and parrot of his immediate 'Family,' but also 'Hares,' 'Foxes,' 'Goats,' 'Pidgeons,' 'Turtle or Tortoise,' and 'Penguins' (p 109), but no dangerous beasts, as he specifically points out when he remarks: 'I found no ravenous Beast, no furious Wolves or Tygers to threaten my Life, no venomous Creatures or poisonous, which I might feed on to my Hurt, no Savages to murther and devour me' (p 132). Gradually Crusoe becomes more and more a part of this animal world, dressing in animal skins, living as the father of his little animal family and as king of the island, and making a glorious, if slightly ridiculous, figure.

When Crusoe comes across the footprint in the sand all his former fears return: '*viz*. That of falling into the Hands of Cannibals, and Savages, who would have seiz'd on me with the same View, as I did of a Goat, or a Turtle' (p 197). The rational and generally happy life he had led is now succeeded by a life of cold fear and 'dismal Imaginations' (p 154), and Crusoe acts for a time like a frightened animal: 'When I came to my Castle, for so I think I call'd it ever after this, I fled into it like one pursued ... for never frighted Hare fled to Cover, or Fox to Earth, with more Terror of Mind than I to this Retreat' (p 154). Crusoe's Christian strength has hitherto been tested only in solitude; now it is to be tested in the infinitely more terrifying world of men. The movement of the second part of the novel and the animal imagery reinforce this pattern, showing the slow and difficult development of Crusoe 'like one pursued' into a man capable of routing the three hundred ravenous wolves at the novel's close.

The wreck of the Spanish ship near the island marks another significant stage in the process which ends Crusoe's isolation, and he is deeply stirred by memories of human society. The sole survivor of the ship, however, is a dog which Crusoe found 'almost dead for Hunger and Thirst' (p 191). 'I gave him a Cake of my Bread, and he eat it like a ravenous Wolf, that had been starving a Fortnight in the Snow,' Crusoe adds, in an unwitting anticipation of the chief episode after his return to Europe in the final section of the novel. The dog comes to Crusoe from the outside world, but he is rescued and brought to the island by Crusoe; he belongs to neither one world nor the other. But he provides a symbolic link between the peaceful animal kingdom of the island and the world with its ravenous wolves to which Crusoe will eventually return.

The ending of *Robinson Crusoe*, the story of the tortuous journey of Crusoe and his fellow travellers across the Pyrenees from Spain to France and the attack on them by wolves, has puzzled commentators who regret that the novel did not end with Crusoe's rescue from the island. But the ending serves an important purpose. In the final portion of the book Crusoe is brought up against the terrors and dangers of furious wild animals in an encounter similar to, but in fact even more perilous than, that which he had faced in Africa. Crusoe's confrontation with the wolves is to be his final test, and its dangers and outcome are essential to the organization and meaning of the book. In the world, as Crusoe rediscovers, man is surrounded by terrible perils, and the devil goes about seeking whom he may devour not as an old goat in a cave, but as three hundred ravenous wolves.

While the terrors are greater than in the earlier episode, the final encounter makes clear Crusoe's skill and confidence in marshalling his little band against the onslaught of the enemy. The tone of the account is highly revealing. Though the dangers are real, Crusoe's facetious admonition to his readers about the proper treatment of a bear takes us back to the island and Crusoe's contrasting description of the nonchalant cat: 'he is a very nice Gentleman, he won't go a Step out of his Way for a Prince' (p 293), Crusoe warns, and if you offer him an affront he will set 'all his other Business aside to pursue his Revenge; for he will have Satisfaction in Point of Honour.' But unlike the impassive cat, which though threatened with a gun was 'perfectly unconcern'd' and later 'march'd off,' the bear, 'once-affronted,' will follow 'at a good round rate, till he overtakes you' and 'has his Revenge.' The difference between the world and the island is suggested by the difference between the revengeful bear and the harmless cat, while at the same time Crusoe's steadiness in this episode and in the attack by the wolves which follows reveals a different man from the one who fled like a frightened hare to cover.

The furious wolves are not merely a pack of ravenous beasts such as most men are unlikely ever to encounter; they are also an image of the wickedness of the world, the rapacious evil that all men meet. Crusoe describes them as 'three hundred Devils' (p 302), and his successful battle against them, as Paul Hunter has pointed out, is Crusoe's 'final victory' in the 'war between good and evil.'[20] Moreover, the wolves suggest the mortal dangers that attack man in the form of other men, as the personification of the wolves and the extended metaphor of military combat suggest: the wolves 'advance,' 'in a Line, as regularly as an Army drawn up by experienc'd Officers'; 'upon firing the first Volley, the Enemy made a full Stop'; 'I found they stopp'd, but did not immediately retreat' (p 298); 'never was [there] a more furious Charge' (p 300); and so forth. Not all men are as rapacious as this picture of the wolves and the metaphor of the 'two-legged Wolves' suggest. Some individuals, the captain of the ship for one, display admirable gratitude and generosity. But Defoe's novels offer a vision of the life of man in which the unaided individual is continually threatened by dangers, both moral and physical. Not least of these is his own weak human nature. By providential intervention Crusoe is for many years set free from such dangers and temptations. But his story is not complete until he returns from that safe haven to the realities of the world. The language and imagery which we have been examining reinforce the structural contrast between the world and the island that gives form to Defoe's vision of the nature of man in society.

3   Moll as Whore and Thief

With *Moll Flanders* (1722) Defoe's vision of the life of man begins to grow darker. Crusoe's cheerful confidence and honest industry give place to Moll's cynical dishonesty and energetic exploitation of deception. Crusoe is a successor to a number of long-suffering biblical figures, the Prodigal Son, Job, Elijah, and the themes of his history, the contest between the two sides of man's nature and the saving order and hope of providence, are worked out within the structural contrast of the world and the island. Moll, on the other hand, in her humiliating discovery of the Elder Brother's deception, early and rapidly grasps the lesson about the nature of man that Crusoe takes so long to learn. Moll is less insistent about providence; she knows that life is a cheat. The knowledge that man is a short-sighted creature leads only to the conclusion that he can be taken advantage of. Where Crusoe is apt to explain things by reference to a sudden and unexpected turn of fortune or else as just punishment for past sins, Moll seeks an explanation in the constant deceptions that human beings practise upon one another for their own ends. While Crusoe is thankful that a merciful providence keeps present dangers and future events hid from our eyes, Moll rejoices that mankind 'cannot see into the Hearts of one another.'[1] The greatest confidence artist of her time, Moll's greatest fear is that of being found out.

The shift in Defoe's social novels towards the darker reaches of his psychology is reflected in the extension of the theme of appearance and disguise which began to be important towards the end of *Robinson Crusoe* and which is a vital shaping influence from *Moll Flanders* onwards. *Moll Flanders* is charged with the ambiguities of appearance and deception established first in the equivocal tone of the 'Author's Preface' and immediately confirmed by Moll's insistence on concealing her name 'till I dare own who I have been, as well as who I am' (p 7). Moreover, the special shape of the novel, fashioned according to Moll's two careers as whore (pp 59–188) and thief (pp 189–272), is informed and developed by the rhythm of concealments and disguises. This structure is supported by ironic motifs such as 'the Deceiver deceived' and the 'double Fraud,' and by a pattern of imagery and language which creates an atmosphere of ensnarement and duplicity.

I

To the reader in the early eighteenth century both Moll's professions would have been suggested by her first name. The *Oxford English Dictionary* gives two meanings in use in the seventeenth and eighteenth centuries for 'Moll' as a female Christian name. One of these, 'a prostitute' or the 'unmarried female companion of a professional thief' (which is probably very much the same thing), is still familiar, at least as recently as the American gangster film. The other meaning, suggesting a woman of no reputation or a thief, is associated with the name of Moll Cut-purse, 'the nickname of a notorious female of the first half of the Seventeenth century,' who appears in Middleton and Dekker's *Roaring Girl* (1610) and in Nathan Field's *Amends for Ladies* (1611). Moll herself is proudly aware of her namesake as she points out shortly after she takes up her new profession: 'I grew as impudent a Thief, and as dexterous, as ever *Moll Cut-Purse* was, tho',' she adds, perhaps with a suggestion of the other meaning, 'if Fame does not belie her, not half so Handsome' (p 201).

Moll's second name, which is ironical, also serves to define theme and structure. Towards the climax of her story, when she is worried about the envious malice of the other thieves, Moll pretends not to know why she was given the name of Moll Flanders by them: 'For it was no more of Affinity with my real Name, or with any of the Names I had ever gone by, than black is of Kin to white ... nor could I ever learn how they came to give me the Name, or what the Occasion of it was' (p 214). Moll's mystification is, of course, assumed since she knows perfectly well, like the sarcastic inmates of Newgate, that 'Flanders'[2] was the name of a fine lace very popular at the time and, along with gold watches and silver plate, one of the most convenient forms of portable property. As Mrs Vixen in *The Beggar's Opera* points out: 'Lace, Madam, lies in a small compass, and is of easy conveyance' (II, iv). The appropriateness of calling a *female* thief by the name of a valuable and expensive lace is obvious, and indeed Moll is closely associated, often ironically, with lace and lace-making long before she becomes a lace-stealer.

As a child Moll is taught to mend laces, an occupation that she naively imagines will enable her to avoid going into service and to become a 'gentlewoman.' In a brilliant short scene of social comment and comedy Defoe ironically anticipates the direction of Moll's life. Moll admits to her nurse that her idea of being a gentlewoman is 'to be able to Work for myself, and get enough to keep me without ... *going to Service*' (p 13): 'for says I, there is such a one, naming a Woman that mended Lace, and wash'd the Ladies Lac'd-heads, she, *says* I, is a Gentlewoman, and they call her Madam' (p 14). The nurse's reply is prophetic: 'Poor Child, says my good old Nurse, you may soon be such a Gentlewoman as that, for she is a Person of ill Fame, and has had two or three Bastards.' Moll's semantic confusion, which the young ladies of Colchester find so amusing, is compounded when her skill with the needle enables her to earn her pocket-money: 'so that now I was a Gentlewoman indeed, as I understood that Word, and as I desir'd to be, for by that time, I was twelve Years old, I not only found myself Cloaths, and paid my Nurse for my keeping, but got Money in my Pocket too' (p 15). Her childhood naivety about the meaning of 'Gentlewoman' throws into relief the appalling choices available in the eighteenth century for a woman with neither a dowry nor independent means. For much of her life Moll is faced with the sad alternatives of either mending lace or stealing it (pp 202, 217, 237).

The name 'Flanders' reflects and defines Moll's place in the criminal world; she is known by her deeds. It is an indication of her success and an intimation of her downfall. That Moll should bear the name of an extremely fine and valuable lace confirms her claim to be 'the greatest Artist of my time' (p 214). Moreover, Flanders lace was contraband, and one of Moll's enterprises during her criminal career is to report a cache of the lace and afterwards share the prize with the customs officers. As she remarks, 'Flanders-Lace, being then Prohibited, it was a good Booty to any Custom-House Officer that could come at it' (p 210). But her name also suggests the inevitability of Newgate. On the second page of the novel Moll tells us, facetiously, that her own mother 'was convicted of Felony for a certain petty Theft, scarce worth naming, (*viz*) Having an opportunity of borrowing three Pieces of fine *Holland*, of a certain Draper in *Cheapside*.' As Moll notes with more than a touch of pride, her own arrest is for stealing much more valuable material –

'two Peices of flower'd Silks, such as they call Brocaded Silk, very rich' (p 272)[3] – but her subsequent conviction and transportation repeat the pattern of her mother's story.

Moll's arrest takes place in a house 'Inhabited by a Man that sold Goods for a Weaver to the Mercers' (p 272), though Moll herself had earlier observed the special danger to the thief from such people (p 208). There is a particular threat to Moll from mercers and drapers, and from the material that they sell, that lingers about the name that her fellow thieves suggestively give her. References to lace, holland, silks, and so forth are particularly frequent during the third section of the novel where Moll is a thief, and they mount to a crescendo just before her arrest. When references to lace, linen drapers and mercers, 'Ells of *Dutch* Holland' (p 240), 'Five pieces of Silks, besides other Stuffs' (p 215), 'a very good Suit of *Indian* Damask, a Gown and Petticoat, a lac'd Head and Ruffles of a very good Flanders-Lace' (p 240) begin to appear on nearly every page, the climax is near.

But 'Moll Flanders' is not, as she points out in the opening sentence of the novel, her real name. 'My True Name is so well known in the Records, or Registers at *Newgate*,' she explains, 'that it is not to be expected I should set my Name, or the Account of my Family to this Work.' Concealing her true name not only from the reader but from the people with whom she works and lives is Moll's basic form of security. It also reminds us that Moll's is a world in which, like that of the professional spy, success comes only to the greatest artists in the arts of false appearance and sudden changes in disguise. Moll is, more than anything else, a consummate actress, able to live almost continually in a world of appearance. Only when, in the end, she comes to believe in her own acts, when appearance becomes reality itself, does that world begin to crumble.

Moll first adopts the name of Mrs Flanders when she is deserted by her linen-draper husband and has to shelter in the Mint. Later it is this name by which she is known among the other thieves and under which she is gleefully received by them in Newgate:[4] 'how did the harden'd Wretches that were there before me Triumph over me? what! Mrs. *Flanders* come to *Newgate* at last? what Mrs. *Mary*, Mrs. *Molly*, and after that plain *Moll Flanders*?' (p 275). Years before, more cautiously, she had kept her identity even from her Lancashire husband Jemy, despite her genuine affection for him: 'I GAVE him a Direction how to write to me,' she allows, 'tho' still I reserv'd the grand Secret, and never broke my Resolution, which was not to let him ever know my true Name, who I was, or where to be found' (p 159). But later her amazing success as a thief becomes unavoidably associated with her name. As Moll proudly boasts: 'the Success I had, made my Name as famous as any Thief of my sort ever had been' (p 262). None the less, though the name of 'Moll Flanders' is becoming notorious, no one is quite sure of her identity. Once, after she has passed 'a Piece of very good Damask' that she had stolen from a mercer's shop to her companion, the other woman is arrested by the mercer's messengers. Moll, meanwhile, has luckily taken refuge in a lace chamber above a near-by house from the window of which she sees the 'poor Creature drag'd away in Triumph to the Justice, who immediately committed her to *Newgate*' (p 221). At length, when Moll's comrade comes to trial she is sentenced to be transported, for although they 'ask'd her where this Mrs. *Flanders* was ... she could not produce her, neither could she give the least Account of' her (p 222). At this point the famous reputation and the actual person of Moll Flanders cannot be identified even by the thieves. Moll explains her success in remaining undetected: 'They all knew me by the Name of *Moll Flanders*, tho' even some of them rather believ'd I was she, than knew me to be so; my Name was publick among them indeed; but how to find me out they knew not, nor so much as how to guess at my Quarters ... and this wariness was my safety upon all these Occasions' (p 222). Eventually, however, after she has been falsely apprehended for stealing goods from a mercer, she is carried before a justice of the peace where, when asked for her name, she admits, 'I was very loath to give [it], but there was no remedy, so I told him my Name was *Mary Flanders*' (p 247). Moll never adequately explains this strange lapse in revealing her name, but the explanation is to be sought, I believe, in Moll's by now complete assumption of the role of the famous thief Moll Flanders. She has been taken in by her own act; the appearance she has so long sustained has become the reality she believes in. She is now terribly proud of being the famous Moll Flanders, and despite her perilous situation she can no longer suppress the desire to be identified.[5] A little later she reflects that she has given in her name to the magistrate: 'I knew that my Name was so well known among the People at *Hick's Hall*, the *Old Baily*, and such Places, that if this Cause came to be tryed openly, and my Name came to be enquir'd into, no Court would give much Damages, for the Reputation of a Person of such a Character' (p 248). From this point her downfall is inevitable,[6] and not long after Moll is arrested and carried to Newgate. After her trial, when she is waiting to be transported to America to re-establish herself as one of the 'new People in a new World' (p 304), significantly she no longer admits to being Moll Flanders. When Moll meets her Lancashire husband again in Newgate she explains to him that she has 'far'd the worse for being taken in the Prison for one *Moll Flanders*, who was a famous successful Thief, that all of them had heard of, but none of them had ever seen, but that *as he knew well* was none of my Name' (p 298). In the emphasis on her success ('famous,' 'successful,' 'that all of them had heard of') there is a lingering pride in her achievement, but Moll is now quite fully aware that it is time to take up a new role and adopt a new appearance. In this name, which symbolizes her immense success as a thief, with its ironic associations with the respectable alternative of lace-mending, its significant link with her mother in Newgate, and its place in the theme of disguise and appearance is illustrated Defoe's rich and complicated way of suggesting theme, and thereby developing structure.

II

The first part of the novel, from Moll's birth to the death of her first husband, casually introduces the themes of family relations and the prison which are to run throughout the novel, but which are intensified at certain points to develop and support the structure of individual sections. The pattern of repetition with variations which we call rhythm may work by establishing symmetry or contrast in either situation or characterization, but when it is successful it generally produces tension and irony. Neither theme is built up exclusively in any one of these ways, though it is probably true to say that the prison theme creates the greater tension, and the family or marriage theme the greater irony. Newgate prison is a threat which hangs over Moll's life from her birth in it, and to it she inexorably moves. Moll stays out of Newgate for so long that the strain, or tension, becomes too great even for her. The more intricate theme of family relations, which also takes its origin from Moll's birth in Newgate where her mother, a transport, has abandoned her, splinters into the related motifs of incest and marriage, child murder, suicide, and madness, and creates ironies of situation and character.[7] Nearly all Moll's important contracts with other people are or become, in varying ways, familial. The only person with whom Moll has extensive dealings who is not related to her either by blood or by marriage is her 'Governess,' but, significantly, Moll learns to call her 'Mother' (p 174). When situations or characters collide, creating coincidence, irony is produced. In *Moll Flanders* irony[8] of this kind is rarely isolated, but rather it derives its special quality from the pressure of preceding actions. Moll's horrible discovery in the midst of her happiness and security in Virginia that her marriage is incestuous and that her mother-in-law is actually her mother is anticipated by her fear that marriage to the younger brother of her first lover would be incestuous and her confession afterwards that, as she says, 'I committed Adultery and Incest ... every Day in my Desires, which without doubt, was as effectually Criminal' (p 59).

An examination of the first fifty pages of the novel reveals Defoe's careful preparation of Moll, and his readers, through the inheritance of Newgate that lingers about Moll's birth and the suggestion of adultery and incest that mars her first marriage, for the shattering revelations of the following sections. The first two pages establish Moll's links with Newgate. She was born there; her name is in its 'Records, or Registers'; and she often expects to leave the world 'by the Steps and the String.' These facts cast over the story an air of disguise and concealment, and, indeed, in the two opening paragraphs Moll brusquely explains that 'it is not to be expected I should set my Name, or the Account of my Family to this Work; perhaps, after my Death it may be better known, at present it would not be proper, no, not tho' a general Pardon should be issued, even without Exceptions and reserve of Persons or Crimes' (p 7). The story we are about to be told is not only criminal, she implies, but shameful, and Moll at the end of her life, writing her 'Memorandums,' knows that she has everything to lose. She is still living, as she has done for most of her life, in disguise. Moll's ties with Newgate not only anticipate her later career as a successful thief and her consequent return to prison, but are also part of the theme of family relations. Moll's mother, herself a thief in Newgate, 'pleaded her Belly' and was 'respited for about Seven Months' before she 'obtain'd the Favour of being Transported to the Plantations' (p 8). Moll is thus not only indirectly responsible for saving her mother's life; she is also the first of the abandoned children in the novel, and like her mother she is destined to go to Virginia. These events, her birth in Newgate and subsequent ignorance of her identity and her separation from her mother, prepare the way for the appalling irony of her marriage to her own brother and the discovery in Virginia of her mother. And these two shaping themes of family relations and the prison are linked, as we will see, not only in their beginning in Moll's birth in Newgate but also because they are worked out within the demands of the larger theme of deception and disguise which imposes conditions on Moll's life that render her successes in marriage and in theft hollow and mocking.

After this foreshadowing of events in the brief account of her origins, the narrative moves to Moll's innocent confrontation with the world of experience illustrated in two episodes, her misunderstanding of the word 'Gentlewoman' and her misunderstanding of the Elder Brother's motives and intentions towards her. Moll's supposition that a gentlewoman is one who earns her own living and her confident choice of the town whore as an example underline her early naivety. By contrast with her later cunning and 'art,' Moll at this point speaks naturally: 'I HAD no Policy in all this,' she explains, 'you may easily see it was all Nature' (p 12). Defoe, like the ladies of Colchester, is amused by Moll's misunderstanding and plays on the equivocation humorously. But in this short episode is displayed his economy of technique. In Moll's insistence that the whore is a gentlewoman and that she 'would be such a Gentlewoman as that' (p 14) Defoe not only ironically antici-pates the true course of Moll's life (she becomes both a gentlewoman *and* 'such a Gentlewoman as that'), but also subtly directs our attention to the conditions of Moll's world, in which, as Moll early learns, things are not necessarily as they first appear to be. In this lesson, which is reinforced shortly afterwards by her sad and bitter experience with the Elder Brother, Moll discovers a deep sense of equivocation in the affairs of men which she later learns to exploit with so much success and which draws her on into a state of chronic mendacity. And, of course, through the exploitation of the techniques of deception, in taking advantage of other people's misunderstanding, Moll fulfils her childhood desire to become a gentlewoman, or at least a woman who passes as a gentlewoman.

On the death of her 'Nurse' Moll is taken into the house of a 'good Gentlewoman' where she picks up a genteel education by imitating the daughters of the house. 'By this Means,' she remarks, 'I had ... all the Advantages of Education that I could have had, if I had been as much a Gentlewoman as they were' (p 18). Moll proudly makes an interesting distinction between the accomplishments of the young ladies, which were largely acquired through education, and her own gifts, which were 'of Nature' (p 18). Moll takes her place in a line of talented bastards who make nature their goddess. It is generally the misfortune of such people to discover that they live in a world where natural endowments are not enough. Her beauty and high spirits recommend her to the Elder Brother, and her vanity and susceptibility to flattery make her his mistress. But he shares the conventional attitude of his sisters, who point out that Moll 'has not a Groat in the World' (p 43), and he refuses to fulfil his promise to make her his wife. Only the honest and simple Younger Brother Robin is prepared to accept the dowry of nature, 'Beauty' and 'good Humour,' in place of the conven-tional dowry of money, and to marry Moll.

In her affair with the Elder Brother Moll exhibits a blindness which ceases to be characteristic of her when the affair is over. She mentions repeatedly her infatuation and short-sightedness and points out that she 'acted as if there was no such thing as any kind of Love, but that which tended to Matrimony' (p 24). It is the momentous realization a little later that there may be love without matrimony as there may be matrimony without love that shapes the whole course of Moll's life. Jilted by the Elder Brother and aware now of hypocrisy and deception, Moll prudently marries Robin, not for love but for money, and in that act begins a pattern that is to inform a significant proportion of her life and her story. Woven into this pattern is the dark thread of incest which first appears when Moll with horror and indignation rejects the suggestion of the Elder Brother that she consider Robin: '*I ask'd him* warmly what Opinion he must have of my Modesty, that he could suppose, I should so much as Entertain a thought of lying with two Brothers? ... I could never entertain a thought so Dishonourable to my self, and so Base to him; and therefore, I entreated him if he had one Grain of Respect or Affection left for me, that he would speak no more of it to me' (p 41). The Elder Brother, with consummate skill and hypocrisy, turns Moll's argument back upon her only a little while later when he protests that he loves Moll as well as ever, 'yet, Sense of Vertue had not so far forsaken him, as to suffer him to lye with a Woman, that his Brother Courted to make his Wife' (p 56). Caught by her own argument and recognizing realistically that she is in danger of being 'turn'd out to the wide World, a mere cast off Whore' (p 56), Moll comes to terms. Yet the theme of incest lingers: I never was in Bed with my Husband,' Moll confesses, 'but I wish'd my self in the Arms of his Brother' (p 59). The incest and adultery that Moll here fears are compounded later when the brother she sleeps with is indeed her own brother, and not merely the brother of her husband. Again the opposition of love and money[9] which marks the difference in Moll's relation with the brothers will later be an important motif in Moll's 'marriage' with her Lancashire husband Jemy, whom she weds for money but whom alone among her husbands she genuinely loves. Moll's love for Jemy and the fortune that she eventually brings him after they are both transported from Newgate to Virginia is one of the major unifying strands of the novel.

There are two other points of interest in this first section which contribute to the development of theme and structure. In the course of her intrigue with the Elder Brother Moll learns to adopt a disguise in order to meet him at a house in Mile End. Moll leaves home 'so that there was not the least Suspicion in the House' in 'no Dress, other than before.' But, she adds, 'except that I had a Hood, a Mask, a Fan and a pair of Gloves in my Pocket' (p 28), all fashionable articles but useful to a woman who prefers to move about secretly. Moll's instinct for disguise (not to mention Defoe's fascination with it), fostered by the need for deception in her liaison with the Elder Brother, develops readily into the indispensable techniques of the successful whore and thief. What begins as a mode of deception is to become a mode of existence.

Moll's forsaking her children is an action that is to be repeated later on, but it also takes us back to her own birth in Newgate where she is deserted when her mother is transported. On the simplest structural level it is necessary for Moll's children to be taken off her hands, as she puts it, if she is to have the freedom of action that the plot requires, but the thematic implications go deeper. Later, in Virginia, her husband-brother is to accuse her of being an 'unnatural Mother' (p 91) because she wants to forsake her children and return to England. Ironically, as we know, Moll is an 'unnatural' mother and an 'unnatural' wife in a sense that her husband does not suspect. Moll's desertion of her children here, as later, may be seen as part of a larger pattern, or theme, of which her fears that her child will be murdered by an unscrupulous nurse and her temptation to murder the young girl whose necklace she steals also form a part.

I have called this theme the theme of family relations because it involves not only the relations of parents and children, but also those of husbands and wives, brothers and sisters, and, ultimately, the whole order of society which Defoe believed was built upon the family.[10] For Defoe a well-ordered and settled society rested upon the foundations of family life which demanded both natural affections and, like society itself, orderly subordination. In this connection it is interesting to note the lack of proper authority in the Colchester family: 'And as to the Father, he was a Man in a hurry of publick Affairs, and getting Money, seldom at Home, thoughtful of the main Chance, but left all those Things [specifically, the question of Moll's marriage with Robin] to his Wife' (p 54). In the non-fiction that he wrote at the same time as the novels Defoe turned his attention to such social questions as family order, religious courtship, the role and position of servants, and the education of children. In the novels he investigates similar themes, but in a darker setting. In the world of Defoe's novels there is an ever-present threat, sometimes carried out, that individuals will slip off the normal road of sanity, family security, natural affections to children, and so forth, not only into a world of bestial desires and ungoverned passions (as in *Robinson Crusoe*), but into a dark world of madness, incest, child murder, and suicide. Such things are part of life's nasty and unexpected turns and the temptations of the devil, a result in part of man's limited sight, and in part of his brutal nature. *Moll Flanders* is a novel about a return – to Newgate – which is the emblem of hell and the punishment for the sins of the heroine. Among the sins for which Moll is surely punished by the return to Newgate is that of having abandoned her children. Yet one of the structural ironies of the novel is that Moll was herself abandoned there.

III

Moll's history, after she is 'left loose to the World' (p 59) by the death of Robin and until she turns thief, is shaped by her four subsequent marriages. Moll announces Robin's death with characteristic abruptness. 'IT concerns the Story in Hand very little, to enter into the farther particulars of the Family, or of myself, for the five Years that I liv'd with this Husband; only to observe that I had two Children by him, and that at the end of five Year he Died' (p 58). Her concept of 'the Story in Hand,' the nearest thing to an authorial remark on narrative method that we can expect to find in the novel, is one shaped by the pressure of life in the world. The momentous change from security to insecurity, signalled by Moll's twice mentioning her fear of being 'left alone in the World to shift for myself' (p 57) – in fact this fear is offered as an explanation for her reluctant first marraige – is brought about by Robin's death five years later. Moll summarizes her changed position in this way: 'I was now *as above*, left loose to the World, and being still Young and Handsome, as every body said of me, *and I assure you, I though my self so*, and with a tollerable Fortune in my Pocket, I put no small value upon my self' (59).

Statements of this kind, which put forward Moll's views on marriage, her own prospects, and the role of women in courtship, provide a context for her various marriages, which seem at times only so many illustrations of her thesis that 'a Woman should never be kept for a Mistress, that had Money to keep her self' (p 61),[11] and amount to what is really a debate on marriage. Moll's newly acquired realism, which characterizes her attitude as she is about to embark on a career of marriage and prostitution, stands sharply in contrast to her naivety a few years earlier. 'I had been trick'd once by *that Cheat call'd* LOVE,' she admits, 'but the Game was over; I was resolv'd now to be Married, or Nothing, and to be well Married, or not at all' (p 60). Her new knowledge she has 'learnt by Experience' in London: '(*viz.*) That the State of things was altered, as to Matrimony ... that Marriages were here the

Consequences of politick Schemes, for forming Interests, and carrying on Business, and that LOVE had no Share, or but very little in the Matter' (p 67).

The marriage debate in *Moll Flanders* is particularly interesting when we consider that Defoe wrote a work on *Religious Courtship* in the same year, a work that reveals some strange parallels as well as contrasts with the novel. The whole area of family relationships, of the duty between parents and children, between husbands and wives, and indeed between masters and servants, preoccupied Defoe during the period in which he was writing the novels. *Moll Flanders* is Defoe's fictional treatment of the marriage theme which is the subject of the sober manual *Religious Courtship* (1722).

Religious Courtship is a consideration of the rights and obligations of both children and parents with respect to courtship and marriage. In a series of dialogues between members of a family Defoe presents two cases which illustrate in different ways his argument that the partners of a marriage ought to be agreed about religion, whether that means that both must be religious (Part I), or that they must have the same religion (Part II). Defoe clearly felt that parental authority was an indispensable force for order in families and society but ought none the less to be exercised only with responsibility and with respect for conscience. The two parts of *Religious Courtship* illustrate in different ways cases of misapplied parental authority. In Part I the father is at fault for exceeding his authority, and his daughter is vindicated in her refusal to marry; in Part II he is at fault for failing in his responsibility for satisfying himself about the religion of his daughter's suitor and, consequently, for not exercising his authority by opposing the match.

The moral and religious arguments of *Religious Courtship*, particularly those of the Eldest Sister, who represents Defoe's own outlook, pass into *Moll Flanders* where they are adjusted to fit Moll's cynical views and where they support the marriage theme. In *Religious Courtship* the Eldest Sister, speaking to her first sister, warns her of the risks of not examining the religious credentials of her suitor: 'I am only arguing, or rather persuading you to inform yourself of things, and know beforehand what you are going to do, that you may not run into misery blindfold, and make your marriage.be, as old Hobbes said of his death, a leap in the dark.'[12] When her sister replies, 'I think all marriages are a leap in the dark in one respect or another,' the Eldest Sister explains that 'It is true there is a hazard in every part of the change of life; we risk our peace, our affection, our liberty, our fortunes, but we ought never to risk our religion' (p 205). The Eldest Sister, who is here mainly concerned with the question of religion, in a similar metaphor extends her argument to emphasize in general the advantage that men take in courtship and the terrible risk the women are exposed to when they are not prepared to find out what sort of men their suitors truly are: 'the times terrify me; the education, the manner, the conduct of gentlemen is now so universally loose, that I think for a young woman to marry, is like a horse rushing into the battle; I have not courage so much as to think of it' (p 123).

In the novel Moll employs the same arguments and even the same images as the Eldest Sister to support her contention that a woman, 'if she manages well, may be Marry'd safely one time or other; but if she precipitates herself, it is ten Thousand to one but she is undone' (p 76). However, marrying 'safely' for Moll is not a religious matter but a financial one, and managing well means that, rather than losing her own money, a woman may come to live as the wife of a well-to-do gentleman and yet preserve her own fortune 'so in Trustees, without letting him know any thing of it, that it was quite out of his reach, and made him be very well content with the rest' (p 73). Moll, like Defoe, feels that 'the Age is so Wicked, and the Sex so Debauch'd' (p 74) and 'the Lives of very few Men now a-Days will bear a Character' (p 75) that women who do not look out for themselves and who rush into marriage are to be pitied as mad:

As for Women that do not think their own Safety worth their Thought, that impatient of their present State, resolve *as they call it* to take the first good Christian that comes; that run into Matrimony, as a Horse rushes into the Battle; I can say nothing to them, but this, that they are a Sort of Ladies that are to be pray'd for among the rest of distemper'd People; and to me they look like People that venture their whole Estates in a Lottery where there is a Hundred Thousand Blanks to one Prize.   (P 75)

'In short,' she adds a little later on, a man 'must have a very contemptible Opinion of her Capacities, nay, even of her Understanding, that having but one Cast for her Life, shall cast that Life away at once, and make Matrimony like Death, be *a leap in the dark*' (p 75). Moll's line of argument in the novel follows the line of argument of the Eldest Sister in *Religious Courtship*, employing the very images of the horse rushing into battle and the leap in the dark and insisting on female independence. The difference lies of course in the total elimination in the novel of the Eldest Sister's religious concern which alone justifies her stand. The perversity of Moll's remarks is that they are distortions of the Eldest Sister's comments.

It has been argued that, although there may be elements of local irony in *Moll Flanders*, there is no pervasive, structural irony because 'there is certainly nothing in *Moll Flanders* which clearly indicates that Defoe sees the story differently from the heroine.'[13] This is true only in the sense that Defoe's imaginative identification with his heroine is so complete that, on the surface, her scheming passes for justifiable common sense and the moral backdrop against which her immoral actions are performed is hard to detect. Lack of aesthetic distance is a fault in a satirist, and in the case of *The Shortest Way with the Dissenters* it had caused Defoe trouble before. But *Religious Courtship* provides evidence that Moll's point of view is not Defoe's, a fact that is confirmed by the widely different results of Moll's convictions and those of the Eldest Sister's. The course of Moll's disastrous marriage career silently confutes her arguments. And since the marriage theme is linked to the return to Newgate, structural irony is indeed established. As the story unfolds and we can see the interdependence and relation of all its parts, the appalling falseness of Moll's doctrine becomes apparent. It is a function of the total structure of the novel to discover the significance of Moll's reunion in Newgate with Jemy. Significantly, the only marriage that is successful and lasting is the one that she remakes, after the expiation of Newgate, out of love and not as the consequence of a politic scheme for carrying on business, and this fact of course gives the lie to her earlier doctrine.[14]

Moll's marriage with Robin is only the first of a series of cheating marriages, and after his death she is resolved, with the enticement of her money, to be 'well Married' (p 60) again. She is prepared to settle for a tradesman, provided he can at least *appear* a gentleman on occasion, and accordingly she marries a draper, an 'amphibious Creature, this *Land-water-thing*, call'd, a *Gentleman-Tradesman*' (p 60). The only adventure with this husband that she records is, suitably enough, their week-long trip to Oxford disguised 'like Quality': 'The Servants all call'd him my Lord, and the Inn-Keepers you may be sure did the like, and I was *her Honour*, the Countess; and thus we Travel'd to OXFORD, and a very pleasant Journey we had' (p 61). And Moll continues, facetiously acknowledging the difference between their fine appearance and the meagre reality, 'not a Beggar alive knew better how to be a Lord than my Husband' (p 61). Moll evidently enjoyed this role-playing and she was doubtless as successful as her husband in her disguise. But Moll's second venture into disguise is a prelude to the disaster brought about by her husband's extravagance, and within a page she is assessing what she has saved from the financial collapse.

Apprehensive about the commissioners who would have seized her residue of portable property in settlement for her husband's debts, Moll decides to go 'quite out of my Knowledge, and go by another Name' (p 64). Having taken lodgings in the Mint, a place of shelter for debtors and a grim portent of Newgate, she once again adopts a disguise by dressing up 'in the Habit of a Widow' and calling herself, for the first time, 'Mrs. *Flanders*' (p 64). Here she meets a widow of a ship's captain with whom she is persuaded to leave and set herself up in a part of town where they are both likely to meet 'some good Captain of a Ship' (p 66). Her experience at this time convinces her that 'the [marriage] Market run very Unhappily on the Mens side' and 'the Women had lost the Privilege of saying NO' (p 67). Although she is doing the same thing herself, Moll indignantly observes that 'the Men made no scruple to set themselves out, and to go a Fortune Hunting, *as they call it*, when they had really no Fortune themselves to Demand it' (p 68). Moll is not at all prepared to accept the male argument that the shortage of men means that the women must take whom they can. 'On the Contrary,' she asserts, 'the Women have ten Thousand times the more Reason to be wary, and backward, by how much the hazard of being betray'd is the greater; and would the Ladies consider this, and act the wary Part, they would discover every Cheat that offer'd' (p 75). The only way to prosper, she has come to believe, is to deceive the deceiver, and that is what she sets out to do.

Moll's third marriage carries her farther along the path of deception. In her marriage with Robin, though she had cheated him in ways he never discovered, Moll could not make any false pretences to a fortune. In her second marriage, although, as she says, 'I was catch'd in the very Snare, which *as I might say*, I laid for my self' (p 60), yet she is worth £1200, a sum which her spendthrift husband quickly reduces by half. But for her third marriage, realizing the world openly says that 'the Widow had no Fortune, and to say this, was to say all that was Ill of me,' Moll resolves to make 'a new Appearance in some other Place where I was not known, and even to pass by another Name if I found Occasion' (p 76). Later as a thief Moll will similarly learn to conceal her true identity in frequent changes of disguise, though then the habit of shape-changing will be more obsessive and necessary: 'generally I took up new Figures,' Moll recalls later, 'and contriv'd to appear in new Shapes every time I went abroad' (p 262). Advised by her good friend the captain's wife, Moll decides to pass as a woman who has a fortune. She points out that in doing this she is only adopting the cheats of the men and therefore that 'it was but just to deal with them in their own way, and if it was possible, to Deceive the Deceiver' (p 77). In this 'unhappy Proposal' Moll commits herself ever more deeply to a pattern of disguise and deception that gradually enmeshes her and drags her at last into Newgate.

By wary management, challenging his declaration of love by asserting that she is poor, Moll so traps her suitor that 'tho' he might say afterward he was cheated, yet he could never say that I had cheated him' (p 80). 'And thus I got over the Fraud of *passing for a Fortune without Money*,' Moll concludes, 'and cheating a Man into Marrying me on pretence of a Fortune; which, *by the way*, I take to be one of the most dangerous Steps a Woman can take, and in which she runs the most hazard of being ill us'd afterwards' (p 84).

But the pattern of deception, which casts a shadow over this marriage, grows more sinister when Moll discovers that it is she who is ultimately deceived. Cheated by life itself into marrying her own brother, Moll suffers one of those unexpected and nasty blows of fortune that come upon us in the midst of our prosperity, and which are an important feature of Defoe's vision of the human condition. Into the unhappy process of Moll's discovery are woven the links between Moll's life and her mother's which increase the pressure of irony upon the shape of the novel. At the centre of the interlinked pattern which joins Moll, her mother, her brother (and husband), and Jemy lies Virginia which Moll visits twice, once in connection with each of her two careers. In Virginia, in conversation with her mother (-in-law), Moll discovers that 'in her younger days she had been both WHORE and THIEF' (p 89), a fact that establishes a further parallel with the life of Moll (who has been a whore, and who will be a thief, and who will eventually be transported, again like her mother, from Newgate to Virginia). Before her first visit Moll is worried that, if she marries her suitor (her unknown brother), she will have to go with him to live on his plantation in Virginia, and she tells him in an ironic anticipation of her second voyage many years later that she 'did not care to be Transported' (p 81). Moll's mother, partly one suspects in proud self-defence, makes the point to Moll that Virginia furnishes an opportunity for the transported criminal to build a new life: 'many a *Newgate* Bird,' in the new world she asserts, 'becomes a great Man' (p 86), an argument that Moll will later use to rouse and sustain the spirits of

Jemy who finds the enterprise ungentlemanly. Defoe is obviously delighted by Moll's mother's point that 'several Justices of the Peace, Officers of the Train Bands, and Magistrates of the Towns they live in ... have been burnt in the Hand' (p 86), but he also takes it seriously enough to make the same point elsewhere.[15] On her second voyage to Virginia Moll is accompanied by her husband Jemy, whom she married while she was a whore, but meets again later in Newgate when she is a thief. Thus Moll's two visits to Virginia are the direct result of her two careers, which are further bound together in this pattern of interlinked persons, places, and careers by the geographical parallel.

Within the structure of the novel Moll's incestuous marriage with her own brother, 'the worst sort of Whoredom' (p 90), extends the theme of incest established by Moll's terrible fear that in marrying Robin she was committing adultery and incest. The element of deception in each of her 'marriages' seems to bear the seeds of its own punishment. The events of the first visit to Virginia are the nadir of Moll's whoredom, and it is somehow fitting that this incestuous marriage ends with an accusation of madness (p 92) and an attempt at suicide (p 104). She returns to a life in England that leads inexorably to Newgate and transportation back to Virginia. Only on the second visit, after the expiation of the hell of Newgate, are her mother's promises for a new life in a new world fulfilled. Both visits span eight years, providing a parallel with the twelve years each that Moll claims she spends as whore and thief. We have already noted the numerical symbolism of *Robinson Crusoe* (the 'strange Concurrence of Days,' p 133), and it seems probable that Defoe intended his readers to see a special connection between the two visits to Virginia.

From the time of her return to England when 'a new Scene of Life' (p 105) opened until that time had passed when she 'might expect to be courted for a Mistress' (p 189), Moll is kept for six years as the mistress of a man she meets in Bath, and is afterwards twice married again. In the first of these episodes Moll emphasizes, negatively, her contention that 'a Woman should never be kept for a Mistress that had the Money to keep her self' (p 61). Unfortunately, in this case marriage is impossible since the gentleman, who clearly has more scruples on this point than Moll, has a wife still living, though 'distemper'd in her Head' (p 109). Once again the shadow of madness darkens Moll's illicit relationship. Oddly, too, the incest theme occurs again when Moll and her friend arrive one night at an inn that has no lodging but a large room with two beds. The explanation of Moll's companion to the innkeeper must have been more poignant to Moll than he could have realized: 'these Beds will do,' he said, 'and as for the rest, we are too near a kin to lye together, tho' we may Lodge near one another.' But Moll seems only concerned with appearances and observes that 'this put an honest Face on the thing too' (p 115).

A number of details in this section point to the growing role of appearance and disguise in Moll's life. When Moll requires the services of a midwife, her landlady and friend, dexterously arranging for Moll to pass as the wife of one 'Sir *Walter Cleave*,' manages to bring Moll off 'with Reputation.' Defoe's fine hand for psychological detail is to be seen in Moll's reaction:

This satisfied the Parish Officers presently, and I lay INN with as much Credit as I could have done if I had really been my Lady *Cleave*; and was assisted in my Travel by three or four of the best Citizens Wives of *Bath*, who liv'd in the Neighbourhood, which however made me a little the more expensive to him, I often expressed my concern to him about it, but he bid me not be concern'd at it.   (P 117)

Moll is, however, not above taking advantage of her lover by laying up 'as much Money as I could for a wet Day, as I call'd it; making him believe it was all spent upon *the extraordinary appearance of things* in my Lying Inn' (p 118, my italics). Later, when her lover is sick and Moll is desperate to have news of him, she visits his house disguised 'like a Servant Maid in a Round Cap and Straw Hat' (p 121), and learns from a maid that the doctors hold out little hope for his recovery. Here Moll goes beyond the pretence of passing for a woman of fortune or a lady of quality for the pure sport of it, into the use of a costume for the specific purpose of obtaining information. Later on her amazing success as a thief will be built upon her skill in constantly changing her appearance and effectively concealing her identity even from her closest companions.

Moll's fourth and fifth marriages together demonstrate her renewed determination to treat marriage as 'the Consequences of politick Schemes, for forming Interests, and carrying on Business' (p 67). Significantly, having had an attractive offer of marriage, she sets out for Lancashire, leaving behind in London her banker 'who I was not so much in Love with, as not to leave him for a Richer' (p 141). Later, after the 'double Fraud' (p 148) of her Lancashire marriage and the subsequent birth of a child, Moll again encourages her 'honest Citizen' (p 141) and marries him. Moll's fourth marriage, which temporarily interrupts the banker's courtship, is her most important marriage, not only because it is part of the structural pattern built up from Moll's two careers and her two visits to Virginia, but also because of the surprising depth of her emotional commitment to Jemy, illustrated in a strange episode of telepathy, which entirely alters the nature of a marriage in which love was meant to have 'no Share ... in the Matter' (p 67).

Like the tragic marriage with her brother, Moll's marriage to Jemy is an attempt 'to Deceive the Deceiver' (p 77). But, once again, the result of her mischief is her own deception, 'a cheat on both Sides' (p 173), as her governess later calls it. Appropriately, both sides are highly skilled in the arts of sham appearance. Moll, on the one hand, first fell into the position of being courted by Jemy because his former mistress and Moll's London landlady, 'a North Country Woman that went for a Gentlewoman' (p 129), 'was always made to believe, as every Body else was, that I was a great Fortune' (p 129). Jemy, on the other hand, who is posing as the brother of Moll's 'Friend, *as I call'd her*' (p 141), makes a dazzling show of accustomed wealth and position. Before she actually reveals the double fraud, Moll's description of Jemy is revealing:

He had to give him his due, the *Appearance* of an extraordinary fine Gentleman; he was Tall, well Shap'd, and had an extraordinary Address; talk'd *as naturally* of his Park, and his Stables; of his Horses, his Game-Keepers, his Woods, his Tenants, and his Servants, *as if* we had been in the Mansion-House, and I had seen them all about me.   (P 143; my italics)

This passage, read without emphasis on the italicized words, seems merely to reflect Moll's wondering admiration and greedy expectation but, like her reference to Jemy's 'sister' – 'she caressed me with the utmost appearance of a sincere, undissembled Affection' (p 141) – an emphasis on the words conveying a sense of appearance reveals both the skill of the deceiver and Moll's (and Defoe's) care in explaining the deception. Understandably, Moll is taken in by the splendid acting of Jemy, who shares with Moll's linen-draper husband the ability to appear 'like Quality' when he wishes. The 'glittering show of a great Estate,' Moll confesses, 'and of fine Things, which the deceived Creature that was now my Deceiver represented every Hour to my Imagination, hurried me away' (p 144). Defoe's preparation for the end of the novel is contained in the development of Moll's genuine love for her Lancashire husband, her proposal that they go to live in Virginia, and her promise that she 'shall have occasion to say more of him hereafter' (p 159). Jemy's answer to Moll's proposal about Virginia, that 'he would then come to me and join in my Project for *Virginia*' (p 159), is another ironic anticipation of events that acquires its full force only when the total structure of the novel is understood.

Moll, unhappily, is not immediately able to recoup the loss of a round in the cheating game of marriage by playing her 'safe Card at home' (p 142), her banker friend in London, since, as she regrets, 'there was no Marrying without entirely concealing that I had had a Child, for he would soon have discover'd by the Age of it, that it was born, nay, and gotten too, since my Parly with him, and that would have destroy'd all the Affair' (p 173). The interlude, brought 'into as narrow a Compass as possible' (p 169), in which Moll gives birth to her child and then farms him out for £15, introduces that 'Dexterous Lady' (p 171) and midwife, Moll's 'Governess,' as she aptly calls her, who forms an essential link between Moll's life as a whore (soon to end) and her life as a thief. This woman, one of Defoe's more vivid and effective helper characters, in her tendency not merely to advise but to direct the heroine, resembles Roxana's maid and companion Amy. Like Amy, she raises the threat – though, unlike Amy, she does not carry it out – of child murder. Earlier the midwife had subtly suggested an abortion, though when Moll is horrified, 'she put it off so cleverly, that I cou'd not say she really intended it' (p 169). None the less, when Moll is considering farming out her child, knowing that 'to neglect them [children] is to Murther them' (p 174), she is prepared to be reassured by her governess that she would not be indulging in 'a contriv'd Method for Murther' (p 173). The debate over the abandoning of children reintroduces the theme of the relationship of parents and children (and especially the responsibility of mothers, who have 'needful Affection, plac'd by Nature in them,' to look after their offspring), complicated now in the direction of irony by the special relationship that grows up between Moll and her governess, 'whom I now learn'd to call Mother' (p 174). The midwife, to strengthen her case, asks Moll is she is sure that she was 'Nurs'd up by your own Mother?' a demand that touches Moll 'to the Quick' for, as she realizes, 'on the Contrary, I was sure I was not' (p 175). 'I have no Murtherers about me,' her governess explains; 'I employ the best, and the honestest Nurses that can be had; and have as few Children miscarry under their Hands, as there would, if they were all Nurs'd by Mothers' (p 174), an explanation, given Moll's early situation in life, that ought to have been less than reassuring. The situational irony that Defoe exploits here is deepened by Moll's repeatedly addressing the midwife as 'Mother' and 'O Mother,' and the midwife's stern advice that Moll 'must e'en do as other conscientious Mothers have done before you; and be contented with things as they must be, tho' not as you wish them to be' (p 176). Moll herself is aware of the midwife's fine irony: 'I understood what she meant by conscientious Mothers, she would have said conscientious Whores' (p 176).

Moll's fifth and final marriage, to her 'Steward,' which provides a treacherous illusion of a 'safe Harbour' for Moll in her 'Stormy Voyage of Life' (p 188), further extends the recurring marriage pattern and deepens the mode of deception. The irony of Moll's deception of this man arises from his ignorance of her situation. (This is a favourite device of Defoe, who probably had frequent occasion to be aware of it as he travelled about England and Scotland spying for Harley.) Moll's banker is a confessed cuckold (his wife having run away with a linen-draper's apprentice), and more than once he flatly explains the nature of his distress and gives to Moll his conviction that 'she that will be *a Whore*, will be a *Whore*.' 'I WAV'D the Discourse,' Moll coolly continues, 'and began to talk of my Business' (p 135). When Moll boldly suggests that he might think of taking a mistress, for his wife 'would not dispute the Liberty with you that she takes herself,' he expresses his repugnance for whores: 'I have had enough of her to meddle with any more Whores' (p 136). The dramatic irony here is increased almost immediately when he asks Moll, as an 'honest Woman,' if she would take him. Her answer is necessarily evasive (the proposal to go to Lancashire being still open), but Moll readily perceives that she is making a very good impression upon the unsuspecting banker. Once again Moll has reason to reflect upon the value of 'Appearance': 'you may see how necessary it is, for all Women who expect any thing in the World, to preserve the Character of their Virtue, even when perhaps they may have sacrific'd the Thing itself' (p 138).

Moll again expresses her deep sense of the irony of her deception, now extended by the escapade of her fourth marriage, when she returns to marry her banker: 'How little does he think, that having Divorc'd a Whore, he is throwing himself into the Arms of another!' Moll senses too that the strands of her past life increase the irony of her last marriage: 'he is going to Marry one that has lain with two Brothers, and has had three Children by her own Brother! one that was born in *Newgate*, whose Mother was a Whore, and is now a transported Thief; one that has lain with thirteen Men, and has had a Child since he saw me? Poor gentleman! *said I*, What is he going to do!' (p 182). Her conclusion, as she thinks about her 'abominable Life for 24 Years past,' goes to the heart of Defoe's own vision of the condition of man in a world of sham, of deceit and false appearance and hypocrisy: 'O! what a felicity is it to Mankind, *said I*, to myself, that they cannot see into the Hearts of one another!' (p 182).[16]

IV

The third part of Moll's history is shaped by the series of robberies that make up her career as a thief and probably reflects, like the first section of *Colonel Jack*, Defoe's growing concern with the rising incidence of street robberies that marked London life in the 1720s. His *Narrative of all the Robberies, Escapes, Etc., of John Sheppard* appeared in 1724, the same year as *Roxana*, and it was followed in 1725 by *The Life of Jonathan Wild* and in 1726 by *A Brief Historical Account of the Lives of Six Notorious Street-Robbers, Executed at Kingston*. In the last few years of his life Defoe published a series of tracts on ways for suppressing robberies, and indeed the last publication of his life, as given by Moore in his bibliography, is *An Effectual Scheme for the Immediate Preventing of Street-Robberies* (1730). The overriding theme of all the writings of Defoe's later years, with the partial exception of his works on magic and superstition, is that of order in society, not only public order and morality (reflected in his concern over such matters as highwaymen and street-robbers and the 'Insolent and Unsufferable Behaviour of Servants in England'),[17] but also private or family order and morality (a concern we have seen expressed in his *Family Instructor, Religious Courtship*, and *Conjugal Lewdness*). In *Moll Flanders* Defoe's deep concern with these two aspects of moral order in society finds expression in Moll's two careers as whore (private immorality) and thief (public immorality).

Defoe makes no very clear distinction, either in his non-fiction or in *Moll Flanders*, between public and private vices because for him they are part of, and inextricably bound up together in, a general decline in the moral fabric of society, a fact that allows for the easy transition in the novel from Moll's 'Matrimonial Whoredom'[18] to the wider world of the professional thief. The happy 'Deliverance' of her fifth marriage, which she refers to, characteristically, as 'this particular Scene of Life' (p 188), ends like the earlier scenes of her life, with the death of her husband. The only significant difference between this 'sudden Blow from an almost invisible Hand' (p 189) and her more youthful disasters is that now Moll, at the age of forty-eight, can no longer 'expect to be courted for a Mistress' (p 189). She frankly admits that her beauty, like her happiness, has been blasted ('the Ruins only appear'd of what had been') and that in 'this dismal Condition' (p 190), without friend or counsellor, she is prey to the temptations of the devil. The only real alternative (other than needlework) for a woman past child-bearing and without money or expectations is theft, and Moll takes to her new career quite naturally. Her carcer of marriages gained through deception is a preparation for the coolness and disguises necessary for her career as thief. In this part of her history the theme of appearance and deception grows until it leads, following Moll's ultimate deception by her own vanity, to Newgate.

Moll's first theft, easy and unplanned, is of a bundle left by a careless maid-servant on a stool in an apothecary's shop, but the second theft, of a child's necklace of gold beads, is one of the most vivid scenes in the novel and imparts the air of an actual experience.[19] Its force derives from its aptness, psychological and realistic, to Moll's situation. Realistically Moll's action here fits into a progressive scheme for her gradual hardening into crime. Stealing a necklace from a child is only a trifle more difficult than stealing an unwatched bundle; Moll after all is only a novice thief at this stage, not yet let into the 'arts' of her profession. But on the psychological level the child, her necklace, and Moll's sudden, terrible impulse to murder have significant links with both earlier and later aspects of her life. The pretty child returning from her dancing lesson may well have stirred in Moll unspoken memories of her own early life in Colchester and her aspiration to be a gentlewoman by acquiring genteel accomplishments such as dancing. The devil-prompted thoughts of 'killing the Child in the dark Alley' (p 194) raise again the spectre of child murder which seems to rise from Moll's guilty mind in moments of dark crisis. Moll's sense of guilt is subtly conveyed in the excuses she makes for herself at the time: 'I only said to my self, I had given the Parents a just Reproof for their Negligence in leaving the poor little Lamb to come home by it self' (p 194). And she adds, 'no doubt the Child had a Maid sent to take care of it, but she, like a careless Jade, was taken up perhaps with some Fellow that had met her' (p 195). Moll's self-justifying reference to the 'careless Jade' follows her reflection on 'the Vanity of the Mother' who had given her child a necklace to wear that she might 'look Fine at the Dancing School,' a remark that not only eases Moll's sense of guilt, but reveals her own deeply felt sense of loss – of something she never had. The necklace in this way symbolizes Moll's aspirations and deprivations. It is not too much perhaps to suggest that it is also a sinister symbol threatening Moll with the fate of so many of her later companions. In eighteenth-century thieves' language the neckless is the halter.

After these first few almost casual thefts and a few more 'purchases' that come her way the pattern of Moll's thieving increasingly involves disguises or what Moll calls 'Shapes.' The strengthening of the pattern of disguise and deception is brought about by that strange creature, Moll's old governess, who has now conveniently 'turn'd Pawn Broker,' that is, become a receiver of stolen goods, and who not only introduces

Moll to 'a School-Mistress, that shall make you as dexterous as her self' (p 201), but who also directs Moll in the various disguises that she adopts. As Moll's luckless companions are caught and taken to Newgate, and as Moll's shifting of disguises becomes more and more necessary, a sense of the inevitability of Newgate sets in. 'Thus,' Moll remarks early in her new career, 'I that was once in the Devil's Clutches, was held fast there as with a Charm, and had no Power to go without the Circle, till I was ingulph'd in Labyrinths of Trouble too great to get out at all' (p 203).

Moll's relationship with her governess is a parody of the natural relationship of mother and child. We have already observed that Moll customarily addresses this woman as 'Mother,' and now, as Moll comes under her guidance, the older woman increasingly calls Moll, who is nearly fifty years old, 'Child' (p 204). The names are, in a sense, merely terms of endearment, but they suggest the symbolic roles the two women adopt, roles which acquire a greater significance through the constant concern with family relations that runs throughout the book. The governess looks after Moll 'like a Mother,' but a mother of the sort that we find in the novel. When Moll is sent out, dressed up by her governess like a child being sent off to school or a party, on expeditions that bring her within the shadows of the gallows, she becomes part of that pattern of exploitation in which children are carelessly neglected or abandoned. Moll, we remember, for her own selfish reasons delivered up her children to various 'Nurses.' Although Moll calls her governess 'Mother' and seems genuinely fond of and grateful to her, she also knows that her governess is a 'Tempter' (p 209), and that she acts the part of the devil. The governess, who is indirectly responsible for Moll's return to Newgate, is a substitute for the mother who abandoned Moll there in the first place. Within the structure of the novel the relationship of Moll and her governess underlines the relationships that Moll has violated in her cheating marriages and the forsaking of her children.

The 'Art' in which Moll proudly claims to have been 'the greatest Artist of my time' (p 214) is picking pockets, for which it is necessary to be well dressed in order to deflect suspicion, 'for you are to observe,' Moll points out, 'that on these Adventures we always went very well Dress'd, and I had very good Cloths on, and a Gold Watch by my Side, as like a Lady as other Folks' (p 211). But when Moll becomes too well known among the other pickpockets she turns to shop-lifting, and now her governess suggests the first of Moll's total disguises: 'this was to Dress me up in Mens Cloths, and so put me into a new kind of Practise' (p 214). Later Moll, constantly directed by her governess, adopts various disguises of which she mentions in particular those of a servant (pp 238–40), a widow (pp 241–53), and a beggar-woman (pp 253–5). Ingenuity has its limits, however, even for Moll who sometimes takes 'the Liberty to play the same Game over again, which is not according to Practice,' though 'generally,' she says, 'I took up new Figures, and contriv'd to appear in new Shapes every time I went abroad' (p 262).

Moll's disguises are as much meant to protect her from the betrayal of other thieves as they are designed to assist her in her thefts. In her disguise as a man, in which Moll passes under the name of Gabriel Spencer, she works with a male companion from whom she effectively conceals her real name and her sex, a fact that is of considerable comfort to her when he is arrested and committed to Newgate. She rejoices that she had the 'Wisdom of ... concealing my Name and Sex from him, which if he had ever known I had been undone' (p 218). None the less, Moll is uneasy ('tho' so well Disguis'd that it was scarce possible to Detect me') that she might be betrayed by her companion in order to save his own life and she goes into hiding until she learns from her governess 'the joyful News that he was hang'd' (p 220). Moll more than once makes the point that her success as a thief depends upon the concealing of her identity and thus upon her artistry in disguise: 'tho' I often robb'd with these People, yet I never let them know who I was, or where I Lodg'd; nor could they ever find out my Lodging, tho' they often endeavour'd to Watch me to it' (pp 221–2).

Moll's attitude towards her various disguises reveals her character. She objects to the disguise of men's clothes because it is 'a Dress so contrary to Nature' (p 215), and she explains that, 'as I did every thing Clumsily, so I had neither the success, or the easiness of Escape that I had before' (p 215). She also objects to her beggar-woman's disguise, not only because she finds that she cannot get near people but because she feels an abhorrence for a costume that reminds her too forcibly of what her life might have been: 'I naturally abhorr'd Dirt and Rags; I had been bred up Tite and Cleanly, and could be no other, whatever Condition I was in; so that this was the most uneasie Disguise to me that ever I put on,' and she adds a little later, 'I thought it was Ominous and Threatning' (p 254). The disguise which suits Moll best is one that not only flatters her aspirations to gentility, but which gives her scope for acting out the part. In 'The Disguise of a Widow's Dress' (p 241) she has all the satisfaction of appearing 'like Quality,' a pleasure that she had first experienced many years before in Oxford, and of knowing that her success in deception rests upon her own cleverness. Moll is the first in a line of fictional heroines leading to such consummate actresses as Becky Sharp and Lizzie Eustace.

Because she is falsely arrested and badly treated by a mercer who had been robbed by another thief also dressed in widow's weeds, Moll, to the delight of her governess, is able to threaten the hapless mercer with a suit at law and eventually to obtain '150 *l.* and a Suit of black silk Cloaths' (p 252). This little scene is shot through with the circumstantial irony that Defoe delights in and handles so well. Moll's indignant repudiation of the charge that she is the thief, though true in fact, glows with the irony that Moll is at once *a* thief, though not *the* thief, disguised as a widow. And ironically, because of the confusion caused by Moll's bold insistence on taking the mercer and his servants before the justice, 'the Woman they had taken, who was really the Thief, made off, and got clear away in the Crowd' (p 246). But the chief delight of the scene lies in the height to which Moll, who is really a thief and in terrible danger from the law if discovered, is prepared to carry out her intimidation of the mercer, an action that gives scope to her acting ability. Advised by her attorney, 'a very creditable sort of Man to manage it' (pp 248–9), she appears before the mercer with 'some State' that he 'might see I was something more than I seem'd to be that time they had me' (p 250). Moll's 'something more' consists in not only a new suit of second mourning and a gold watch, but also 'a good Pearl Neck-lace, that shut in behind with a Locket of Diamonds.' Moll mentions only casually that the necklace was one that her governess 'had in Pawn,' but this fact deepens the irony of her pretence. To increase the 'State' of her arrival, Moll comes with a maid and in a coach, and when she returns to collect the money, she is accompanied by her governess, 'dress'd like an old Dutchess, and a Gentleman very well dress'd, who we pretended Courted me, but I call'd him Cousin, and the Lawyer was only to hint privately to him, that this Gentleman Courted the Widow' (p 252). This scene, which could be straight out of Restoration comedy, displays Moll's unabated zest for role-playing. But it is significant that the whole episode with the magistrate and the mercer which Moll carries to such daring heights of dissimulation is one of those 'Broils' which made Moll known and which, she realizes, was 'the worst thing next to being found Guilty, that cou'd befall me' (p 241). Newgate means for Moll not merely the misery and humiliation of that 'hellish' place, but the discovery of her identity, the place where the other thieves finally, and triumphantly, call her Mary Flanders. It is the end of a life of crime based on the success of her art of deception.

V

The movement of the third section of the novel, Moll's career as thief, culminates in her return to Newgate, 'the Place that had so long expected me, and which with so much Art and Success I had so long avoided' (p 273). It is clear that Moll sees Newgate not merely as the culmination of her career as a thief but as the climax of the whole structure of her life, which she has been recounting. It is thus also for her 'the Place where my Mother suffered so deeply, [and] where I was brought into the World.' Her last twelve years of theft take their place within the larger pattern of her life. She sees the movement of her life as cyclical, shaped by the inevitability of her return to Newgate, where she expects to die an infamous death: 'it seem'd to me that I was hurried on by an inevitable and unseen Fate to this Day of Misery, and that now I was to Expiate all my Offences at the Gallows' (p 274). In Newgate the two themes of family relations and the prison, which support Moll's two careers as whore and thief, finally come together.

The pattern of return is characteristic of the final portion of Moll's story and draws attention to a secondary structure in the novel, lying behind the main organization of Moll's two careers and strengthening the structural irony and the unity of the novel. This is the structure, or system, of interconnected persons and places, built from the links that join Moll, her mother, Newgate, Jemy, and Virginia. Newgate is thus a pivotal point, the place where the two systems of organization in the novel touch.

The pattern of return begins when Moll goes back to Colchester shortly before her final arrest. This return helps to prepare the reader for the events that are soon to follow by creating the impression that the story is drawing to an end. Moll begins to speak at this point of the utility of her story which, 'duly consider'd, may be useful to honest People, and afford a due Caution,' and of the moral, which 'is left to be gather'd by the Senses and Judgment of the Reader' (p 268). After Colchester Moll returns once more to London and the end is in sight:

Upon my return, being hardened by a long Race of Crime, and Success unparalell'd, at least in the reach of my own Knowledge, I had, as I have said, no thoughts of laying down a Trade, which if I was to judge by the Example of others, must however End at last in Misery and Sorrow. (P 269)

In Newgate itself the cyclical movement of the story intensifies. As we have seen, Moll is deeply struck by the fact that Newgate is the place of her birth and of her mother's suffering. It thus serves to connect her not only with the events of her early life, but also with her mother and the tragic discovery of her marriage to her own brother in Virginia. But, further, while she is in Newgate, her Lancashire husband Jemy, who is actually a highwayman, is brought in. Years before Moll had been puzzled when he would not accompany her any nearer to London than Dunstable (p 159). After she meets him again in Newgate and has an account of his life Moll finally understands Jemy's good 'Reasons.'

A grasp of Jemy's role in the novel is essential to an understanding of Defoe's fairly complex structural patterns. He alone of all Moll's husbands represents the possibility of a true marriage, for, although the marriage was contracted on both sides as a business arrangement, yet there soon grew up between Moll and Jemy a deep and genuine affection that characterized their relationship even in the face of the discovery of the double fraud. This is why, after both have been punished by their stay in Newgate, Jemy can be brought back and reunited with Moll. The fourth section of the novel, with its returns to Colchester, Newgate, and Virginia, repeats in brief the pattern of Moll's life. In her reunion with Jemy and their successful attempt to make a new life in the new world the marriage theme is completed. In his *Conjugal Lewdness* Defoe defines 'Matrimonial Whoredom' (which Moll practises so often throughout the novel) as 'Marriage without Love' and calls it 'the compleatest Misery in Life.' 'Besides,' he adds, 'I must say, it is to me utterly unlawful, and entails a Curse upon the Persons as being wilfully perjured, invoking the Name of GOD to a Falshood.'[20] Moll is fully punished for all her illicit marriages, and her crimes bring down a curse on much of her life. The most terrible curse is that of incest, and it is significant that in her new marriage with Jemy Moll returns once more to Virginia where her brother-husband is still living. But now the curse has been lifted. Moll finally comes into the legacy left to her by her mother; she sees once more her son, who treats her with great kindness and regard; and with Jemy she grows prosperous and, so far as we can tell, happy. Jemy draws our attention to the fulfilment of the structural pattern when he finds, ironically, that he has after all married a fortune: 'why who says I was deceiv'd, when I married a Wife in *Lancashire*? I think I have married a Fortune, and a very good Fortune too' (p 341). In a marriage properly based on mutual affection Moll discovers that she can have all those things that her years of false marriage and of theft had denied her. The final page of the novel is spent in regularizing Moll's life. With the death of her brother she can at last publicly own her marriage to Jemy. She is forgiven by her son, who assures her that her marriage to his father and her brother was 'a Mistake impossible to be prevented.' And in the closing paragraph Moll announces her return to England where she is now living with her husband 'in good Heart and Health' and, as she appears to believe, 'in sincere Penitence, for the wicked Lives we have lived.'[21]

VI

The symbolism of *Moll Flanders* is less contrived than that of *Robinson Crusoe*; the effect of the vocabulary and imagery is not to support a neat, symmetrical structure, as in *Robinson Crusoe*, but to suggest a world of equivocation and hypocrisy. Moll's world is one which runs on deception, and the language of the novel reflects and intensifies the mood of disguise and dissimulation. What images there are (e.g., the snare, the hook, and the halter) work as metaphors suggesting the quality of life rather than as symbols defining the moral theme. Moll leaves the moral of her story 'to be gather'd by the Senses and Judgment of the Reader' (p 268).

Although Moll's two visits to Virginia retain something of the deliberate symbolic contrast of Crusoe's movement towards and then away from the island, the shape of *Moll Flanders* as a whole, like the language and imagery which help to create it, is less mechanical and, to the confusion of the critics,[22] less clear than in *Robinson Crusoe*. What *Moll Flanders* loses in sharpness of profile, it gains in the increased subtlety of its presentation of the complexities of human life. The editor's comment that Moll was not afterwards so extraordinary a penitent as she was at first – a master-stroke of characterization – establishes a tone of mild cynicism that is part of the vision of life in the novel. This tone is sustained by the language and imagery that we come now to examine.

Central to the vision of Moll Flanders are two closely related metaphors for human life: life as a play and life as a cheat. Moll's idea of herself as the greatest artist of her time, her customary references to new 'Scenes' of her life, her use of fan, mask, and hood on several occasions, and her constant sense of role-playing help to establish an analogy with the stage, an analogy that is first suggested by the editor in the preface to the novel:

THROUGHOUT the infinite variety of this Book, this Fundamental is most strictly adhered to; there is not a wicked Action in any Part of it, but is first or last rendered Unhappy and Unfortunate: There is not a superlative Villain brought upon the Stage, but either he is brought to an unhappy End, or brought to be a Penitent.

Upon 'this Foundation' he recommends the book to the reader and also suggests that, if plays were likewise devoted to the reformation of manners by never failing 'to recommend Vertue, and generous Principles, and to discourage and expose all sorts of Vice and Corruption of Manners,' much too 'might be said in their Favour.' The idea that life is like a play is as old as the theatre, which returns the compliment when it proposes that life is the test of art. It is interesting, however, to observe that Defoe's emphasis within this traditional metaphor is not on the brevity or futility of life (as with Shakespeare's 'poor player who struts and frets his hour upon the stage and then is heard no more') but on duplicity and 'appearance.' It is clear that the stage Defoe had in mind was that of Restoration comedy, with its vigorously theatrical use of pretences and disguises (especially the paraphernalia of masks, fans, hoods, paint, etc), lost relations who turn up unexpectedly, fraudulent marriages for money, and a concept of manners which Congreve called the Way of the World.

It is because life resembles this kind of drama that life is a cheat. In a world in which all action is pretence and every word affectation, in which a 'plain and Honest' man (p 30) will marry his brother's whore, the clever, who are distinguished not by their plain-speaking but by their wit, will practise the arts of deception and equivocation. In the introduction to the second *Family Instructor* Defoe falls into the metaphor of the stage to emphasize the pitfalls of life:

If we would but duly reflect upon the different scenes of human life, and the several stations we are placed in, and the parts we act, while we are passing over this stage; we should see there are follies to be exposed, dangers to be cautioned against, and advices to be given.[23]

Like Moll, Defoe here cautions extreme wariness against the cheats of life. Moll in one of her reflective moments, speaking out strongly as a successful professional thief, expresses a similar opinion about human nature:

On the other hand, every Branch of my Story, if duly consider'd, may be useful to honest People, and afford a due Caution to People of some sort, or other to Guard against the like Surprizes, and to have their Eyes about them when they have to do with Strangers of any kind, for 'tis very seldom that some Snare or other is not in their way.   (P 268)

The snare is the image Moll customarily uses to draw attention to life's dangers and cheats. Snares may be either the deceits of other people or the human weaknesses of pride, vanity, and ambition that go before a fall. Moll's vanity is the original cause of her ruin, and she first employs the image of the snare to suggest how the Elder Brother flattered her vanity to draw her into 'his Net':

he began with than unhappy Snare to all Women, (*Viz.*) taking Notice upon all Occasions how pretty I was, as he called it; how agreeable, how well Carriaged, and the like; and this he contriv'd so subtilly, as if he had known as well, how to catch a Woman in his Net, as a Partidge when he went a Setting.   (P 19)

This simile recalls the imagery of ensnarement and imprisonment in *Robinson Crusoe*, there generally used in connection with the animals that Crusoe traps for food. Hereafter Moll uses the image more abstractly, without specific reference to animals, though its origin in a device for trapping animals and birds should not be forgotten.

The image is extended for some pages and helps to epitomize Moll's relationship with the Elder Brother. After this, Moll says, he 'baited his Hook, and found easily enough the Method how to lay it in my Way' (p 20). She speaks, too, of being clasped in his arms: 'I struggl'd to get away, and yet did it but faintly neither, and he held me fast' (p 22). The effectiveness of the vocabulary of ensnarement rests upon the continuing image of the struggling animal or bird caught in a trap that runs throughout Moll's account of her affair with the Elder Brother, as we are remined by such phrases as 'an opportunity to catch me again' (p 22) and 'fail'd not to catch me all alone' (p 29). The family of the Elder Brother, who are deceived by both Moll and her lover, naturally look upon Moll as the (fortune) hunter and the Elder Brother as the victim: 'we have all look'd upon you as a kind of a Snare to my Son' (p 51), the Mother explains to Moll in a confidential chat. Later, after she has married Robin, Moll realizes that the Elder Brother is still a snare, though in a different sense: 'his Brother being so always in my Sight ... was a continual Snare to me; and I was never in Bed with my Husband, but I wish'd my self in the Arms of his Brother' (p 59). Now not Moll's vanity but her love has become the bait of the snare.

The image of the snare continues to appear, reflecting Moll's attitude to the human condition and deepening the atmosphere of cheating and deception. For example, she looks upon her gentleman-tradesman husband as a snare 'which, *as I might say*, I laid for my self' (p 60). The fear of being an old maid is a snare to women who as a result marry in haste. The snare, although not specifically mentioned, lurks behind Moll's comment about her third husband, that 'I had him fast both ways; and tho' he might say afterwards he was cheated, yet he could never say that I had cheated him' (p 80). She sees and freely acknowledges that she has been a snare to her Bath lover and she is aware that she is the wrong creature for the North Country Woman's trap: 'IF this Woman had known my real Circumstances, she would never have laid so many Snares, and taken so many weary steps to catch a poor desolate Creature that was good for little when it was caught' (p 130). When she is about to embark on her second career as a thief, Moll partially justifies her actions in this manner:

BUT there are Temptations which it is not in the Power of Human Nature to resist, and few know what would be their Case, if driven to the same Exigences: As Covetousness is the Root of all Evil, so Poverty is, I believe, the worst of all Snares.   (P 188)

Sometimes it is the devil himself who sets the snare. Moll's first theft is a bundle of clothes left unguarded by a careless servant. 'THIS was the Bait,' Moll explains, 'and the Devil who I said laid the Snare, as readily prompted me' (p 191). Similarly the little child wearing a necklace of gold beads is, for Moll, a snare 'of a dreadful Nature indeed' (p 194) which the devil lays in her way. Another version of the snare image is that of the fisherman's hook, and the fisherman is often the devil. Towards the end of her career as a thief Moll begins to think that she ought to retire, but by now she has been hooked fast by the devil: 'but my Fate was otherwise determin'd, the busie Devil that so industriously drew me in, had too fast hold of me to let me go back' (p 203). One of the interesting differences between the nature of Moll's life as thief and as whore can be seen in the imagery. As a thief it is Moll who is often the victim of the devil's snares and hooks. As a whore it is Moll who generally acts the devil's part: 'I had hook'd him so fast, and play'd him so long,' she says of her third husband (her brother), 'that I was satisfied he would have had me in my worst Circumstances' (p 82).

The ultimate snare is of course the hangman's noose, the halter. On the first page of the novel Moll informs us that she often expected to go out of this world 'by the Steps and the String,' a phrase that seems to emphasize the sinister snare-like quality of the gallows. Moll often repeats her fear that she would 'certainly come to be hang'd at last' (p

196), and she sees all the snares that the devil puts in her way as steps to the gallows, as indeed an eighteenth-century thief might wisely do. Just as the devil sets snares for the unwary, so he also lurks behind the gallows itself. At the moment of 'utmost horror,' when Moll is in Newgate and under sentence of death, she can think of nothing 'Night or Day, but of Gibbets and Halters, evil Spirits and Devils' (p 277). Closely associated with the threatening image of the gallows is Newgate, itself part of the imagery of ensnarement. Moll habitually speaks of her fear of being 'caught' and 'taken,' of her comrades who 'ran themselves into Newgate,' and of her own wariness which was such that she 'always got off.' As snares and traps are little prisons placed by the devil in Moll's path, so is the great prison of Newgate the very home of the devil; as such it appeared to Moll 'an Emblem of Hell itself, and a kind of an Entrance into it' (p 274).

The atmosphere of deception in a world of sham and hypocrisy that the imagery suggests and then concentrates into the terrible symbol of Newgate is reinforced and extended by a language of equivocation. Earlier we noticed Moll's confusion about the meaning of the word 'Gentlewoman' which was in a sense the beginning of all her troubles. That little episode inculcates in Moll the early realization that being a gentlewoman – or for that matter anything else – rests so very much on 'Appearance.' In *The True-born Englishman* and *The Compleat English Gentleman*, as elsewhere in his writing, Defoe scoffs at the idea that gentility has anything very much to do with innate qualities, with 'blood.'

It is a strange Folly in the best of Mankind to Cap Pedigrees; since as the tallest Tree has its Roots in the Dirt; and the Florists tell us the most beautiful Flowers are raised out of the grossest mixtures of the Dunghill and Jakes; so the greatest Family has its Beginnings in the Throng, and the Search brings it to Nothing.[24]

While the vehemence of his argument perhaps betrays his own social insecurity, this point of view is completely in line with his customary way of thinking. Defoe argues that a gentleman who claims social position and political power by virtue of his ancestry and who is not educated (*The Compleat English Gentleman* is, after all, a treatise on education) is not truly a gentleman, and therefore has no real right to his privilege. Tradesmen, runs a constant theme in his works, can become gentlemen, and are often more *truly* gentlemen than the debased sons of ancient families. The section of the novel in which Moll passes herself off as a woman of fortune in order to make various advantageous marriages is a satire on the contemporary respect for gentility. The irony lies in the fact that a woman born in Newgate of a mother shortly afterwards transported, who is later to be a notorious thief and herself transported, is readily accepted as a gentlewoman, even though, in fact, she has very little money. Moll's passing as a countess when she visits Oxford and the splendid first appearance of Jemy who knows so well how to look like a gentleman (while actually he is a highwayman) are particularly high-spirited examples of Defoe's satire.

Moll herself frequently draws our attention to the need for keeping up one's appearance or reputation. For example, in her courtship with the banker whom she eventually marries Moll repeatedly emphasizes her techniques for making a good impression: 'I knew that the way to secure him,' she explains, 'was to stand off' (p 138). Part of her appearance is to show that she is independent: 'I CAME the next Evening accordingly, and brought my Maid with me, *to let him see* that I kept a Maid' (p 138). There may also be need for polite protest, for 'saving face': 'after we had Supp'd, I observ'd he press'd me very hard to drink two or three Glasses of Wine, which however I declin'd; *but Drank one Glass or two*' (p 139, my italics). The last clause of this sentence makes it clear to us with great economy that Moll's initial polite protest is part of her policy of standing off. At the end of her visit, after the banker had threatened to make 'a Proposal,' Moll begins to put on her gloves and prepares to go, though she adds, typically, 'at the same time I no more intended it, than he intended to let me' (p 139). At one point Moll explains at large:

However, I ventur'd that, for all that the People there, or thereabout knew of me, was to my Advantage; and all the Character he had of me, after he had enquir'd, was, *that I was a Woman of Fortune*, and that I was a very modest sober Body; which whether true or not in the Main, yet you may see how necessary it is, for all Women who expect any thing in the World, to preserve the Character of their Virtue, even when perhaps they may have sacrific'd the Thing itself. (P 138)

The vocabulary of equivocation is not only reflected in Moll's habitual concern with reputation but pervades the entire narrative and lends weight to the fundamental idea that things generally are not what they appear to be. The pervading duality of Moll's world, which begins with her confusion over the meaning of the word 'Gentlewoman,' is carried on by the play on appearance and reality that characterizes Moll's thinking and the tone of the novel. One of her favourite phrases points out that something both is and is not at the same time. After her linen-draper husband has left her, she realizes that she is 'a Widow bewitch'd' for, as she explains, 'I had a Husband, and no Husband' (p 64), meaning, of course, that she cannot legally marry again even though her husband has left her and left England forever. After her return from Virginia, when she sets herself up in Bath, she says that she is '*as it were*, a Woman of Fortune, tho' I was a Woman without a Fortune' (p 106), a remark that calls attention to her fine appearance in the world and the meagre reality behind it. Of her lover in Bath she says that 'he had no Wife, that is to say, she was as no Wife to him' (p 120). Similarly, her banker, when she first met him, 'had *a Wife*, and *no Wife*' (p 133; cf p 134), though in his case it is because his wife is an adulteress rather than a madwoman. And her governess at one point reassures her that 'to have a Husband that cannot appear, is to have no Husband' (p 162). Again, after the unprofitable theft of a horse Moll comments, 'this was a Robbery and no Robbery' (p 254). What these phrases[25] reveal is Moll's mind at work when, characteristically, she wants to find a way around a reality that she cannot entirely deny. Of course she *is* a wife, and her various husbands *are* already husbands, and the theft of a horse *is* a real, and potentially fatal, theft. But Moll's movements would be too restricted by a scrupulous adherence to the truth (e.g., that she has a husband) and she seeks and finds another 'truth' (e.g., that she has no husband) that relies for its usefulness very often on other people's ignorance of all the facts. There is one truth that operates in the conscience or at moments of self-accusation, but there is another 'truth' that exists only in the world of appearance and deception. Occasionally Moll is forced to face things as they really are, for example, when she sees that she is to be turned out by the Elder Brother, 'a mere cast off Whore, *for it was no less*' (p 56), but the usual state of her mind is more complicated, as we see in this sentence in which Moll comments on her governess's advice to farm out her baby to a nurse:

I understood what she meant by conscientious Mothers, she would have said conscientious Whores; but she was not willing to disoblige me, for really in this Case I was not a Whore, because legally Married, the Force of my former Marriage excepted. (P 176)

Moll knows (1) that she is a whore, but she protests (2) that in this particular case she is not a whore, as long as we forget (3) that her second husband who deserted her many years ago is not known to be dead. The irony (first gently suggested by 'conscientious Whores') that

this kind of double-thinking produces and the language of equivocation in which it is expressed pervade the novel and heighten and qualify
the vision of life as a cheat.

The effect of Moll's acceptance of the 'reality' of appearance is an
emphasis upon externals in the novel. Both Moll and Crusoe, like their
creator, know that we cannot see into the hearts of one another, and
thus the way people appear, in both their clothes and their manners,
becomes all the more important. All Defoe's heroes and heroines are
greatly concerned about their clothes. Crusoe takes care to let us know
how he is dressed and how it is that he can provide European clothes
for Friday. Moll frequently mentions her clothes ('I lov'd nothing in the
World better than fine Cloths' [p 112], she confesses); and both Colonel
Jack and Roxana are equally concerned about their appearance in their
clothes. The details of the clothes are rarely important except in so far
as they emphasize the general appearance that the effect of the clothes
produces. Moll refers, in general terms, to 'a great many very good
Cloaths, and Linnen in abundance' (p 312) or to 'a Widows dress' (p
250) or to 'the best Cloths' (p 296), or says that she dressed herself 'to all
the Advantage possible' (p 235) or in 'very good Cloaths' (p 211). We
are given more details only if the accumulation of details will give
greater emphasis to her point about 'appearance.' Thus, to demonstrate her righteous prosperity at the end of her story, she enumerates
the things she is able to buy for her husband:

HERE we had a supply of all sorts of Cloaths, as well for my Husband, as for
myself; and I took especial care to buy for him all those things that I knew he
delighted to have; as two good long Wigs, two silver hilted Swords, three or
four fine Fowling peices, a fine Saddle with Holsters and Pistoles very handsome, with a Scarlet Cloak; and in a Word, every thing I could think of to oblige
him; and to make him appear, as he really was, a very fine Gentleman. (P 340)

The significance of Moll's list lies in her emphasis on the effect of the
clothes which make Jemy *appear* a very fine gentleman, a remark that
takes us back to her first meeting with him when he had 'the Appearance of an extraordinary fine Gentleman' (p 143). But there is an
important play on the two kinds of appearance, in Lancashire and in
Virginia, of Moll's husband. His first 'Appearance' was a deception, as
indeed 'appearance' often is; his second 'Appearance' as a gentleman is
backed up by the reality of his newly acquired wealth. Moll's mother
(her *real* mother) on Moll's first visit to Virginia had pointed out that
transported criminals can become gentlemen in the new world, and

Jemy by the end of the book has become an illustration of this thesis. Yet both 'appearances' are described by Moll in the same way – in terms of clothing. Moll's quick shift from 'make him appear' to 'as he really was, a very fine Gentleman,' like her remarks earlier about her marital status, is indicative of the shifting ambiguities of appearance and deception in the novel.

The language of equivocation underscores the theme of shape-changing. The growing importance of shape-changing, and the sort of 'reality' it permits Moll to accept, explains the ending and gives to the novel its ultimate unity. Defoe is careful to show how Moll comes to a gradual realization of the illusory nature of appearance and to the possibility and advantage of changing one's shape (or appearance) in the world. The laughter of the young ladies of Colchester over her confusion about the word 'Gentlewoman' is Moll's first lesson, and her affair with the Elder Brother, in which she learns the value of disguise, of both manner and dress, is her second. When she is living in the Mint and looking for a husband, Moll, then only a novice in the arts of deception, remarks, 'I resolv'd therefore ... that it was absolutely Necessary to change my Station, and make a new Appearance in some other Place where I was not known, and even to pass by another Name if I found Occasion' (p 76). Later on she will become used to changing her appearance not once but every time she goes out, and her decision to pass by another name will not be qualified by 'even.' As a 'matrimonial Whore' Moll widens her experience of deception and shape-changing, but it is as a thief that her shape-changing becomes almost frenzied. She more than once points out that she had 'several Shapes to appear in' (p 238) and that she 'generally ... took up new Figures, and contriv'd to appear in new Shapes every time I went abroad' (p 262). In Newgate Moll changes shape in another and more alarming way:

like the Waters in the Caveties, and Hollows of Mountains, which petrifies and turns into Stone whatever they are suffer'd to drop upon; so the continual Conversing with such a Crew of Hell-Hounds as I was with had the same common Operation upon me, as upon other People, I degenerated into Stone; I turn'd first Stupid and Senseless, then Brutish and thoughtless, and at last raving Mad as any of them.   (P 278)

The powerful image of the transforming power of water in mountain caves is central to the imagery, the language, and the structure of the novel. This passage marks the lowest point in Moll's life, her descent into the hell of Newgate. She has, after all her shape-changing, turned finally into stone, a state of being in which further change is barely possible. It is only the arrival of Jemy that shakes her out of her degeneracy, and brings her again to a realization of the 'horrid detestable Life' she has led and her abhorrence of Newgate. She concludes, significantly in another image of shape-changing: 'in a word, I was perfectly chang'd, and become another Body' (p 281). This fundamental change, brought about by her descent into Newgate seen as hell and her return as 'another Body' through the realization of her responsibility in Jemy's misfortune, prepares the way for the ending. Both Moll and Jemy are now ready for the last and most important change of shape which is brought about through their transportation to Virginia, itself a symbol of the possibility of renewal. Moll describes Virginia to Jemy as a place where 'we should live as new People in a new World' (p 304). In the final portion of her story, which epitomizes her life as a whole, Moll leaves Newgate at the age of 61 for the second time in her life and goes, in 'poor and mean' clothes, once again to Virginia. Within eight years through hard work and good fortune she is able to return once more to England, transformed finally, so it would seem, into the gentlewoman that she has always wanted to be.

The pattern of change and appearance continues to the end of the novel, but in its new emphasis gives meaning to what has gone before. Moll never gives up her disguises, but she turns them to new ends. She relinquishes the constant shifting of costumes and the unending petty deceptions of others for the more fundamental and important change away from a life of crime and matrimonial whoredom to a 'new Life in a new World.'

4 Jacobite and Gentleman

Colonel Jack (1722),[1] which appeared in the same year as *Moll Flanders*, is in several respects the male version of the story of Moll.[2] Both Moll and Jack are illegitimate orphans who early in life become obsessed with the notion of gentility, which they eventually obtain largely by means of disguise and deception. Moreover, both make two visits of several years' duration to Virginia, a place in the world of Defoe's novels where sins are expiated and men and women grow rich. Each finally returns, married and prosperous, to London. Their stories are recommended to the reader as exemplary histories of wicked lives repented. In their reflection of Defoe's vision of the life of man in society these two novels are midway between the qualified optimism of *Robinson Crusoe* and the ultimate despair of *Roxana*. Of course there are also important differences between them, mainly in the character of the protagonists and the time of their reform. Since Moll remains in mortal danger of discovery until near the end of her story, and since her repentance takes place in Newgate (and even then, according to the preface, is qualified), she retains a vitality and energy throughout which animates her story. Jack, like Crusoe, repents and reforms early in life, but there is not the extraordinary situation of total isolation on an island to supply interest. Although he keeps up his disguises and deceptions, they are often largely for his own amusement and do not spring from any pressing need, as in *Moll Flanders*. As a result Jack is often a more shadowy and less engaging character than Moll.

Although in *Colonel Jack* there is some falling off from the thematic and structural coherence of the two earlier major novels, the novel does not deserve the charge brought against it by Ernest Baker in his history of the novel: 'the first part is a realistic and sympathetic study of manners and social conditions; but the later career of the hero is a series of aimless and insipid adventures.'[3] Baker's judgment finds an echo in an article by W.H. McBurney, written almost thirty years later, in which he speaks (mistakenly) of 'the two-volume form'[4] and of that 'structural flaw [which] is practically a trademark of Defoe's novels,' namely, the 'anticlimactic section dealing with Cuban and Mexican trading.'[5] Yet it was McBurney who first identified the theme of gentility in *Colonel Jack* and suggested that by means of it Defoe manages to make 'an organic whole' of a very loosely constructed narrative. Michael Shinagel[6] accepts the notion of gentility at face value and argues that Jack (like his creator) becomes a true gentleman in every sense of the word.[7] Certainly the theme of gentility is central to the organization of the novel, but in a rather complex way. McBurney's motif of gentility, in fact, is part of a larger preoccupation with the ambiguities of identity and disguise, reality and illusion, and with the irony that gentility itself may be a mode of deception.

I

That the theme of gentility is to be treated ironically by its association with disguise and deception is suggested by the hero's name.[8] On the title page[9] we learn that the hero is 'The Truly Honourable Col. Jacque,' and the story records how Jack acquires the attributes of a gentleman, thus justifying his childhood name, 'Colonel Jack.' The facetious innuendo in 'Truly Honourable' and the foreign spelling (actually misspelling) of 'Jacque' suggest the falseness of Jack's social position in much the way that 'Moll' and 'Roxana' underline the bad eminence of those heroines.

Several meanings of the word 'jack' current in the eighteenth century suggest Jack's roles in the novel. At the beginning of the novel, when the hero calls himself 'Poor Boy Jack' or 'one of the Three Jacks of Rag-Fair,' his name bears the connotation primarily of the second meaning in the *Oxford English Dictionary*: 'A man of the common people; a lad, fellow, chap; *esp.* a low-bred or ill-mannered fellow, a knave.' Jack's shame in being a 'jack' motivates his driving ambition to become a gentleman, while the lack of education and worldly sophistication imposed on him by the circumstances of his birth hampers his attempt and qualifies his achievement.

A second meaning of Jack's name implies something false or assumed: in the eighteenth century the phrase a 'Jack-gentleman' means 'a man of low birth or manners making pretensions to be a

gentleman, an insolent fellow, an upstart.'[10] This is precisely what Jack
becomes when he returns to London and passes himself off as a French
gentleman. His rise in the novel from a jack to a jack-gentleman is thus
accompanied by the transformation of Jack into Jacque.[11] But the
social difficulties in courtship and marriage that Jack experiences as a
would-be gentleman draw attention to his perennial naivety, and constantly threaten to expose his assumed social position. The air of
pretence and pretentiousness that his childhood name of 'Colonel Jack'
has helped to create lingers about the hero and ironically underlines his
false gentility.

In the last part of the novel Jack's name bears another meaning. In
addition to being a low-born fellow and a would-be gentleman, Jack is a
Jacobite,[12] a meaning of his name that would not be lost to the reader of
1722. Significantly Jack's rise to gentlemanly rank, which is the controlling motif of the first part of the novel, is almost shattered by his
Jacobitism in the latter part; Jack the gentleman is nearly undone by
Jack the Jacobite. It is only by means of a clever disguise that Jack, living
as a 'gentleman' in Virginia, escapes discovery as a Jacobite Jack. All this
acquires greater force when we remember Defoe's attitude to the
Jacobites whom, particularly after the Jacobite rebellion of 1715, he
considered to be a group of deluded men, nourishing vain hopes, and
taken in by French ambitions. Jack's Jacobitism is the political expression of the naivety that runs throughout his entire career.

Defoe's treatment of Jacobitism in *Colonel Jack* is one of the didactic
aims of the work.[13] Opposition to Jacobitism was Defoe's strongest and
most constant political conviction, expressed tirelessly in the pages of
the *Review* and numerous tracts, particularly towards the end of the
reign of Queen Anne, when the succession was unsettled, and during
and immediately after the 1715 rebellion. Defoe's strategy in the *Review* and elsewhere is to argue that the Jacobites are deluded because
they have been tricked into thinking that the cause of the Old Pretender is genuinely supported by the French. Defoe maintains that
'*Jacobitism* is a Branch of *French* Power'[14] used by Louis xiv to weaken
England. The French king supports the Jacobite faction just enough to
keep England unsettled, but never enough to ensure a Jacobite victory.
In the *Review* and the various Jacobite tracts Defoe consistently refer-
red to Jacobitism as a 'meer whim,' 'this *Chimera*,' 'an Imposture,' and so
forth.[15] Yet Jacobitism was sufficiently powerful to attract a substantial
number of followers, even though, as Defoe argued, there had been
ample opportunity to discover that belief in either the Pretender or his
chance of success was a snare. Consequently Defoe accused his country-

men of being a 'Blinded Infatuated People, a Nation that may be drawn into a Snare' even though the snare is spread 'in your sight.'[16] The nation had been caught in the snare of Divine Right once before and now appeared to be in danger of running headlong into it again. In this way his countrymen would be 'below the Sylliest Species of the whole Field, who are never caught twice in that Snare they have been once intangl'd in.'[17] Defoe also contended that some men were Jacobites not solely because they expected French support but out of conscience, because they really accepted the notion of Divine Right. Of this belief Defoe says:

It is hard to say, whether there are any Delusions in *Popery* itself more gross, and in which more Sophistry, and Artifice to Cheat and Abuse the World has been made use of, and with more Success: There are a Thousand *Innocent Tories* lead away by this Chimera, to profess themselves *Jacobites* upon meer Principles of Conscience, perfectly jingled into it by the Harangues of the Jugling Emissaries of *France*.[18]

In maintaining that Jacobitism was a lost cause, and one moreover that was being used by England's enemies, Defoe was attacking Jacobitism by playing down its strength and its appeal. If the Jacobite cause were thought to have any chance of success, it might well attract men with lingering sympathies for the 'legitimate' monarch, as well as those who would hope to receive rewards at the accession of James III. Defoe, in other words, took the Jacobites seriously enough to want to minimize their claims of strength and support.

As well as attacking Jacobitism directly in political tracts and journals Defoe used Jacobitism as a fictional theme before he wrote *Colonel Jack*. In 1718 he wrote *The Memoirs of Majr. Alexander Ramkins*, a work that is interesting not only for the light it throws upon Defoe's attitude to the Jacobites (here too represented as the victims of a great deception) but also as an example of his use of fiction for didactic ends. The technique that Defoe used in the *Memoirs* was to show a man sympathetic to the Jacobite cause awakening from his delusion. The following passage is typical of the way in which Defoe suggests that even a born Jacobite, if he is reasonable, must see through the French pretence:

There was a Time when *France* gloried in the Ostentatious Title of being the Assylum of distres'd Monarchs, and I remember I was once dispos'd to have almost deify'd their Monarch upon that Score; but when I took the Frame of his Politicks, and examin'd every Wheel and Spring by which they moved, I rescued myself from the Prejudices I had been nurs'd up in; and though I always pursu'd the same End, yet I was a constant Enemy to their Method, which I was convinc'd were all directed another Way, and that a Restoration upon a French Footing was a Chimerical Project, and that if it had taken Effect by their Arms, *England* must have had another Doomsday-Book, and have suffer'd once more under an Arbitrary Discipline, more dreadful than that of *William* the Conqueror.[19]

The cunning of this sort of fictitious memoir is that, unlike the more obviously polemical tracts,[20] it might be taken as a genuine Jacobite memoir[21] and therefore be read by men with Jacobite sympathies. Hence, Defoe probably enlarged his audience to include those he most wanted to reach and convert.

In *Colonel Jack* Defoe employs similar techniques to accomplish his didactic purpose. Jack's Jacobitism is presented as part of a pattern of delusions. It is a momentary infatuation springing from his political inexperience, and, as the Pretender has promised to make him a colonel, an ambitious affectation arising from his desire for gentility. Jack first took up the military life which was to lead to his joining the Pretender when he joined an Irish regiment and fought in the opening campaign of the War of the Spanish Succession in northern Italy. As a captain in an Irish regiment serving the French king, Jack fought against the Austrians, and also, therefore, against the interest of England. But Jack's motives were not political. Rather, having left England and his troublesome wife, he was at loose ends and simply 'fell into Company with some *Irish* Officers' (p 207). He was really concerned with improving his social standing by becoming an officer. Years before in his brief career as a foot soldier he had 'Dream't of nothing but being a Gentleman Officer' (p 105), and now he is able to realize that dream: 'I was exceedingly pleas'd with my new Circumstances, and now I us'd to say to my self, I was come to what I was Born to, and that I had never till now liv'd the Life of a Gentleman' (p 207).

As an officer (in fact, by this time a lieutenant-colonel) in the Irish regiment Jack finds that the easiest way of advancing his military career and leaving the war in which he has been fighting for some seven years is to join the Old Pretender. As a Jacobite Jack takes part in the unsuccessful attempt of the Pretender to land with French support in Scotland in 1708. Jack's attitude towards this 'invasion' is, like Defoe's, that it is really an attempt by Louis xiv to use the Jacobites for his own interests, 'meditating nothing more than how to give the *English* a Diversion' (p 222). Although, as he tells us, he 'pretended a great deal of Zeal for his Service,' Jack does not at this time 'much consider the Cause, of one Side or other,' and claims that he was 'not only insensibly drawn in, but was perfectly Voluntier in that dull Cause' (p 223). Of course Jack hopes that in joining the Chevalier de St George (as the Old Pretender was known in Jacobite circles) he may 'have the *Chevalier's* Brevet for a Colonel, in Case of raising Troops for him in *Great Britain*, after his arrival' (pp 222–3).

By 1715, however, Jack is much more committed to the Jacobite cause. When in Scotland the Earl of Mar proclaims the Old Pretender James III and VIII and begins the invasion of England from the North, Jack is 'all on Fire on that Side' (p 250) and joins the rebels, passing as a French officer. Jack offers to lead a detachment to defend 'the Pass between *Preston*, and the River and Bridge' (p 265). When his advice is not followed, he gives the rebels up for lost and escapes from them. By doing so he also escapes the battle of Preston in which his comrades are all either killed or taken prisoner. His part in the events at Preston is the occasion for the final portion of the novel, since the arrival in Virginia of some of the Preston rebels, who would have been able to recognize Jack, causes his hasty departure in disguise for 'Nervis or Antegoa' in the Leeward Islands.

Finally, having recognized his political delusions and rejected Jacobitism, Jack is pardoned by a royal 'act of Grace, *that is to say, a General Free Pardon*' (p 276) and becomes a loyal subject of George I. Defoe thus shows George I to be a gracious monarch with sufficient wisdom to win the undying affection of those, like Jack, whom he forgives:

AND here let me hint, that having now as it were receiv'd my Life at the Hands of King GEORGE, and in a manner so satisfying as it was to me, it made a generous Convert of me, and I became sincerely given in to the Interest of King GEORGE; and this from a Principle of Gratitude, and a sense of my Obligation to his Majesty for my Life; and it has continu'd ever since, and will certainly remain with me as long as any Sense of Honour, and of the Debt of Gratitude remains with me. (P 276)

Whatever Defoe may have thought of George I in other respects, he clearly approved of the policy of pardoning Jacobite rebels.[22]

Defoe's didactic message about Jacobitism does not occupy as prominent a place in the novel as this outline of its function inevitably suggests. References to the Jacobite interlude in Jack's career, although important, are infrequent and the whole sorry episode is treated by

Jack with a casualness that is part of Defoe's understated purpose. Defoe wants to make the Jacobites appear a marginal and largely ineffective political force which attracts drifters like Jack. Jack's irrepressible desire to appear the gentleman remains the centre of the novel, and his Jacobitism is perceived as only one of the false means by which he hopes to obtain that goal. At the same time Jack's flirtation with Jacobitism offers us a valuable clue to the way Defoe wants us to think of his hero and his hero's story. Jacobitism in *Colonel Jack* is not merely of topical or incidental interest; Defoe makes Jack's Jacobitism an integral part of the characterization of the hero and of the pattern of delusions that informs and ironically qualifies the straightforward story of Jack's social ascent.

From what we have seen about Defoe's attitude to the Jacobites it is clear that a hero attracted to their cause must be politically naive. And Jack's naivety does not begin with his political inexperience. Jack in fact is carefully presented by Defoe throughout the novel in a deliberately ambiguous fashion; Jack is capable and ambitious, but also naive and easily deluded. Much of the time, particularly in the central scenes set in London, Jack is not so much a gentleman, as someone dressed up to look like a gentleman. Jack is almost as deluded about gentility as he is about Jacobitism.

The naive side of Jack's personality not only accounts for his early drifting from innocence into criminality ('and thus I was made a Thief involuntarily' [p 19], he observes), but also explains his later social, marital, and political misadventures. Moreover, and more significantly, this aspect of Jack's character conditions the novel's central theme; the quest for gentility is often ironically misdirected. At one stage Jack confuses becoming a gentleman with being a 'Gentleman Thief' (p 62). And when he learns, especially in France, how to 'look like a Gentleman' (p 200), he forgets to learn how to defend his honour and so betrays his appearance. Defoe's characterization of the innocent boy who 'was made a Thief involuntarily' finds a logical fulfilment in the naive man who is 'insensibly drawn in' to the Jacobite cause.

Jack's attraction to the cause of the Old Pretender is really the culmination of the pattern of delusion that springs from his naivety and social pretensions. By means of his military career and his profession of Jacobitism Jack hopes to acquire a right to the titles of 'gentleman' and 'colonel' which he has so long employed but realizes that he has failed to live up to. As an officer Jack thinks that at last he has acquired the social position that he 'was Born to' and believes that he is now living 'the Life of a Gentleman' (p 207). But when he drifts into

Jacobitism, partly at least to advance his career and enhance his social status, Jack again emphatically demonstrates his perennial naivety. Becoming a Jacobite colonel may seem to Jack to add to his appearance as a gentleman, but in fighting against his own king and serving the Pretender's 'dull Cause' Jack necessarily fails to meet Defoe's standards of gentlemanly conduct. He does not act like a man of honour but, like the Polish nobility that Defoe castigates in *The Compleat English Gentleman*, Jack is prepared to play 'Jack a both sides, to-day for and to-morrow against.'[23]

Moreover, since the Jacobites stand no chance of success (as Defoe is always careful to make clear in his writings), Jack dangerously deludes himself when he commits high treason in order to further his advancement to gentility. Even the zeal which Jack feels before Preston does not compensate for the dishonour of his Jacobite service or the foolishness of thinking that Jacobitism offers a short cut to gentility. Although Jack eventually becomes an officer and a gentleman – of sorts – Defoe clearly thinks that there is something suspect about gentility derived from serving in a Jacobite army. Defoe shows that Jack comes to realize the naivety of his supposition when he renounces the Pretender and submits to George I. And Jack is further made to recognize the delusion of the Jacobite promise when his position in Virginia is threatened by the near discovery of his earlier Jacobite service.[24] By showing us that Jacobitism is a delusion, and at the same time extending the characterization of Jack as naive and unthinking, Defoe's use of Jacobitism in the novel serves didactic and fictional ends at once.

The Jacobite theme is linked, moreover, to the theme of gratitude in the novel. In so connecting it Defoe manages to suggest that the royal policy of securing the loyalty of former Jacobites by pardoning them is not only prudential but springs from a humane and perceptive knowledge of human nature. The most notable instance of the theme of gratitude occurs in the long passage set in Virginia in which Jack demonstrates that it is better to encourage his master's Negro slaves to work out of gratitude than from fear of the lash: 'So that the Gentle usuage and Lenity, with which they had been treated, had a Thousand times more Influence upon them, to make them Diligent, than all the Blows and Kicks, Whippings, and other Tortures could have, which they had been us'd to' (p 149). The argument that Defoe advances through Jack in this episode reflects his belief that there is a 'Principle of Gratitude' in all men and that 'Nature is the same, and Reason Governs in just Proportion in all Creatures' (p 143). Four years earlier in the *Family Instructor* Defoe had argued that treating slaves with 'rage and fury' was aimed only at 'breaking the spirit': 'there is neither concern for soul or body expected in the master; no love to his slave's person, or concern for his future state; nothing in view but to have his work done, and his command be without reserve obeyed.' On the contrary, Defoe maintains, 'the nature of correction, as it respects a father to a child, or a Christian master to a servant, is quite different; passion can bear no share in it.'[25] The Christian relationship between superior and inferior is based on firm but gentle correction from the one, and gratitude for leniency from the other. Defoe's discussion of Jack's treatment of the slaves, particularly Mouchat, illustrates this idea.[26]

And it is not only the slaves who demonstrate the reciprocal benefits of gentle usage. Jack is himself the recipient of kind treatment and has reason to be deeply grateful to his master. The master, impressed with Jack's demonstration of the efficacy of calculated kindness and the value of gratitude, decides to show 'the same Principle of Gratitude to those that serv'd him, as he look'd for in those that he serv'd; and particularly to me' (p 150). The 'Principle of Gratitude' works in both directions, Defoe suggests, and establishes a chain of gratitude that now reaches from the slaves, through Jack, to his master.

Through the theme of Jacobitism Defoe extends this concept of the 'Principle of Gratitude' to the highest power, the king. Just as Jack's slaves out of their gratitude had become diligent in his service, so Jack himself from his 'Debt of Gratitude' becomes a loyal subject of George I:

for Gratitude is a Debt that never ceases while the Benefit receiv'd remains, and if my Prince has given me my Life, I can never pay the Debt fully, unless such a Circumstance as this should happen, that the Prince's Life should be in my Power, and I as generously preserv'd it.   (P 276)

Ironically, the lesson that he had long before so laboriously taught Mouchat now comes home to Jack. The royal act of grace should be seen, then, as part of the proper Christian relationship which governs parents and children, master and servants, rulers and subjects.[27] The Jacobites are really like rebellious children who must be firmly but gently corrected and then forgiven. This wise treatment restores an appropriate relationship and makes the reformed Jacobites loyal out of gratitude. The Jacobite interlude and its outcome, the royal pardon and Jack's debt of gratitude, thus extend and complete the theme of gratitude.

II

The reference in the preface of the novel to a 'wicked mispent Life' has sometimes seemed in conflict with Jack's early reform when he gives up his life as a thief. McBurney, for example, suggests that when he reforms Jack 'does a *volte-face*' and his 'personality, therefore, is transformed.'[28] Although it is true that Jack gives up his life as a petty thief because 'a strange Rectitude of Principles remain'd with him' (p 1), yet for many years as an adult he is guilty of a crime, equally odious and treated with the same severity by the law, namely, the political crime of treason. We have already noted that Jack is ultimately converted away from Jacobitism, but as he is forced because of his political crime to leave his 'apparent Tranquility' and to go 'wandring into the World again' (p 264), just as earlier he had been trepanned and sent as an indentured servant to Virginia 'as a Punishment for the Wickedness of my younger Years' (p 119). Both Jack's crimes, one as a youth, the other as an adult, spring from his ignorance. Jack is equally deluded by the attraction of the 'gentleman thief' and by the appeal of Jacobitism. And both may be said to arise from the fact that Jack, as a boy, lacked 'the Advantage of Education' (p 1).

Jack's lack of schooling as a child and the dismal fate that might easily have overtaken him (as the parallel stories of Major Jack and Captain Jack clearly show) reflect another of Defoe's didactic purposes in the novel, namely, his argument for 'publick Schools, and Charities ... to prevent the Destruction of so many unhappy Children, as, in this Town, are every Year Bred up for the Gallows' (p 1). The argument for orphanages and for charity education is carried over from the same concern expressed earlier that year in *Moll Flanders* (where it has less point), and takes its place in the context of the contemporary debate on the value of such institutions. Moll attributes her sad fate, being left 'a poor desolate Girl without Friends, without Cloaths, without Help or Helper,' to the lack of an insitution which she has heard of ('whether it be in *France*, or where else, I know not'), where the children of transported or hanged criminals can be cared for and 'put into an Hospital call'd the *House* of *Orphans*' (pp 7 and 8).

The origin of the controversy over charity schools antedates by a few years the publication of *Moll Flanders* and *Colonel Jack*. Orphans and children of parents too poor to pay for education were the objects of charity throughout the eighteenth century. And as charity schools were considered pious foundations, they were often supported by influential clergymen. Every year from 1704 to 1728 a sermon was preached 'on Thursday in Whitsun-Week' to the 'Aniversary Meetings of the Children Educated in the Charity Schools in and about the Cities of London and Westminster.' The preachers on these occasions were 'the Right Reverend the Bishops, and other Dignitaries.'[29] One of these sermons, by Thomas Sherlock, DD, Dean of Chichester, 'Preached in the Parish-Church of St. Sepulchre, May the 21st 1719,' is accompanied[30] by figures which suggest the extent of charity school education. At that time there were 130 schools in London; 1182 in other parts of Great Britain; and 130 in Ireland. A total of some 29,533 boys and girls were being educated in such institutions. Charity schools were not, however, as kindly looked upon as these figures might suggest. The year before at a special service in Chislehurst, Kent, according to Defoe's account, Sir Edward Bettison and Captain Farrington interrupted the service at the collection designed for the charity school and alleged that 'the money should not be given, as it was pretended, to the poor Children, who were Vagrants in the Eye of the Law, and were sent about Begging for the *Pretender*; and therefore it behov'd his Majesty's Justices of the Peace vigorously to oppose them.'[31] In the battle which ensued (Defoe's description of it is masterly) the rector and the preacher, the Reverend Mr Hendley, as well as the three men who took up the collection were arrested and bound over to the Quarter-Sessions at Maidstone as 'Rioters and Vagrants.'

The best-known tract in the charity-schools controversy was published the year following *Colonel Jack*. In 1723 Bernard Mandeville brought out the second edition of his *The Fable of the Bees*, accompanied now by a new 'Essay on Charity and Charity-Schools' in which he attacked the whole notion of attempting to educate poor children and maintained that instead they ought to be kept in ignorance for the sake of their religion. On 15 June 1723 a letter was published in the *British Journal* which also vigorously attacked the concept of charity education. This point of view met with opposition from clergymen anxious to defend charity as a Christian virtue. On 6 March 1723/4 William George Barnes, by appointment of the Bishop of Norwich, preached a sermon at St Martin's Palace, Norwich. In this sermon, entitled 'Charity and Charity Schools Defended,' Barnes endeavours 'to vindicate those who are careful to maintain Good Works, from those heinous Crimes charged upon them by their wicked Adversaries.' A rather more pragmatic argument is made by the Reverend William Hendley (the preacher of the inflammatory sermon at Chislehurst in 1718) in a tract published in 1725 and entitled *A Defence of Charity-Schools*. In this tract (as we learn from the full title, 'The many false, Scandalous and malicious Objections of those *Advocates* for *Ignorance* and *Irreligion*, the Author of *The Fable of the Bees*, and *Cato's* letter in the *British Journal*, June 15. 1723. are fully and distincly answer'd; and the USEFULNESS and EXCELLENCY of such *Schools* clearly set forth') Hendley argues that the charity schools discourage idleness and encourage industry, and from 'Industry Wealth is encreased.' In the face of national wickedness, he says, 'we cannot have too many Nurseries of Piety and Religion' (p 99).

Colonel Jack illustrates, against the background of the controversy over charity schools, the ill effects upon a good boy of the lack of education, which first turns him into a thief and later into a Jacobite. Clearly themes such as these shape the form of the novel, creating a resemblance in the first part to the 'rogue biography' and in the second part to the 'memoirs' of a disillusioned Jacobite. But the structure of the novel is more complex than an explication of Defoe's major didactic themes can convey. *Colonel Jack* is constructed, like all Defoe's novels, around a loose four-part arrangement, and unified by the ironically handled theme of gentility.

III

Four main sections of the novel are suggested by the four forms or meanings of Jack's name, and the divisions imposed upon the story by his two journeys to the New World. These four sections are (1) Jack's early career as a 'jack,' a boy and a thief; (2) his years in Virginia where, growing wealthy, he becomes a 'jack-gentleman' and so returns to Europe; (3) the period in which he acquires the name 'Jacque,' fights for the Pretender, becomes a colonel, and marries four times; and (4) his return to Virginia from which, fearing recognition as a Jacobite, he flees and spends some years trading with the Spanish in Cuba and Mexico. In each section Jack has a different career or careers; he is first a thief, then a planter, afterwards a soldier and a lover, and finally a trader. And the rhythm of his journeys to and from Virginia reinforces the theme of gratitude in the double pattern of crime, punishment, and rehabilitation.

The first section establishes the central unifying theme of gentility which is associated with appearance and developed by the symbolic use of changes of clothing. Jack knows that his father had been a gentleman and he conceives an overwhelming desire to become a gentleman too. Jack is not at all certain what a gentleman is, and throughout this section his notion of gentility undergoes several transformations. At first being a gentleman is nothing more to Jack than having a pair of shoes and stockings or a good hot supper. Later on he is overjoyed to find that his handsome physical appearance sometimes causes people to wonder if he might not have been better born. At one point, hearing an 'old Gentleman' say that true gentlemen would not indulge in the 'hateful Practice' of swearing, Jack discovers that 'from that time forward I never had the least Inclination to Swearing' (p 61). Experiences of this sort increase in Jack's mind that 'strange original Notion, as I have mentioned in its Place, of my being a Gentleman' (p 60). For a while he is led astray by the enticing idea of the 'Gentleman Thief,' and he joins a gang when he is told by his companion Will that 'we shall be all Gentlemen' (p 59). But he soon realizes that as a thief he is on the 'High Road to the Devil' and that this conflicts with his desire to live 'the Life of a Gentleman' (p 67). This section of Jack's life ends with his 'reform'; he returns stolen money to a poor woman of Kentish Town. But not long afterwards on a journey to and from Scotland he is kidnapped and sent as an indentured servant (the farthest remove from gentlemanly status) to Virginia. Meanwhile, having briefly become a soldier on his northern journey, Jack is taken up with the ambition of becoming a 'Gentleman Officer' (p 105), a desire that is not to be fulfilled until his return to Europe after his experiences in the New World.

In Virginia Jack becomes a Planter and a 'Gentleman' or, by Defoe's lights, a jack-gentleman, since, although he was in a sense a 'born Gentleman,' because he lacked education he was not a 'bred Gentleman.' In *The Compleat English Gentleman* Defoe points out that:

there are two sorts or classes of men who I am to be understood to speak of under the denomination of gentleman:
  1. The born Gentleman
  2. The bred Gentleman.

But the 'complete Gentleman ... will take them in both.'[32] Colonel Jack, although he is illegitimate, may have been well born, but he is not yet a complete gentleman. Moreover, he is deeply aware of the deficiency of his education and resolves to set this straight. He is able to buy a potted library when another planter dies and so he has the 'Opportunity of Reading some very considerable [books] such as *Livy*'s Roman History, the History of the *Turks*, the *English* History of *Speed*, and others; the History of the *Low Country* Wars, the History of *Gustavus Adolphus*, King of *Sweden*, and the History of the *Spaniard's* Conquest of *Mexico*, with several others' (p 157). And to his knowledge of history Jack is able to add Latin which he learns from one of his own servants who is an educated man.

Moreover, he discovers that he has acquired 'a solid Principle of Justice and Honesty.' He cannot explain how this is, but only that 'That Original something, I knew not what, that used formerly to Check me in the meannesses of my Youth, and us'd to Dictate to me when I was but a Child, that I was to be a Gentleman, continued to Operate upon me NOW, in a manner I cannot Describe' (p 155). The realization that he has become an honest man is a 'secret Satisfaction' and 'an inexpressible Joy' to Jack because his definition of a gentleman now includes the idea 'that to be a Gentleman, was to be an *Honest Man*, that without Honesty, Human Nature was Sunk and Degenerated, the Gentleman lost all the Dignity of his Birth, and plac'd himself, even below an Honest Beggar' (p 156). His newly found moral rectitude makes him hopeful that he is turning into a gentleman, that, as he puts it, while his honesty and repentance for past wrong are the 'Foundation of my new life,' that 'this was not the Superstructure, and that I might still be born for greater things than these' (p 157).

But his education serves only to teach him how little he knows of the world: 'I look'd upon my self as one Buried alive, in a remote Part of the World, where I could see nothing at all, and hear but a little of what was seen' (p 172). Virginia had enabled Jack to improve his position in the world, to become wealthy and educated, but he is still bothered by his 'old Reproach.' Jack wants to be a gentleman and that means being in Europe. However much opportunity for social and economic advancement Virginia may offer, Jack is plagued by the reflection that 'even this was not yet, the Life of a Gentleman' (p 172). He resolves to return to England, and his story 'begins a new Scene.'

Jack finally arrives home after a short series of adventures which takes him for some time to France. In England he finds he has 'the Reputation of a very considerable Merchant' and decides to pass 'for a Foreigner and a *Frenchman*' (p 185). He is concerned about concealing himself from his old criminal acquaintances, but this he discovers 'was the easiest thing in the World to do.' He has 'grown out of every Body's knowledge' (p 184) and his two brothers, both unreformed criminals to the end, have been executed. This news, of his brothers' dishonourable deaths, must have borne home to Jack the advantages of repentance and the degree of his subsequent advancement. The passage of time and the change in social class are in themselves sufficient disguise and Jack's pretending to be French reveals a love of role-playing typical of all Defoe's protagonists. 'I was infinitely fond of having every Body take me for a *Frenchman*,' he confesses 'so I went constantly to the *French-Church* in London, and spoke *French* upon all occasions, as much as I could, and to compleat the appearance of it, I got me a *French* servant to do my Business' (pp 185–6). Going now by the name of Colonel Jacque, he so successfully passes himself off not as an English but as a French gentleman that even the lady in the house opposite, whom he courts, takes him for a Frenchman. The orphan boy and former thief and indentured servant is now able to carry on a fashionable courtship, to take intimate suppers, to play at cards, and to dance, for as he points out, 'in *France* I accomplish'd myself with every thing that was needful, to make me what I believ'd myself to be even from a Boy, I mean a Gentleman' (p 191).

However, although he has the 'appearance' of a French gentleman, his position is false, and Jack is soon exposed since, for all his recently acquired polish, he has failed to learn the gentlemanly accomplishment of handling a sword. When a 'Gentleman' comes to collect a bill drawn upon his estranged wife and Jack refuses to pay, the other man, threatening to draw his sword, puts Jack into a dreadful fright: 'I must now own that tho' I had learn'd a great many good things in *France, to make me look like a Gentleman*; I had forgot the main Article, of learning, how to use a Sword, a thing so universally practis'd there' (pp 200–1).[33] Significantly Jack recognizes that he is not really a gentleman; rather he merely looks like one. When Jack refuses to fight, the bill collector taunts him, suggesting that he is neither a gentleman nor a Colonel: 'they say, you are a Gentleman, and they call you Colonel; now if you are a Gentleman, I accept your challenge, Sir' (p 201).[34]

In this section[35] of his story Jack gives us the history of his four marriages which, with the exception of the final alliance, are uniformly disastrous. Each of his wives disappoints him. One is vastly extravagant; another takes to drink; a third is unfaithful. Even Moggy, who is frugal, sober, and faithful, turns out to have 'made a Slip in her younger Days' (p 249). When Moggy dies and the small pox carries off three of his children, Jack concludes that, in spite of his fear of being buried alive, heaven has summoned him to 'retire to *Virginia*, the Place, and as I may say, the only Place I had been bless'd at, or had met with any thing that deserv'd the Name of Success in' (p 250).

In the final section of the novel, set entirely in the New World, Jack is punished for the political crime of Jacobitism; he meets again his first wife, whose story reinforces the pattern of his own history; and he becomes a Spanish gentleman. Although he had 'reformed' after 'Six and Twenty Years' as a thief, Jack continues in several ways to lead a life of 'levity' and 'Wickedness.' When he arrives again in Virginia, it is 'after a Ramble of four and Twenty Years' (p 251), a misspent period, as he concludes penitentially at the very end of the novel when he reflects that he had 'for 24 Year together liv'd a Life of levity, and profligate Wickedness' (p 308). In spite of the hero's early reform *Colonel Jack* conforms to the pattern of Defoe's novels in which the protagonist, after more than twenty years of isolation or of wickedness, ends his history with remorseful reflections upon his wretched life.

For his second quarter-century of bad behaviour Jack is punished by his fear of discovery and the gallows and by exile from his wife and home. Years before Jack had deliberately chosen the 'Life of a Gentleman' rather than the 'High Road to the Devil' (p 67) which leads to the gallows; now by an irony of fate the terrible fear of the gallows, which had frightened him as a thief, returns to frighten him as a respectable planter. Once more Jack adopts a life-saving disguise and he leaves Virginia, the home of his success and the place where he first became a 'gentleman.' Although he soon learns the good news that he is not excluded from the king's 'General Free Pardon,' yet, as a result of his flight, his situation is unhappy. Just as Jack had been 'brought into this miserable Condition of a Slave by some strange directing Power, as a Punishment for the Wickedness' (p 119) of his notorious cheats in London, even so retributive justice punishes him again for his crimes against the king. My wife, he laments, 'was gone, and with her, all my good Fortune, and Success in Business seem'd to have forsaken me; and I had another Scene of Misery to go thro', after I had thought that all my Misfortunes were over, and at an end' (p 277).

The repetition of the theme of crime and punishment in Jack's history is underlined by the coincidence of the story of his first (and therefore only legal) wife, who reappears on Jack's own plantation as his housekeeper.[36] When Jack fails to recognize her, she falls at his feet saying, 'O! Sir ... I see you don't know me, be merciful to me, I am your miserable divorc'd Wife!' (p 255). After separating from Jack, who had refused to support her extravagance, she had been 'deluded into Gay Company' which 'betray'd her to several wicked Courses' so that at last she 'fell in among a Gang of Thieves' and was transported to Virginia. In short, like Jack, she became a thief and was punished for it. After a suitable punishment and repentance in Virginia she is changed from a wretched servant into the wife of a plantation-owner. Jack's kind treatment of her in Virginia, when he takes her once again as his wife, not only ties up one of the loose strands of the novel, but also allows

Defoe to illustrate in yet another way the theme of gratitude. Immediately afterwards Jack has reason to be grateful to his wife, who is responsible for his safe escape from Virginia: 'it was by her Direction that I took every Step that follow'd for the extricating my self out of this Labrinth' (p 268).

Jack's desire to be a gentleman, which motivates his behaviour throughout the novel, runs into a new channel in the closing pages of the novel. Having first become a gentleman in Virginia, then a French gentleman in London, and a 'Gentleman Officer' under the Pretender, Jack finally passes as a Spanish gentleman under the splendid name of '*Don Ferdinand de Villa Moresa*, in *Castilia Veja*' (p 301). When he is captured near Cuba by the Spanish Jack passes some time there in an enforced visit during which he discovers that it is possible to trade privately with the Indies and Mexico, in spite of the Spanish monopoly of trade. Eventually, of course, he is nearly caught and has to be hidden by his Spanish friends, and so finds himself longing for his liberty, but in 'a most happy, and comfortable Retreat, tho' it was a kind of Exile' (p 307). Because he happens to speak Spanish well, the merchants find it easy to have Jack 'pass for a natural *Spaniard*' (p 298). Finally Jack escapes, not to his plantation in Virginia, but, by passing as a Spanish merchant, to Spain, and thence to London.

The final section of the novel emphasizes and clarifies the irony in Defoe's treatment of Jack's desire to be a gentleman. In the earlier sections of the novel, while Jack does indeed acquire gentlemanly attributes – such as wealth, education, polite manners – his social position continues to be based on pretence. His colonelcy is granted by the Pretender; his pose as a French gentleman is successfully challenged by a bill-collector; his three marriages to middle-class women fail. Finally, at the end of the novel, he makes a faintly comic figure, richly dressed 'like a *Spaniard* of the better sort,' but in an exile which he compares with the penitence experienced 'under the Discipline of a Transported Criminal as my Wife and my Tutor, or under the Miseries and Distresses of a Shipwreck'd wanderer, as my Skipper or Captain of the Sloop' (p 309). He reaches the melancholy conclusion that his has been 'a long ill-spent Life' and that he has never seen clearly into things, that he has been constantly deluded by appearance. Ironically even his fear of discovery by the Preston Jacobites, the cause of his final voyages, proves to have been illusory for when he meets them again 'there was not a Man of them, that ever took the least notice of me' (p 292). 'It would have been a singular Satisfaction to me,' he says, 'if I could have known so much as this of them before, and had saved me all the

Fatigue, Hazard, and Misfortune that befel me afterwards.' But, like all Defoe's main characters, he realizes that it is not the lot of man to penetrate the deceptiveness of fate: 'Man, a short sighted Creature, sees so little before him, that he can neither anticipate his Joys, nor prevent his Disasters, be they at ever so little a Distance from him' (p 292).

Jack's gentility is very largely a mode of appearance in which he is as much deceived as deceiver. His search for gentility has led him, finally, into the curious exile in Cuba in which he is at once a gentleman and a prisoner. Years before in conversation with his 'Tutor' in Virginia he had realized that he had 'hitherto gone on upon a Notion of things founded only in their appearance' (p 168). The story of Jack's desire for gentility is really the story of his failure to follow up this realization. In his Cuban exile he returns to these reflections upon the course of human life and the 'invisible over-ruling Power' of providence that he had briefly touched upon before:

I WHO had hitherto liv'd, as might be truly said, *without God in the World*, began now to see farther into all those Things, than I had ever yet been capable of before, and this brought me at last to look with shame and blushes, upon such a Course of Wickedness, as I had gone through in the World: I had been bred indeed to nothing of either religious, or moral Knowledge.   (P 308)

Jack's quest for gentility proves to have been a false quest; no one has been more deceived than Jack himself.

In this final portion of the novel Defoe subtly suggests the way in which a mode of deception may recoil upon the deceiver. Jack had avoided the Preston Jacobites and escaped from his plantation by pretending to be lame of the gout. In the closing pages he tells us that he was aided in writing his memoirs by 'the Benefit of a violent Fit of Gout, which as it is allow'd by most People, clears the Head, restores the Memory, and Qualifies us to make the most, and just, and useful Remarks upon our own Actions' (p 307). It is Defoe's final little irony that Jack's pretended gout, by which this section began, has now become both real and painful.

IV

The manner in which the theme of gentility is rendered in the novel and the characterization of Jack as naive and easily deceived are reinforced by the novel's imagery and language. Defoe characteristically associates the movement towards gentlemanly status with symbolic changes of clothing. Jack is constantly preoccupied with clothing and with changes of clothing throughout the novel. It is significant that as a boy he is well known as 'one of the three *Jacks* of *Rag-Fair*' (p 77), the cheap clothes market in Rosemary Lane. His first purchase as a successful young thief is a pair of Rag-Fair stockings and shoes which produce a delight in his own appearance that we recognize as typical of Jack: 'I found myself so refresh'd with having a Pair of warm Stockings on, and a Pair of dry Shoes; things, I say, which I had not been acquainted with a great while, that I began to call to mind my being a Gentleman; and now I thought it had come to pass' (p 15). A dinner taken at 'a boiling Cook's in *Rosemary-Lane*' confirms this impression, especially when 'the Maid and the Boy in the House every time they pass'd by the open Box where we sat at our Dinner, would look in, and cry, Gentleman Do ye call? and do ye call Gentlemen?' This, Jack adds characteristically, 'was as good to me as all my Dinner' (p 16). Although he realizes, as he looks back later, that his childish idea of his then being a gentleman was 'utter Ignorance,' yet the lesson that gentility cannot be gained by outward appearance is one that Jack never learns. His belief in appearances is strengthened by the remarks of a woman who owned an old clothes shop in Whitechapel and who asserted that Jack 'may be as good a Gentleman's Son for any thing we know, as any of those that are well dress'd.' And, Jack adds, 'she pleas'd me mightily to hear her Talk of my being a Gentleman's Son, and it brought former things to mind, but when she talk'd of my being not Clean, and in Rags, then I cry'd' (p 27). However, provided with a hat and breeches, Jack is easily able to believe his change of clothing to be a change in status: 'I thought my self a Man now I had got a Pocket to put my Money in' (p 28).

Perhaps the most socially significant change of clothing, and certainly the most dramatic, comes with his elevation on the plantation in Virginia from the rank of indentured servant to the position of overseer. When the good news is first given him Jack expresses his reaction sartorially: 'ALAS! *says I*, to him, I, an Overseer! I am in no Condition for it, I have no Cloaths to put on, no Linnen, nothing to help myself' (p 126). However the warehouse-keeper supplies Jack with 'several Suites of Cloths ... three good Shirts, two Pair of Shoes, Stockings and Gloves, a Hat, six Neckcloths, and in short, every thing I could want' (p 127). And then, indicating a changing-room, the warehouse-keeper adds dramatically: 'go in there a Slave, and come out a Gentleman.' Here becoming a gentleman is made part of a larger preoccupation with changing outward appearance, with disguise, with deception and self-deception within the novel. In Jack's transformation into a 'gentleman' the emphasis is placed upon his clothes, upon outward appearance, and the overseer gives him 'Joy of my new Cloths.' At this point and for some years to come Jack still makes judgments 'upon a Notion of things founded only in their appearance.' Defoe suggests the falseness in the assumption that good clothes make the gentleman, and at the same time gives further emphasis to the characterization of Jack as naive.

The density of the description of the 'Suites of Cloths' allowed to Jack is rare in *Colonel Jack*, though it is the sort of passage that is generally cited as an example of Defoe's verisimilitude. Samuel Holt Monk has rightly drawn our attention to the thinness of description in Defoe.[37] For example, although Jack and Moll enumerate the streets they use for their escape routes after a theft, we cannot visualize those streets from their descriptions. When Defoe does occasionally give us details, he usually has in mind a definite purpose, which is something more than authenticity. In the plantation episode Jack is casting off the rags of a servant, but he is not yet about to put on the fashionable clothing of a French gentleman. The description of the clothing – 'plain but good'; 'good Broad cloth, about 11s. a Yard'; 'Shoes, Stockings and Gloves, a Hat, six Neckcloths' – is designed to let us know exactly how far Jack has moved along the path that leads to gentlemanly status.

Similarly Defoe uses the device of describing a change of clothing to underline a change in social position in the case of Moggy, 'an innocent Country Wench,' to whom Jack gives his former wife's clothes when he marries her, or again in the case of his first wife whom he discovers on his plantation in Virginia working as a housekeeper. Out of compassion Jack orders that a complete set of clothes be provided for her, 'especially Head Cloaths, and all sorts of small things, such as Hoods, Gloves, Stockings, Shoes, Petty-Coats, &c. and to let her chuse for her self; also, a Morning-Gown of Callico, and a Mantua of a better kind of Callico, *That is to say*, to new Cloath her' (p 256). Mixed with his compassion is Jack's sense of triumph over his termagant wife: 'WHEN I came to the House which was the third Day, she came into the Room I was in, *cloath'd all over with my Things*, which I had ordered her, and told me she thank'd God, she was now my Servant again, and *wore my Livery*, thank'd me for the Cloaths I had sent her; and said it was much more than she had deserv'd from me' (p 257; my italics). Here the humility and repentance of Jack's wife is conveyed through her sense of gratitude for her clothes, which she calls livery.

In a similar, though rather more obvious, way the theme of money charts Jack's social rise from childhood beggary to adult prosperity.

But in Defoe's treatment of this theme Jack does not want money merely because it releases him from poverty and starvation, or later because it brings him considerable material comfort. Rather, Defoe emphasizes the ways in which money permits the transformation of Jack, a thief and later a traitor, into someone who appears to be a gentleman. Money, like good clothes, is valued by Jack primarily as a correlative of gentility.

As a young boy Jack is deeply impressed by the fact that the possession of money and decent clothing brings with it gentlemanly treatment (p 16). But as a thief Jack is never so much in love with money for its own sake that he is not capable of returning it (to the poor Woman of Kentish Town, p 67) when he realizes that his life of crime is 'not the Life of a Gentleman.' Money soon becomes really another form of disguise, and is associated with disguise throughout the novel. In the little scene in which Jack appeals to his 'Benefactor, the Clerk, at the *Custom-House*' (p 75) to look after his £30 for him, he finds that having money itself requires a disguise – 'that he might not wonder how I came by so much Money.' Jack puts on livery and pretends to be in service to a gentleman in the country in order to explain his new wealth.

Like most of Defoe's fictional protagonists Jack eventually becomes far richer than need requires or prudence dictates. In the final section, dealing with his Mexican trading adventures, Jack dreams of 'immense Treasure' and believes that he has found 'the way to have a Stream of the Golden Rivers of *Mexico* flow into my Plantation of *Virginia*' (p 296). But Jack's succumbing to the pursuit of wealth for its own sake acts as a prelude to his final realization that in pursuing wealth he has 'liv'd a Life of levity, and profligate Wickedness' (p 308). In his repentant mood he recognizes that what he has thought of as his own achievements are an illusion, since 'an invisible over-ruling Power, a Hand influenced from above, Governs all our Actions of every Kind, limits all our Designs, and orders the Events of every Thing relating to us' (p 308).

The importance given to clothing and to money, and therefore to appearance, in the world of Defoe's novels – one thinks of Crusoe's verbal self-portraits, of Moll's various costumes, of Roxana's masquerade dress – underlines a view of life in which 'Things are to us as they appear to be,'[38] while at the same time that view is criticized and qualified by Defoe's radical sense of human deceptiveness and the central idea that man is a short-sighted creature who rarely understands even his own motives and springs of action in 'the various Changes, and Turns' (p 307) of his affairs.

This view of the life of man in the world is reinforced and extended, as in *Moll Flanders*, by a vocabulary of equivocation which helps to create and sustain an atmosphere of trickery, sham, and hypocrisy. Often of course it is Jack who is the agent of dissimulation as he emphasizes by his frequent use of the verb 'to pass,' suggesting his skill at deception. In the early pages of the novel he 'pass'd among my Comrades for a bold resolute Boy ... but I had a different Opinion of my self' (p 7). Later, with what success we have seen, he 'pass'd for a Foreigner, and a *Frenchman*' (p 185). Among the Preston Jacobites he 'pass'd ... for a *French* Officer, and a Man of Experience' (p 265). Finally, at the end of the work, he is able to 'pass for a natural *Spaniard*' (p 298). Jack's choice of phrases in all parts of the novel intensifies the mood of appearance and dissimulation, as in the following examples: 'some Reputation, for a mighty civil honest Boy' (p 8); 'took up the air of what my Habit did not agree with' (p 114); 'brought my self off with my Tongue' (p 7); 'The Captain for all his smooth words must be a Rogue' (p 123); 'she had a Charming Tongue' (p 259); 'to make me look like a Gentleman' (p 200). But because 'we do not always Judge ... things by the real Temper of the Person, but by the Measure of our Apprehensions,' part of the vocabulary of deception is, specifically, of self-deception: 'I fancy'd myself Brave' (p 208); 'I believ'd myself Abus'd' (p 226); 'I reason'd and talk'd to my self in this wild manner so long, that I brought my self to be seriously desperate' (p 245).

In addition to the symbolic suggestiveness of clothing and changes of clothing *Colonel Jack* also shares with *Moll Flanders* the three images of life's cheats, the snare, the hook, and the gallows, which help to make vivid the forces operating against Jack and the traps that lie in the path of the naive and unwary. Often of course it is the devil himself who sets the snares and baits the hooks that lead to the gallows. As a young thief Jack suffers from a moral confusion designed by the diabolic fisherman: 'the subtile Tempter baited his Hook for me, as I was a Child, in a manner suited to my Childishness, for I never took this picking of Pockets to be dishonesty' (p 19). Even after Jack 'reforms' and is no longer in immediate fear of the gallows, he still remains in danger of the hook and the snare. Thus it is that the ale-house keeper in New Castle was a 'Subtil Devil, who immediately found us proper Fish for her Hook' (p 108); that the 'Tempter baited his Hook for me' (p 19); and that Jack's tutor warns him against 'such Snares as Human Nature cannot resist' (p 163). One of the greatest snares of Jack's life was laid for him by the devil and his first wife, who considered Jack 'a kind of Catch, for she manag'd all by Art, and drew me in with the most resolute backwardness, that it was almost impossible not to be deceiv'd by it' (p 187). Indeed, the entire conduct of that courtship is described in the vocabulary of deception – 'Witch-Craft in the Conversation,' 'ensnar'd,' 'drawn-in,' 'the Cheat,' 'out-witted,' 'meant not one Word,' 'the utmost Art and Subtlety,' and so forth. The last and most fearsome hook or snare is the gallows, literally both a hook and a trap, but figuratively part of the imagery of ensnarement. Just as Jack habitually sees the actions of others (though never of himself) in terms of the imagery of the hook or snare, he is also possessed by the image of the gallows whenever his actions bring him to the edge of disaster. 'I was in the uttermost Consternation,' he tells us when Will is arrested, and 'my Head ran upon nothing but *Newgate*, and the Gallows, and being Hang'd' (p 75). Later, as a Jacobite in fear of detection by the Preston soldiers, he 'thought of nothing, but being discover'd, betray'd, carried to *England*, hang'd, quarter'd, and all that was terrible' (p 269). In Colonel Jack's world of deception the gallows is a trap for those unlucky or unskilful enough to run into it, which is why Captain Jack, 'ignorant and unteachable from a Child,' dies upon it, while Colonel Jack manages by his disguises and pretences to escape.

The language of the novel is permeated with verbs such as 'disguise,' 'appear'd,' 'betray'd,' 'made as if,' 'conceal,' 'pretend,' 'bilk'd,' 'contriv'd,' 'deceiv'd,' 'out-witted,' 'drew-in' which help to define the quality of life in which speech is equivocation and appearance is deception. The accumulation of nouns suggesting deception – 'Pretence,' 'Wariness,' 'Craftiness,' 'Art,' 'Cunning,' 'Guile,' 'Grimace,' 'Masquerade,' 'Mask,' 'Costume,' 'Shape,' 'Cheat,' 'Game,' 'Fraud,' 'Trick,' and so forth – similarly reflects and intensifies the atmosphere of disguise and dissimulation. The themes of the novel, Jack's striving for gentility and his discovery of the moral and religious myopia which is the inheritance of the human condition, are worked out in a vocabulary that helps to explain the conclusions that Jack reaches in the final pages of the novel. Life for Defoe, as for Defoe's protagonists, is 'a Condition full of Hazards, and always attended with Circumstances dangerous to Mankind, while he is left to choose his own Fortunes, and be guided by his own short sighted Measures' (p 264).

5 Roxana's Secret Hell Within

Roxana (1724)[1] is Defoe's darkest novel. In *Robinson Crusoe*, with its traditional Christian emphasis on the fallen nature of man, repentance and redemption are possible. *Robinson Crusoe* is conditioned by a providential form. In the novels between *Robinson Crusoe* and *Roxana* repentance and reform are still possible, though they are less central to the structure of the novel than in *Robinson Crusoe*. But in Defoe's final novel both the heroine's capacity for struggling against calamitous misfortune and the possibility of her repentance and redemption are reduced. Roxana is Defoe's only protagonist who is passive in the face of disaster, a fact that helps to account for the increased importance of her confidante and servant, and the novel ends not after Roxana expiates her sins and returns to England, but after a 'Blast of Heaven' and her departure for Holland. There is no period of spiritual awakening, and the novel closes with the heroine's dispirited observation that 'my Repentance seem'd to be only the Consequence of my Misery, as my Misery was of my Crime.'

The reader of Defoe's fiction encounters in *Roxana* motifs and themes made familiar by the earlier novels, though he often finds them in forms that are significantly different. Jack's delight in his splendid appearance and his French accent, which facilitate his entry into fashionable society on his return to London, is repeated in a higher sphere in Roxana's decision to return to London and to pass as a wealthy, beautiful, and titled French lady. In Roxana Defoe takes up again the debate on marriage introduced in *Moll Flanders*, but what in the earlier novel is only an argument about a woman's need to be independent and to drive a hard bargain in courtship ('as the Market run very Unhappily on the Mens side,' p 67) becomes in the later novel an argument against marriage at all for a woman of means ('*I was as well without the Title*, as long as *I had the Estate*,' p 167). Finally, from *Robinson Crusoe* Defoe takes the theme of the relation of parents and children, which is also important in *Moll Flanders*, but in *Roxana* blame is shifted from the prodigal son to the profligate mother. In Defoe's first novel the hero attempts to recreate a family and a miniature society to replace the one he has lost. In *Roxana* the heroine attempts to preserve her 'Liberty' at the expense of the love and obligations she owes to her daughter.

I

In addition to the themes from the earlier novels carried over into *Roxana*, in his last novel Defoe broadens his attack on what he sees as the moral decline of his age to include both the highest and lowest elements of society. Consequently we have in *Roxana* a novel in which the heroine moves easily in all ranks of society, making a companion of her maid and becoming the mistress of the king. All of Defoe's lengthy social tracts, which we have examined earlier, are directed at abuses of morals and behaviour in his age, but if there is one theme which is common to most of his social criticism it is the need for social order. As he wrote in the preface to *The Family Instructor* of 1718: 'Doubtless there are duties in all our relative stations one to another; duties from parents to children, and from master to servants, as well from children to parents, and from servants to masters.' Virtually everything Defoe wrote in the area of social criticism is an extension of this doctrine. As the reign of George 1 advanced there seemed to Defoe to be less and less order and responsibility throughout the fabric of society. Two important aspects of *Roxana* reflect Defoe's concern about the two social extremes, servants and the court. In his conception of the servant Amy and her relations with her mistress Roxana he draws upon ideas that were to emerge in *The Great Law of Subordination Consider'd* (or, 'The Insolence and Unsufferable Behaviour of Servants'), published a month after the novel, while in the important central scenes describing Roxana's masquerade party he obliquely attacks the fashionable public masquerades attended by all classes of society and supported by royalty. These two themes have an important effect upon the structure of the novel.

In his consideration of *The Great Law of Subordination* Defoe regrets the weakening of the authority of masters and the increasing equality and extravagance of servants. In particular he comments on 'the gaiety, fine Cloaths, Laces, Hoops, Etc, of the Maid Servants, nay, even to

Patches and Paint.' And he goes on to suggest that 'it would be a Satyr upon the Ladies, Such as perhaps, they would not bear the reading of, should we go about to tell, how hard it is sometimes to know the Chamber-maid from the Mistress; or my Lady's Chief-Woman from one of my Lady's Daughters' (pp 14–15). His conclusion about this and similar offences is that 'in a word, Order is inverted, Subordination ceases, and the World seems to stand with the Bottom upward' (p 17).

In the light of works such as *The Great Law of Subordination* Defoe's attitude to the position of Amy and to Roxana's crime in elevating her servant to a position of equality becomes clearer. Roxana's casual remark that it is 'no great Difficulty to make *Amy* look like a Lady' (p 194) gives a warning of the moral and social disorder in the world of the novel in which 'Order is inverted' and 'Subordination ceases.'

Amy first plays the part of a gentlewoman on her own initiative. When Roxana's landlord, who is shortly afterwards to make Roxana his mistress, first comes to dinner Amy, although she waits at the table during dinner, afterward appears in another station: 'and as soon as Dinner was over, *Amy* went up-Stairs, and put on her Best Clothes too, and came down dress'd like a Gentlewoman' (p 31). Later on, however, it is Roxana who takes the initiative in making Amy her equal, in this case not socially but morally. In a salacious passage, highly uncharacteristic of Defoe, Roxana forces Amy to go to bed with her own lover: 'So I fairly stript her, and then I threw open the Bed, and thrust her in' (p 46). By the time that Roxana has become mistress to the prince, Amy's social elevation from time to time is casually accepted. When Roxana and the prince set out on their tour, Amy is left in charge at home: 'he [the prince] order'd a good honest ancient Man and his Wife, to be in the House with her, to keep her Company, and a Maid-Servant, and Boy; so that there was a good Family, and *Amy* was Madam, the Mistress of the House' (p 100). At the height of her success, and of her wickedness, Roxana lives in luxurious apartments in Pall-Mall, 'handsome Lodgings indeed, and very richly furnish'd,' and now, significantly, the versatile Amy is raised by Roxana to the position of 'Companion' and is 'dress'd like a Gentlewoman' (p 165). It is at this period that Roxana's daughter Susan, abandoned years before with her other children, is, unknown to Roxana, employed in the house as a servant. Truly 'the world seems to stand with the bottom upwards' when 'my Lady's Chief-Woman' and 'one of my Lady's Daughters' occupy each other's proper place.

Curiously *Roxana* is the only novel of Defoe's in which a secondary character is introduced at the beginning and maintains her importance to the end, or virtually to the end. It is highly typical of Defoe's first novels that the protagonist-narrator's viewpoint is dominant and exclusive. In *Roxana*, for the first time, the interplay between the two leading characters is often at the centre of our attention. All of Defoe's earlier heroes and heroines are self-obsessed, highly independent, and individual, and often acutely lonely (it is significant in this regard that Defoe's first novel is about a man's twenty-eight years of isolation). The stories they tell are their own. Other characters cut across their lines of vision but, once they are out of sight again, they no longer seem to impinge upon the action. The insignificance of the husbands and wives of Defoe's leading characters, once the story has moved on from them, is a striking example of his usual method. All of Defoe's early protagonists, moreover, complain of the lack of a friend in need, of a confidante, of someone to unburden themselves to and to receive advice from. Moll Flanders, for example, laments that she had 'no Help, no Assistance, no Guide' (p 128): 'I had no adviser ... and above all, I had no Body to whom I could in confidence commit the Secret of my Circumstances to, and could depend upon for their Secresie and Fidelity; and I found by experience, that to be Friendless is the worst Condition, next to being in want' (p 128). In *Roxana* Defoe for the first time supplied his protagonist with an adviser and confidante who plays a major role in the structure of the novel. And it may not be insignificant that he names her Amy, which suggests her place in the story.

I do not mean to suggest that Amy develops *ex nihilo*. Both Friday and Moll's governess are important, though temporary, secondary characters. Moll's governess, in particular, is a forerunner of Amy for she gives advice which the protagonist takes. (Friday, of course, does not.) Further, like Amy, she is capable of playing the devil's part and drawing the leading character into sin. But the governess appears about half-way through the novel and disappears before its end. Amy's real importance is that she shares the centre of the stage with Roxana throughout the novel, and the relationship between them is part of the form of the novel.

Indeed, it is often Amy who is the instigator of the action of the novel. When Roxana's 'fool husband' deserts her, leaving her penniless, it is Amy who cleverly contrives to get rid of Roxana's five children while Roxana, as she confesses, leaves 'the Management of the whole Matter to my maid *Amy*' (p 19). It is generally Amy, 'a diligent indefatigable Creature' (p 198), who is resolute while Roxana passively allows others to arrange her life for her. Amy's resoluteness and Roxana's passivity help to bring into focus Roxana's moral dilemma. Generally Amy does in deed what Roxana only wishes in thought. Amy in this way is the agent of Roxana's desires, even when they are only partially articulated. But Roxana's way of looking at things is always more complicated than Amy's. Roxana is clearly worried about her own responsibilities – to her children, for example, and to conventional morality. Roxana sees the need to abandon her children, and later realizes that her security is very much threatened by her daughter, but she is not herself prepared to forsake the children or to murder Susan. Roxana's relation with Susan at the end of the novel is particularly revealing on this point. Roxana is deeply torn by her fear of Susan's persistence in claiming her as mother and her desire to establish a relationship with her:

I cannot but take Notice here, that notwithstanding there was a secret Horror upon my Mind, and I was ready to sink when I came close to her, to salute her; yet it was a secret inconceivable Pleasure to me when I kiss'd her, to know that I kiss'd my own Child; my own Flesh and Blood, born of my Body; and who I had never kiss'd since I took the fatal Farewel of them all, with a Million of Tears, and a Heart almost dead with Grief, when *Amy* and the Good Woman took them all away, and went with them to *Spittle-Fields*: No Pen can describe, no Words can express, *I say*, the strange Impression which this thing made upon my Spirits; I felt something shoot thro' my Blood; my Heart flutter'd; my Head flash'd, and was dizzy, and all within me, *as I thought*, turn'd about, and much ado I had, not to abandon myself to an Excess of Passion at the first Sight of her, much more when my Lips touch'd her Face; I thought I must have taken her in my Arms, and kiss'd her again a thousand times, whether I wou'd or no.

But I rous'd up my Judgment, and shook it off, and with infinite Uneasiness in my Mind, I sat down: You will not wonder, if upon this Surprize I was not conversable for some Minutes, and that the Disorder had almost discover'd itself; I had a Complication of severe things upon me; I cou'd not conceal my Disorder without the utmost Difficulty; and yet upon my concealing it, depended the whole of my Prosperity; so I us'd all manner of Violence with myself, to prevent the Mischief which was at the Door.   (P 277).

It is not usual for a character in Defoe to experience such a 'Complication of severe things.' Amy's function in the novel is to throw into relief the complexity of Roxana's emotions by the contrasting simplicity of her own reactions. *Roxana* is not of course in any sense a 'psychological' novel, but in this last novel Defoe moved towards a greater concern with the mind, and an analysis of the emotions, of his narrator.[2]

Amy serves as a projection of Roxana's mind and also of her sense of guilt. Because Roxana is often morally troubled – about her responsibilities to her children, or about becoming the mistress of her landlord – and because Amy tends to sweep aside these worries, Roxana is concerned that Amy should bear with her the burden of guilt. Roxana's determination that Amy will sleep with her lover reflects Roxana's own guilty knowledge that she has become a whore: 'but as I thought myself a Whore, I cannot say but that it was something design'd in my Thoughts, that my Maid should be a Whore too, and should not reproach me with it' (p 47). Roxana thrusts the burden of responsibility, in this case of sexual promiscuity, upon Amy because it was Amy who had first encouraged Roxana to sleep with her landlord. Part of Amy's claim to social equality with Roxana is that she is a partner in Roxana's 'Wickedness.' The moral disorder in Amy's position is thus doubled.

II

From Defoe's point of view the social and moral disorder of his age is reflected just as much in the court and fashionable society as in the behaviour of ambitious or vainglorious servants. After 1715 he has frequent occasion, as we have earlier observed, to refer to the moral decline of his age, which he contrasts unfavourably with the reigns of William III and of Anne when there was a climate of moral reform. The age of George I seemed to have as its closest parallel the age of Charles II, when 'Lewdness and all Manner of Debauchery arrived at its Meridian: The Encouragement it had from the Practice and Allowance of the Court, is an invincible Demonstration how far the Influence of our Governors extends in the Practice of the People.'[3] These words were written in 1698, but four years after the accession of George I Defoe wrote in a letter in *Mist's Journal*: 'we are now running headlong, not into the same vile debauch'd Taste of King Charles the Second's Reign, but into as much worse as Thought can conceive.'[4] The signs of the time were the reappearance of royal mistresses, a Prince of Wales at strife with his father, flourishing theatres and opera-houses, the presence in London of innumerable 'mountebanks' and 'Merry-Andrews,' wild financial speculation and uncertainty[5] such as gave rise to the South Sea Bubble, and, above all perhaps, the introduction of large public masquerades which were taken by many of Defoe's contemporaries as symptomatic of, and in a measure responsible for, the growing atheism and immorality.[6]

Defoe's desire to draw a parallel between his own age and that of

Charles II accounts for the unusual form of *Roxana*, which in appearance resembles the prose fiction written in this period by other hands.[7] The romances of Mrs Haywood, Mrs Manley, and Penelope Aubin, which bear titles such as *Court Intrigues*[8] or *The Perplex'd Dutchess: or, Treachery Rewarded*[9] allowed their readers a glimpse into an exotic, and erotic, aristocratic world far above them, rather in the way that the movie magazines of today profess to tell about the secret lives of famous film stars. Defoe's novel, which bears the typical romance title[10] of *The Fortunate Mistress*, claims to be a 'History of the Life and Vast Variety of Fortunes of Mademoiselle de Beleau, afterwards called the Countess de Wintselsheim in Germany Being the Person known by the Name of the Lady Roxana in the time of Charles II,' although in the preface Defoe takes pains to distinguish his book from the contemporary romances since, unlike other 'Modern Performances of this Kind,' 'the Foundation of This is laid in Truth of Fact.' And Roxana is clearly aware of the romantic appearance of her story when she tells us that to repeat all the kind things her lover said to her would make her story 'look a little too much like a romance' (p 72). The special advantage to Defoe in creating a novel that resembled a romance was that, in addition to its immense contemporary popularity, the romance provided for an aristocratic setting and the revelation of aristocratic vices. And, more important, since many of the romances were set in the court of Charles II, Defoe was able to adopt the political expedient of criticizing the court of his own time under the cover of a description of the court of Charles II, and at the same time to suggest a moral comparison between the two.

Roxana probably owes something too to the various biographies of Mary Carleton, as Ernest Bernbaum pointed out many years ago. Bernbaum's point is that Defoe's writing grew out of the 'twilight zone' between journalism and literature 'from the days of Elizabeth to those of the Georges' in which we find 'the flourishing of imposture,' and not from the direct fictional imitation of truthful records, as Walter Raleigh had earlier suggested.[11] Certainly Mary Carleton, like Roxana, was a mistress of the arts of disguise and deception, and the author of one of these narratives of Mary Carleton's life, *The Memoirs of Mary Carleton, commonly stiled, the German Princess* (1673), might as easily have been describing Roxana: 'a person of very quick Apprehension, she being Mistris of as many Languages as there are Liberal Arts; but to do Justice on all sides (give the Divel his due) as to Legerdemain, or any other ingenious contrivance of that nature, nothing ever went beyond her' (p 4). Mary Carleton owed much of her success to her transformation of herself into a German princess on her arrival in England from Holland. Again, there is a parallel not only with the personality but also with the techniques of Roxana, who transformed herself into a great French lady on her arrival from Holland and who was later, if we are to believe the title-page, a German countess. However, there is a satiric purpose in alluding to the success story of a German noblewoman since readers of *Roxana* would readily think of the two unpopular German mistresses of George I, Charlotte Sophia, Baroness von Kielmannsegge, later Countess of Darlington, and Ehrengarde Melusine, the daughter of Gustavus Adolphus, Count of Schulenburg, who replaced Kielmannsegge as the king's first favourite and was created Duchess of Kendal in 1716.[12]

Roxana's exotic name, a further indication of the novel's resemblance to the court romances, may owe its origin to yet another memoir of the reign of Charles II, namely the *Memoirs of the Life of the Count de Grammont: Containing, in Particular, the Amorous Intrigues of the Court of England In the Reign of King Charles II* (1714) by Anthony Hamilton, Count de Grammont: 'The Earl of *Oxford* fell in Love with a handsom, graceful Player, belonging to the *Duke's Theatre*, who acted to Perfection, particularly the Part of *Roxana*, in the *Rival-Queens*, insomuch that she afterwards was call'd by that Name' (p 246). Maximillian Novak, in a survey of the possible origins of Roxana's name, mentions Grammont's *Memoirs* which 'has usually been suggested [as] the source of the name' Roxana, but he insists that 'an attempt to identify Roxana with any single person would be an error.'[13] Novak argues persuasively that in *Roxana* Defoe 'was aiming at a quintessential courtesan rather than any specific person' and suggests that Roxana is really 'a mélange of all of Charles's mistresses.' What Novak does not suggest is that a royal mistress with a German title might at the same time remind contemporary readers of the mistresses of George I.

Whatever the origin of Roxana's curious name, and Novak, I believe, is right about its deliberate vagueness, it seems clear that Defoe was attempting to present a fictitious work which resembled the romances set in the court of Charles II.[14] At the same time, it would be unlike the author of the *Journal of the Plague Year* to set his story in the reign of Charles II without having some more devious purpose in mind. The *Journal of the Plague Year* was so convincingly set in 1665 that it has often been taken as a genuine historical document; yet it was prompted by a fear of a return of the plague to England after the news of an outbreak in Marseilles in 1721 and may well have been written, as John Robert Moore suggested, as a justification for Walpole's quarantine policy.[15]

Similarly, two years later when Defoe wrote *Roxana* he set the story in the reign of Charles II – it was of course politically expedient to do so – but his real interest was in immediate contemporary events. Defoe is concerned in *Roxana* with the decline in social morality *in his own age* which he attacks under the guise of its resemblance to the notorious age of Charles II. Public masquerades were a prominent feature of the period in which Defoe was writing, and the vividness of the masquerade scenes in *Roxana* suggests that Defoe was drawing upon interest in a contemporary phenomenon. While these scenes ostensibly represent a condemnation of the licentiousness of the time of Charles II, they are intended as a specific, though slightly veiled, attack upon the contemporary masquerades which were once again providing the occasion for a rise in immorality.

Masquerades were introduced to London early in the reign of George I, shortly before the beginning of the government's South Sea scheme, by the manager of the Haymarket Opera House, the celebrated Swiss promoter J.J. Heidegger, and at once became vastly popular. A letter of advertisement in *The Weekly Journal, or Saturday Post* for 15 February 1718, reckons that seven hundred people were present at a masquerade in the Haymarket 'on Tuesday, last Week ... with some Files of Musquitiers at Hand, for the preventing any Disturbance might happen by Quarrels, &c. so frequent in Venice, Italy, and other Countries, on such Entertainments.' Gaming-tables[16] were provided for those who pleased to play, 'while Heaps of Guineas pass about,' and sweetmeats and wine were available from 'divers Beaufetts, over which is written the several Wines therein contain'd, as Canary, Burgundy, Champaign, Rhenish, &c. each most excellent in its kind; of which all are at Liberty to drink what they please.'[17] At eleven o'clock a cold supper was provided in an adjoining room; 'the whole Diversion continuing from Nine o'Clock till Seven next Morning.' The masquerades received royal patronage from the Prince of Wales, who is said to have given £1000 for their support.[18] At any rate, he certainly favoured Heidegger and, after he became king, appointed him Master of the Revels, in which capacity Heidegger had the management of the chief private and public entertainments.

The particular attraction of the masquerades seems to have resided in the opportunity they inevitably provided, through the disguise of costumes and masks, for an indiscriminate mixing of classes and a considerable degree of sexual licence. *The Weekly Journal* for 25 January 1724, about a month before *Roxana* was published, reports that:

The Humour of the Company appears chiefly in dressing in Characters different from their Rank in Life; I talk'd with a Chimney-Sweeper, whom I discover'd to be of no less Quality than a Duke; and a Person in the rich Habit of a noble Venetian, who, taking off his Mask, I knew to be an Apprentice to a Tallow-Chandler.

Although these assemblies were guarded, prostitutes, pickpockets, and sharpers of all kinds gained admission, and the masquerades, apparently scenes of debauchery, theft, and quarrels, rapidly acquired a scandalous reputation which brought on the attacks of newspapers, pamphleteers, and clergymen. An unsuccessful attempt was made to suppress them by a bill in Parliament, but eventually a royal proclamation was issued against masquerades, after which they were called 'ridottos' or balls.[19] Understandably they were a natural target for Hogarth's satirical pen and in 1724 he engraved *Masquerades and Operas* (No. 1), which depicts a satyr and Folly (said to be the Prince of Wales, later George II), on a road before Burlington House, Piccadilly, leading a group of masquerade revellers into a colonnade labelled 'MASQUERADE,' while, from a window, Heidegger, indicated by an 'H,' overlooks the scene. In the centre foreground there is a woman who is calling 'Waste Paper for Shops' and pushing a wheel-barrow filled with volumes marked 'Congrav, Dryden, Otway, Shakspere, Foe, Pasquin No. xcv, Addison.'[20] In the same year a cartoon, entitled *Hei Degeror. O! I am undone*,[21] satirized the director of masquerades whose name is scarcely concealed in the title. This cartoon probably takes its rise from a sermon[22] against the masquerades preached on 6 January 1724 by Edmund Gibson, the Bishop of London, before the Societies for the Reformation of Manners. Six weeks later, on 29 February 1724, *Roxana* was published.[23]

There can be no doubt that the masquerade scenes in *Roxana* should be seen in the context of the general attack on the age in the early 1720s, and, in particular, the attack on the masquerades which were, for many of Defoe's contemporaries, both symbol and cause of an alarming decline in morals. It was a period that had just witnessed the folly that preceded, and the frenzy that followed, the bursting of the South Sea Bubble. Both King George I and the Prince of Wales were thought to be keeping mistresses; the theatres, always a beam in the eye of the reformers, were flourishing; the vogue of the Italian opera was approaching its height, and the extravagant rivalry of Francesca Cuzzoni and Faustina Bordoni was soon to divide the fashionable part of the town into two camps. In addition, quacks, mountebanks, and charlatans,[24] the parasites of a gullible people, abounded. In 1728 Gay, in the immensely successful *Beggar's Opera*, pointed out that great cheats, such as politicians, flourished, while lesser cheats, such as highwaymen, were hanged. It is all a matter of skilful deception. 'Thus we live in a general Disguise,' Defoe wrote in 1726, 'and like the Masquerades, every Man dresses himself up in a particular Habit.'[25]

Defoe readily saw the parallel between his own time and the days of Charles II and made use of it in his conception of the central scenes of *Roxana*. What Defoe is attacking is not only the immorality of the Restoration, which I rather think he took for granted, but the moral laxness of his own time which, he suggests by his comparison, resembles that of the Restoration all too closely. The masquerades in *Roxana* take place simultaneously in the reign of Charles II and of George I, as the double time scheme of the novel makes clear. Ostensibly, the novel is set in the seventeenth century. The title refers to 'the Person known by the Name of the Lady Roxana in the time of Charles II'; Roxana invites the reader to confuse her with Nell Gwyn by calling herself a 'Protestant Whore' (p 69);[26] and her often mentioned financial adviser, Sir Robert Clayton, prominent in the reigns of Charles II and James II, died in 1707. But the implication that the story is set in the Restoration is contradicted by the first pages of the novel where we learn that Roxana, born in France, was 'brought over hither' (that is, to England) at 'about ten Years old' by her parents in 1683. A few pages after the description of the masquerades she writes:

I held this wicked Scene of Life out eight Years, reckoning from my first coming to *England*; and tho' my Lord found no Fault, yet I found, without much examining, that any-one who look'd in my Face, might see I was above twenty Years old, and yet, without flattering myself, I carried my Age, which was above Fifty, very well too.

I may venture to say, that no Woman ever liv'd a Life like me, of six and twenty Years of Wickedness, without the least Signals of Remorse. (Pp 187–8)

If she was 'about ten Years old' in 1683 we can readily deduce that she must therefore have written the passage just quoted in about 1723.[27] It follows from this that she met her landlord the jeweller in 1697 ('six and twenty Years of Wickedness' earlier), left England three years later in 1700,[28] and returned in 1715 'eight years' before 1723), at exactly the right moment[29] to allow her 'large Apartments in the *Pall-Mall*' to be used for masquerade balls by important persons in the court and society.

Roxana's masked ball, although attended by a large number of people unknown to her, was a relatively private affair, while the masquerades described in the newspapers and satirized by Hogarth were public assemblies. Roxana's masquerade party might almost have been attended by the writer of *The Weekly Journal*[30] for 18 April 1724: 'We did not go directly to the *Hay Market*, we made a Stop by the way, and went into the House of a certain Person of Quality, who, upon those Nights, receives Company in Masks.' At the same time, the resemblance between Roxana's masquerade and the public assemblies is remarkably close. Roxana does not organize the ball herself; rather it is managed by others (as is the masquerade at the Haymarket). Food and drink are provided, as well as gaming tables; a 'strong Party of Guards' is necessary; and the party lasts through the night until six the next morning.

Defoe is writing fiction, not a pamphlet, and his attack on the great public masquerades is kept properly veiled by time ('the time of Charles II') and setting ('a large Apartment in the *Pall-Mall*'), though the target to the readers of 1724 would have been abundantly clear. That his intended comparison of the reign of George I with the time of Charles II will not be missed, Defoe provides a direct link between the two periods in Roxana's frank summary of her daughter Susan's description of the party she witnessed as a maid in Pall-Mall: 'yet, *after all she cou'd say*, her own Account brought her down to this, That, *in short*, her Lady kept little less than a Gaming-Ordinary; or, *as it wou'd be call'd in the Times since that*, an Assembly for Gallantry and Play' (p 290, Defoe's italics). The masquerade scenes are, of course, a brilliant evocation of the atmosphere of the court of Charles II, and, like the *Journal of the Plague Year*, have a life of their own. But in the very vitality of his fictional creation and the vividness of his moral comparison lies also the strength of Defoe's commentary upon the morality of his own day.

III

Roxana differs from the earlier novels, not only in the emphasis given to social criticism by the attack on both ambitious servants and the dissolute court, but also in a new concern for the person of the heroine herself. Here the most instructive comparison is naturally with *Moll Flanders*. In the earlier novel Moll's dance of life is so energetic that she rarely has time to cultivate her emotions or contemplate her despair. Lover follows lover, and when that 'Game' is over, theft follows theft. Moreover, Moll succeeds in her two careers by remaining essentially uninvolved with other people. She operates alone and is eminently able to take decisions. And although she is apparently capable of deeply felt emotions, as in the strange case of mental telepathy with Jemmy, she realizes that her achieved social place depends on the suppression of private emotions. What keeps us reading *Moll Flanders* is our fascination with the heroine's extraordinary ingenuity, energy, zest for life in the wide variety of her experiences. Here, in a word, is the abundance of comedy.

This is not the case with *Roxana*. Several changes may be noted. The most significant, as we have observed, is the introduction of a confidante and friend. Amy is not only the agent of Roxana's wishes: she is also a projection of Roxana's mind. In this sense the struggle in Roxana's soul – between her timidity and her vanity, her irresolution and her ambition – is dramatized in a way that anticipates Hardy's more complicated dramatization of the two sides of Jude's personality through his love for the passionate Arabella and the intellectual Sue Bridehead. Unlike Moll Roxana is frequently incapable of action, and her moments of indecision permit her to examine her own life. The torment that Roxana suffers from her troubled conscience is an important theme in the novel. In the world of *Roxana* past actions impinge upon the present. Children cannot simply be abandoned. Confidantes cannot be let into vital knowledge without consequences, a fact that Moll understands thoroughly, but which Roxana does not. Moll always works out her problems alone, but Roxana works out her problems with the help of Amy, and generally with a far greater awareness of the social and personal implications. Roxana persistently examines her motives, and she never completely learns Moll's lesson that her social position depends upon the suppression of private emotions. Roxana lacks the irrepressible energy of Moll, but the reader's attention is held by the growing sense of tragic suspense. Far more than in the earlier novel every action leads towards the final action. The abundance of comedy gives way to the tighter structure of tragedy.

Roxana is herself aware that the outcome of her actions imposes a shape upon the story she tells: 'I might have interspers'd this Part of my Story with a great many pleasant Parts, and Discourses, which happen'd between my Maid *Amy*, and I; but I omit them, on account of my own Story, which has been so extraordinary' (p 83). Of course in the earlier novels, particularly *Moll Flanders*, the narrators sometimes have occasion to remind us that they are telling only their own stories, but when Roxana makes similar remarks, it is generally with a heightened sense of the direction of her tale. 'I could dwell upon the Subject a great-while; but my Business is History,' she insists at one point; 'I had a long Scene of Folly yet to run over' (p 133). And while Moll eliminates extraneous material because it is too dull, Roxana does so because interesting diversity would detract from the story of crime and punishment. She refuses to give us details of her journey in Italy, for example, because 'it would be too full of variety' (p 103). About half way through the novel these remarks about the need for narrative economy are replaced by comments which emphasize the coming disaster: 'my Measure of Wickedness was not yet full' (p 159); 'an Introduction to my Ruin' (p 160); 'in a very unlucky Hour, and in the very Crisis of my Affair' (p 232); 'in *an evil Hour*' (p 234); 'the Clouds began to thicken about me' (p 296); 'the Crime going before, the Scandal is certain to follow' (p 298); 'this wou'd, at last, all end in my Ruin' (p 312). Roxana is Defoe's only protagonist who is passively evil, and it is part of her character that she recognizes in these and many similar remarks the operation in the world of powerful forces which she cannot control. Her reflection on the inevitability that the prince will one day drop her is typical of her resigned attitude in the face of destructive and deceitful forces; 'the highest Tide has its Ebb; and in all things of this Kind, there is a Reflux which sometimes also is more impetuously violent than the first Aggression' (p 107).

Formally tragedy provides for greater introspection on the part of the protagonist than comedy (as we witness in the difference between *Clarissa* and *Pamela*). The tragic protagonist, like Roxana, grows aware of his fate and turns in upon himself as a result. Throughout the novel Roxana is presented with difficult and disturbing moral choices, such as the alternative between virtuous poverty and sinful prosperity, and far more emphasis is put upon the debate over what to do than in Defoe's previous fiction. In the dialectic of sin it is Amy who argues the devil's cause, as Roxana specifically points out to her. You 'argue for the Devil, as if you were one of his Privy-Counsellors' (p 37), Roxana says when Amy tries to persuade her that she might sleep with her landlord the jeweller since she had been so long deserted by her husband. But while the devil's arguments are put into the mouth of Amy, Roxana later comes to acknowledge the fact that Amy merely puts boldly what she (Roxana) thinks to herself: 'It is true, this Difference was between us, that I said all these things within myself, and sigh'd, and mourn'd inwardly; but *Amy*, as her Temper was more violent, spoke aloud, and cry'd, and call'd out aloud, like one in an Agony' (p 126). The moral choice is really an internal debate, a struggle in Roxana's mind, which is externalized when Amy argues on the side of vice and thereby allows Roxana to be persuaded to do what she really wants to do.

Roxana is, as Novak has ably demonstrated, 'a novel of moral decay.'[31] But what makes it so unusual among Defoe's novels is the attention paid to the interior drama of moral deterioration. There are several stages in Roxana's moral downhill path, each of which corresponds to a rise in her financial and social position. At first, even after having faced starvation and want, she repulses the suggestion of her benefactor that they live together as husband and wife. Moreover, she is able for a while to resist Amy's more persuasive 'Rhetorick' (p 39) but is eventually won over by that 'Viper, and Engine of the Devil' and agrees to cohabit with her landlord 'from a Principle of Gratitude' (p 38). What Roxana emphasizes about this first step is that, not merely afterwards but at the time, she was fully aware that they 'were no more than two Adulterers, in short, a Whore and a Rogue' (p 43). She does evil, and knows that she does evil, as she points out: 'In this I was a double Offender, whatever he was; for I was resolv'd to commit the Crime, knowing and owning it to be a Crime' (p 41). No other protagonist in Defoe is so deeply, if only occasionally, troubled by conscience: 'there was, and would be, Hours of Intervals, and of dark Reflections which came involuntarily in, and thrust in Sighs into the middle of all my Songs; and there would be, sometimes, a heaviness of Heart, which intermingl'd itself with all my Joy, and which would often fetch a Tear from my Eye' (p 48).

In her first temptation and fall it can be said of Roxana that she attempts to withstand the arguments of the devil; that she can plead the desperation of poverty and the claims of gratitude; and that she recognizes clearly that she has done wrong. When the jeweller, her second 'husband,' is murdered, she is courted by a French prince and soon agrees to become his mistress. Her measure of wickedness is increased. She is no longer poor ('I had now no Poverty attending me; on the contrary, I was Mistress of ten Thousand Pounds,' p 65); she is flattered by the attentions of a nobleman who appeals to her 'Vanity'; and she is dazzled by 'Great Things.' Roxana is now not merely a common-law wife; she is a mistress and is kept, significantly, by a prince – his high rank and foreign title suggesting aristocratic, and continental, profligacy and dissipation. At this point she has an opportunity to repent and to reform. The prince, conscience-stricken by the death of his wife, leaves Roxana, who shortly afterwards finds herself courted by a respectable and kindly Dutch merchant who wants her to become his wife. It is interesting to observe here how Defoe uses difference of class to underscore the advances and retreats in Roxana's moral decline. With her middle-class suitors Roxana is a wife, is asked to become a wife, or is able to pass as a wife. With the aristocrats (the French prince, the king, and an English lord of unspecified rank) Roxana is always a kept mistress.

Roxana's refusal to become the wife of the Dutch merchant is, as Robert Hume has pointed out, 'the key to her fall.'[32] Both Roxana and the merchant are free to marry. Amy had written to Roxana to report (falsely) that her real husband, the brewer, had died. But Roxana is now so entranced with the immoral way of life she has been led into that she confounds the Dutch merchant by agreeing to become his mistress, but not his wife. This is the crucial error. 'If I had not been one of the foolishest, as well as wickedest Creatures upon Earth,' she confesses, 'I cou'd never have acted thus' (p 158). By rejecting an honourable marriage with the merchant, Roxana rejects respectability, morality, and a middle-class life. Close to the end of her affair with the Dutch merchant Roxana tells us that she has resolved to try her luck in London as a whore of the most ambitious sort: 'I was not at a Loss how to behave, and having already been ador'd by Princes, I thought of nothing less than of being Mistress to the King himself' (p 161). Roxana's success in this ambition marks the height of her immoral achievement and the summit of one of the two contrasting paths open to her. The choice between living 'like a Queen' (here as the king's mistress) and living as the wife of a wealthy merchant is emphasized at significant points in the story. As the mistress of the French prince Roxana tells us that she 'liv'd indeed like a Queen,' though, she adds a little ruefully, as 'the Queen of Whores' (p 82). When she rejects the merchant she throws away not only 'an opportunity to have quitted a life of Crime and Debauchery' but also an opportunity, ironically, to have 'liv'd like a Queen, nay, far more happy than a Queen' (p 159). A little later Sir Robert Clayton recommends to Roxana that she marry 'some eminent Merchant' who would maintain her 'like a Queen' (p 170). To Roxana Clayton's remarks must have seemed heavily ironic since she had left her Dutch merchant only a short while before. And Clayton's comments on the true gentility of merchants adds to the irony of the scene. He insists that 'a true-bred Merchant is the best Gentleman in the Nation; that in Knowledge, in Manners, in Judgment of things, the Merchant out-did many of the Nobility.' Although Roxana professes to agree with this advanced point of view (which, of course, is Defoe's), she is overwhelmed by 'the Title of Highness' and rejects the merchant a second time when she learns that the prince is seeking her again. It is not surprising that, as she confesses later, she can understand mad women who imagine themselves queens: 'I have wonder'd since, that it did not make me Mad; nor do I now think it strange, to hear of those, who have been quite *Lunatick* with their Pride: that fancy'd themselves Queens, and Empresses, and have made their Attendants serve them upon the Knee; given Visitors their Hand to kiss, *and the like*' (p 235). Roxana's tragedy is that at the crucial moments of her life she fancies herself a queen and, until it is too late, rejects the merchant who might really have given her a life in which she could openly and honourably have lived 'like a Queen.'

The debate over the two paths, honourable marriage or the glamorous but immoral life of a whore, reflects the central question of Roxana's life and suggests something of the inner turmoil she endures. Although she argues with the Dutch merchant against marriage, yet one part of her still longs for respectability: 'poor Gentleman! thought I, you know little of me; what wou'd I give to be really what you really think me to be!' (p 137). Roxana's presentation of the advantages of the mistress over the wife ('a Wife is look'd upon, as but an Upper-Servant, a Mistress is a Sovereign,' p 132) and her long debate with the Dutch merchant on the same topic (pp 145–57) underline the moral decay of a woman who earlier had to be coaxed by her servant to take the first step into 'Wickedness.' At the same time the very fact that the debate goes on, and that the role of Amy as instigator and encourager does not diminish, reveals the still troubled mind of Roxana. Even after she has been a dazzlingly successful hostess in London and mistress to the king, Roxana is frequently unsure of herself and irresolute. For five weeks after she has accidentally caught sight of the Dutch merchant in London, she 'suffer'd a hundred Thousand Perplexities of Mind ... *in a word*, I was at a perfect Loss how to act, or what to do' (p 220). When Amy returns, it is to urge Roxana to abandon all thought of the Dutch merchant for the prince who is seeking her. We are reminded by Roxana that Amy always encourages the side of Roxana that prefers the glamorous and immoral to the dull and conventional: '*Amy*, an ambitious Jade, who knew my weakest Part, *namely*, that I lov'd great things, and that I lov'd to be flatter'd and courted; said abundance of kind things upon this Occasion, which she knew were suitable to me, and wou'd prompt my Vanity' (p 231).

In short, the drama of Roxana's moral decay, which defines the tighter structure of the novel, is conducted in terms which permit a greater insight into the troubled conscience of the protagonist than in any previous novel by Defoe. As the story builds towards the tragic conclusion, and Roxana at last, but too late, attempts to recover her respectability and to return to a life of conventional morality by finally accepting the Dutch merchant's proposal of marriage, the reader is not surprised to find that Roxana speaks once more of 'the Blast of a just Providence,' 'the Justice of Heaven,' and 'the Reflections which at some certain Intervals of time, came into my Thoughts' (p 260). Let 'no-body conclude,' she warns, that 'I either was happy or easie':

No, no, there was a Dart struck into the Liver; there was a secret Hell within, even all the while, when our Joy was at the highest; but more especially *now*, after it was all over, and when according to all appearance, I was one of the happiest Women upon Earth; all this while, *I say*, I had such a constant Terror upon my Mind, as gave me every now and then very terrible Shocks, and which made me expect something very frightful upon every Accident of Life. (P 260)

It is the 'secret Hell within,' the damaging consequences for the individual of the sacrifice of personal integrity for worldly opportunity, that marks Roxana off from the earlier protagonists. I do not want to suggest that what we have here is in any sense a psychological novel, or even a very perceptive analysis of inner moral deterioration. But Defoe finds in the torment of this woman a theme that seems to cast a long shadow forward to the tragic themes of Dickens, Hardy, Conrad, and James.

IV

In Defoe's novels verbal patterns – the vocabulary of appearance and of hypocrisy, the metaphors for the 'snares' and 'cheats' of life, the constant reference to disguise and dissimulation – reinforce and qualify a vision of human life as uncertain and insecure. Nowhere is this truer than in *Roxana* where unusual stress, even for Defoe, is placed upon speech. Moreover, the attention paid to non-verbal elements, such as clothing, which we noticed in the earlier novels is once again important here.

    Roxana is probably the only novel by Defoe that employs idiosyncrasies of speech for the purpose of characterization. It is a frequently observed feature of many novelists, Fielding in *Joseph Andrews*, Jane Austen in *Pride and Prejudice*, Dickens in practically everything he wrote, that their characters may be readily identified by the way they speak. Defoe's novels generally reveal by contrast the limitations of the early novel and the remarkable achievement in this area that later English fiction was to be capable of. Roxana, however, is the exception, for her speech both betrays her French birth and suggests that she has fallen easily into the fashionable affectation of using French phrases in what she would herself have called the '*Beau Monde*' (p 84).

In the first two pages of her story Roxana twice tells us that she 'retain'd nothing of *France*, but the Language.' And knowledge of the French tongue is to be crucial to her plans when later in Paris she decides to pass as the French wife of the English jeweller. But she assures us that she did not 'so much as keep any Remains of the *French* Language tagg'd to my Way of Speaking, *as most Foreigners do*, but spoke what we call Natural *English*, as if I had been born here.' Like all Defoe's protagonists Roxana has a facility for learning languages (she picks up Turkish from a slave girl, for example), and there is no reason to doubt her claim to speak English naturally and fluently. But it is simply not true that she has managed to keep 'the Remains of the *French* Language' out of her speech. Within a few pages of this claim she describes her husband as 'a conceited Fool, *Tout Opiniâtre*' (p 8) and throughout the course of the novel she makes frequent and familiar use of French phrases. She describes the 12,000 livres in bills that she claims after the death of the jeweller as an '*Amende*' (p 56) for the 30,000 livres she had brought him. And near the end of the novel she reports that the Dutch merchant offered his long search for her as 'an *Amende Honorable*, in Reparation of the Affront given to the Kindness of my Letter of Invitation' (p 227). She thrice refers to her morning dress as '*une Deshabille*' (p 64), or 'a *Dishabille*' (pp 283, 287), and to her hair as '*Tout Brilliant*' (p 247). At her masquerade party there is a dance '*a la Comique*' (p 173) and music '*a la Moresque*' (p 175). Her first husband, after he had deserted her, had become a trooper in 'the *Gensd'arms*' (pp 86, 94); while her son by the prince later becomes 'an Officer of the Guard *du Corps* of *France*' (p 82). The Dutch merchant refers to her way of arguing as '*a la Cavalier*' (p 153) and to himself as '*Une Miserable*' (p 228). Roxana refers to 'a *Gasconade*' (p 232) rather than to a tall story, describes the prince's manservant as an '*Homme de Parole*' (p 237), and compares herself in her mad desire to be a princess to a '*Malade Imaginaire*' (p 238). In France she 'was known by the Name of *La Belle veuve de Poictou*' which, she explains, means 'The pretty Widow of Poictou' (p 57), but when the prince, a couple of pages later, says to her '*Levez vous donc*' (p 61) and calls '*Au Boir*' (p 62), she doesn't bother to translate. Indeed, except in the one instance when her vanity compels a translation, Roxana never gives us the English for these phrases, but rather uses them with the assurance and unconscious familiarity of one whose mother-tongue is French.

The care that Defoe takes over details such as the characterization of Roxana by her use of French phrases is reflected in the attention paid to financial references in the novel. In *Robinson Crusoe* we have noticed how Crusoe's concern, or lack of concern, about money, helps define his changing attitude to the world. And in *Moll Flanders* Moll's marital fortune-hunting underscores the moral themes of the novel. Similarly money, and Roxana's attitude towards it, reinforces and deepens the meaning of Roxana's decline into wickedness. Roxana's moral decay is accompanied by a corresponding growth in wealth and social position, so much so, indeed, that she gives us a reckoning up of her fortune after each affair. References to her wealth, calculated in terms of money (pounds, pistoles, rixdollars, livres), plate, jewels (diamonds, rings, necklaces), gold and gold watches, fine furniture, linen, clothing, and other 'Household-Stuff' (p 56), securities, investments, mortgages, capital stock, estates, ships and cargoes are very much part of the texture of the work. Roxana is by far the wealthiest of Defoe's pro- tagonists, and all her wealth is the product of her high-level prostitu- tion. 'I had so long habituated myself to a life of Vice, that really it appear'd to be no Vice to me; I went on smooth and pleasant; I wallow'd in Wealth' (p 188), she confesses. But the more Roxana casts up her accounts and points out the degree of her wealth, the more she emphasizes the needlessness of her prostitution, as she is herself aware: 'for the common Vice of all Whores, I mean Money, was out of the Question, nay, even Avarice itself seem'd to be glutted' (p 182). Finally even Roxana, now worth 'fifty Thousand Pounds' (p 202) a year, sees that she can make no more excuses to herself. As she puts it, 'Avarice cou'd have no Pretence' (p 202). And with all this money she is forced to demand of herself: '*What am I a Whore for now?*' It is because her wealth so thoroughly strips her of any need, and therefore of any excuse, for her 'Life of Vice' that Roxana is so culpable. Like the debate over the choice between being a wife and being a whore, the frequent references to Roxana's ever-growing (and carefully invested) wealth foreshadow the tragic ending. Again the comparison with *Moll Flanders* is instruc- tive. In the earlier novel Moll triumphantly ends her story by revealing to her husband the extent of her wealth and the fact that he has, after all, 'married a Fortune.' But in a similar position Roxana's concern is to spare her husband the 'Blast of a just Providence, for mingling my cursed ill-gotten Wealth with his honest Estate' (p 260).

Money and other forms of wealth are so important in this novel that the language of finance permeates the way in which characters think of

themselves and of their relations with others. When Roxana offers to
pay the Dutch merchant for his assistance in preserving her from the
machinations of the Jew, he warmly refuses, saying that he kept her 'for
a deeper Reckoning,' that they would 'talk it over another time, and
ballance all together' (p 140). At first Roxana is not sure whether 'so
many Circles, and round-about Motions' (p 141) are financial
metaphors for a 'Matter *of Love*' or whether he is really speaking of a
'Matter of Money.' But the merchant eventually proposes marriage to
Roxana in the same imagery: 'seeing Providence had (as it were for that
Purpose) taken his Wife from him, I shou'd make up the Loss to him' (p
141). The comical periphrasis of this shy and rather awkward suitor
subtly characterizes him as a man more at home in the world of business
than of love. (This trick of characterization is a common feature of
English fiction – though the amorous and aging suitor is generally a
military or nautical figure, such as Uncle Toby or Commodore
Trunnion.) Roxana is also capable of thinking of herself in terms of
money, or rather, of silver plate, through the fact that she does so
points to something deeper – not familiarity with the world of business
but corruption by excessive and 'ill-gotten' wealth. When her affair
with the king is over, Roxana once more assesses her 'incredible
Wealth' – her 'near 5000 Pounds in Money ... besides Abundance of
Plate, and Jewels,' her 'five and thirty Thousand Pounds Estate,' and
her savings of '2000 *l.* every Year' (p 182). But then she continues:

After the End of what I call my Retreat, and out of which I brought a great deal
of Money, I appear'd again, but I seem'd like an old Piece of Plate that had been
hoarded up some Years, and comes out tarnish'd and discolour'd; so I came out
blown, and look'd like a *cast-off Mistress*.

The simile is remarkable simply because it is casual and off-hand.
Roxana sees herself, if only for a moment, in terms of her own vast
fortune, itself a symbol of her moral decay.

Roxana's wealth contrasts with and underlines her moral poverty,
but is also part of the pattern of appearance and disguise within the
novel. Roxana's money gives her unusual freedom – 'the Dignity of
Female Liberty' (p 225) as she tellingly calls it – to live where and how
she wishes and at any social level. By means of money Roxana can adopt
those Proteus-like changes in appearance that Defoe was himself often
accused of. When, for example, Roxana wants to retire from her high
life, she has only to follow Amy's advice to 'transform ourselves into a
new Shape.' 'I have found a Scheme,' Amy reports, 'how you shall, if

you have a-mind to it, begin, and finish a perfect entire Change of your Figure and Circumstances, in one Day; and shall be as much unknown, Madam, in twenty-four Hours, as you wou'd be in so many Years' (p 209). Roxana moves to the other side of London, takes lodging with a Quaker woman, and, on her own initiative, adopts the 'perfect Disguise' (p 211) of the Quaker's dress. The ease of changing outward appearance and therefore of deceiving others, which Roxana's wealth helps make possible, is part of the familiar pattern of disguise and dissimulation that in Defoe's fiction creates and supports a vision of human uncertainty and insecurity.

The language of the novel at every point suggests the degree of deception which human beings practise upon one another. Here are only a few of the countless words and phrases which, by constant repetition and variation, establish the conditions of Roxana's world of the cheat, the sham, and the snare: 'put on a Face of Business' (p 9); 'suspected her of some Contrivance' (p 20); 'acted to the Life' (p 22); 'to outward Appearance' (p 49); *I have not deceiv'd you with false Colours* (p 72); 'in its own natural Colours; when no more blinded with the glittering Appearances, which at that time deluded me' (p 79); 'All this, the *Jade* said with so much Cunning, and manag'd and humour'd it so well, and wip'd her Eyes, and cry'd so artificially, that he took it all as it was intended he should' (pp 89–90); 'made as gay a Show as I was able to do' (p 165); 'change your Liveries, nay, your own Cloaths, and if it was possible, your very Face' (p 208); 'my real Design was, to see whether it wou'd pass upon me for a Disguise' (p 211); 'but a Copy of my Countenance' (p 233); 'all Grimace and Deceit';[6] a Piece of meer Manage, and fram'd Conduct, to conceal a pass'd Life of Wickedness' (p 300).

Much of Defoe's fiction is concerned with cases of conscience, as G.A. Starr's study of Defoe and casuistry[33] has shown, but nowhere is this truer than in *Roxana*, which devotes a remarkable amount of space to Roxana's moral dilemmas, to Amy's role as persuader, and to the vocabulary of hypocrisy. The language of persuasion, of which Amy is mistress, is part of the emphasis put on speech in this novel. In arguing that Roxana should live with her landlord as his wife, Amy, we are told, 'represented all those Things in their proper Colours; she argued them all with her utmost Skill.' But, says Roxana, she had 'too much Rhetorick in this Cause' (p 39). Time and again Roxana points out Amy's special abilities in argument, in wit, in talk, and in dialogue. And to show her skill Roxana twice gives us verbatim reports of Amy's conversations, once with Roxana herself (pp 28–9), and once with

Amy's brewer husband (pp 88–9). Roxana's Quaker friend is also mistress of a subtle tongue, which is one of the reasons Roxana likes her. Another of the dialogues, reported with name tags (i.e., *Qu.* and *Girl*) to identify the speakers, displays the Quaker's skill in evading the searching questions of Roxana's daughter. The Quaker, as Roxana points out more than once, suffers from the handicap of not permitting herself to tell a direct lie, a fact that makes an ironic contrast with Roxana and Amy.

The vocabulary of deception and hypocrisy is reinforced by the image of the devil's snare (already familiar to Defoe's readers from *Moll Flanders* and *Colonel Jack*) and by the association of the devil with verbal cunning, particularly with Amy's fatal persuasiveness. Sometimes other people appear to Roxana to be instruments in the hands of the devil designed to bring her to ruin and destruction; at other times she acknowledges that she is herself the 'Bait' or the 'Snare.' Thus, when Roxana owes a debt of gratitude to the jeweller, Amy points out that 'he knows your Condition ... he has the surest Bait in the World to take you with' (p 28). And the image of the devil as both diabolic hunter and diabolic fisherman lies behind Roxana's realization a little later that 'all the Bounty and Kindness of this Gentleman, became a Snare to me, was a meer Bait to the Devil's Hook' (p 38). Similarly she refers to the 'hellish Snare' which she believes the Jew is setting for her; explains that the course of her career as a whore is set and 'manag'd by the Evil Spirit' (p 201); and wonders (when her daughter reappears as the 'Sister' of the ship's captain's wife) whether 'the Devil had any Snare at the Bottom of all this' (p 275). But while Roxana readily and characteristically sees the devil's hand behind the actions of others, she is also capable of recognizing the degree to which she herself has become 'the Devil's Agent' (p 48). Looking back upon her affair with the prince, for example, she wonders how she could 'be the Snare of such a Person's Life; that I should influence him to so much Wickedness; and that I should be the Instrument in the Hand of the Devil, to do him so much Prejudice' (p 102). And she more than once lacerates herself with the thought that she has ruined Amy: 'I had been the Devil's Instrument, to make her wicked' (p 126). What is perhaps particularly interesting about this pattern of images as it is worked out in Defoe's last novel is Roxana's sense of the devil's place in her own thoughts. In the mental struggle between conscience and the devil, the latter generally succeeds, as in her affair with the prince where, Roxana points out, 'the Devil had play'd a new Game with me, and prevail'd with me to satisfie myself with this Amour, as a lawful thing' (p 68). From hindsight she sees how apt we are to persuade ourselves to do what we really long to do:

It cannot be doubted but that I was the easier to perswade myself of the Truth of such a Doctrine as this, when it was so much for my Ease, and for the Repose of my Mind, to have it be so.

     In Things we wish, 'tis easie to deceive;
     What we would have, we willingly believe.   (P 68)

In his *The Political History of the Devil* (published in 1726, two years after *Roxana*) Defoe comments on the devil's subtle method: 'he never wants a handle; the best of men have one weak place or other, and he always finds it out, takes advantage of it, and conquers them by one artifice or another.'[34] Roxana's weak places, as she emphasizes several times, are her vanity and her avarice: 'These were my Baits, these the Chains by which the Devil held me bound; and by which I was indeed, too fast held for any Reasoning that I was then Mistress of, to deliver me from' (p 202). The real devil's snare for Roxana does not come from without; it is her mind, her ability to distinguish between right and wrong, that is ensnared.

V

The conclusion of Roxana's history within the tragic form we have been examining demands special attention. It has all the appearance of an 'added' ending (like the apparently anticlimatic endings of *Robinson Crusoe* and *Colonel Jack*), yet it is actually a logical completion of the pattern of wickedness which begins with the abandoning of her children by means of a 'Contrivance,' is developed through all the pretences and disguises and deceptions of the following years, and forms a symbolic core for the novel in the masquerade scenes. Two paragraphs after telling us about 'the secret Hell within' (p 260) Roxana says that she 'left *England* again.' Apart from dark hints later about 'a dreadful Course of Calamities,' the story is not carried forward in time beyond this point. Instead, the final section of her history is devoted to what Roxana calls 'the Story of my two Daughters,' and she turns from the sorrowful contemplation of her own wretchedness to this story with the awkward sentence: 'I must now go back to another Scene, and join it to this End of my Story, which will compleat all my Concern with *England*, *at least*, all that I shall bring into this Account' (p 265).

    When we examine the relation of the conclusion to the first three-quarters of the novel, the link between Roxana's crimes and her terrible punishment becomes clear. The consequence of Roxana's initial wickedness and her taking up a life lived by disguise and deception is that one of her own daughters becomes her servant; witnesses her mother's 'Turkish' dance and therefore the bestowal of the name 'Roxana'; and finally, attempting to re-establish a normal relationship with her mother, is murdered by the servant who has both usurped her station in life and taken her place in her mother's affections. The central coincidence upon which the mutual discovery by Roxana and Susan of each other's identity rests is the fact that Susan is a servant in Roxana's house, a symbol, as we have seen, of the moral disorder in the novel.

After her return to England Roxana is eager to know what has happened to the five children she had 'turn'd out, as it were to the wide World, and to the Charity of their Father's Relations' (p 188), and she entrusts Amy with the task of seeking them out and assisting them if possible. Significantly, the children have been made 'little better than Servants in the House' (p 189) of their aunt, and later have become servants in fact and have been separated from each other. Amy is able to trace only one of these children, a son, and she arranges that he should be taken from his apprenticeship to 'a mean Trade' and made a merchant. Then, nearly a year later, Amy, discovering that one of the maids has come home 'crying bitterly' from a visit to the city to see some friends, seizes an opportunity to question her about her misery:

The Maid told her a long Story, that she had been to see her Brother, the only Brother she had in the World; and that she knew he was put-out Apprentice to a ———; but there had come a Lady in a Coach, to his Uncle ———, who had brought him up, and made him take him Home again; and so the Wench run-on, ... till she came to that Part that belong'd to herself; and there, *says she*, I had not let them know where I liv'd; and the Lady wou'd have taken me, and they say, wou'd have provided for me too, as she had done for my Brother, but no-body cou'd tell where to find me, and so I have lost it all, and all the Hopes of being any-thing, but a poor Servant all my Days; and then the Girl fell a-crying again.. (P 196)

Amy realizes, after some further questioning, that, as Roxana says, 'this was no other than my own Daughter.' But Amy's discovery throws into relief Roxana's moral dilemma, which is to grow in importance as the novel advances. She realizes that Roxana will be torn between her emotions and her prudence, or, as Roxana puts it, the 'great Perplexity between the Difficulty of concealing myself from my own Child, and the Inconvenience of having my Way of Living be known' (p 197). Since Amy clearly cannot act as Roxana's agent ('for as she [Susan] had been Servant in the House, she knew *Amy*, as well as Amy knew me'), Roxana arranges for another woman to let Susan know that 'something would be done for her.' Naturally, after Susan has 'fit herself to appear as a Gentlewoman,' she pays a visit to Amy to tell her of her good fortune, and Susan and Amy 'began an intimate Acquaintance together.' In the course of subsequent conversations Susan casually, and possibly cunningly, mentions that she had never seen her mistress (Roxana) except in a disguise: '*'twas very strange*: Madam, *says she to* Amy, but tho' I liv'd near two Years in the House, I never saw my Mistress in my Life, except it was that publick Night when she danc'd in the fine *Turkish* Habit, and then she was so disguis'd, that I knew nothing of her afterwards' (p 206). It is this fact that at first puts Roxana's mind at rest, but which will eventually lead to her discovery.

The Turkish habit, the masquerade costume in which Roxana performed her celebrated Turkish dance and which Susan mentions in conversation to Amy, is an important motif in the novel and becomes by the end a symbol of all that which is wrong in Roxana's life – her shameful life as a courtesan, her need for concealment, her fear of her own daughter. Roxana's familiarity with Turkish dancing is mentioned as early as her visit to Italy with the prince: 'Here my Lord bought me a little Female *Turkish* Slave, who being taken at Sea by a *Malthese* Man of War, was brought in there; and of her I learnt the *Turkish* Language; their Way of Dressing, and Dancing, and some *Turkish*, or rather *Moorish* Songs, of which I made Use, to my Advantage, on an extraordinary Occasion, some Years after, as you shall hear in its Place' (p 102). The dress itself is introduced at the masquerade party as the 'Habit of a *Turkish Princess*; the Habit I got at *Leghorn*, when my *Foreign Prince* bought me a *Turkish* Slave' (p 173), and is described in considerable detail. Significantly it is her Turkish dance and Turkish dress that lead to her being christened 'Roxana,' a name that comes to symbolize her position as a courtesan or, as she puts it later on, 'a meer Roxana' (p 182), an equivalent, at a higher social level, of a 'Moll.'

We hear of the Turkish dress once more when Susan mentions it to Amy, and then again, not long afterwards, when Roxana has gone into retirement, taken up the Quaker mode of speech and manner of dressing, and married the Dutch banker. On one occasion, in the week following her marriage, Roxana desires to entertain her husband by dressing 'in one kind of Dress that I had by me, that he would not know his Wife when he saw her, especially if any-body else was by' (p 246).

After taking the precaution of making her husband promise that he will never ask her 'to be seen in it before Company,' Roxana puts on her Turkish costume. Of course both the Quaker and her husband are delighted: 'The QUAKER was charm'd with the Dress, *and merrily said,* That if such a Dress shou'd come to be worn here, she shou'd not know what to do, she shou'd be tempted not to dress in the QUAKERS Way any-more' (p 247), and her husband is 'surpriz'd, and perfectly astonish'd.' The promise that Roxana has extracted from her husband is demanded on the grounds that it is 'not a decent Dress in this Country, and wou'd not look modest ... for it was one Degree off, from appearing in one's Shift,' although in fact her real reason, as she in at pains to emphasize, is one of concealment: 'there was good Reason why I shou'd not receive any Company in this Dress, *that is to say,* not in *England*; *I need not repeat it*; *you will hear more of it*' (p 248).

The ending of the story thus carefully prepared for is centred on Susan's discovery of Roxana's identity by means of the Turkish dress, and in this way links Susan as servant in the central section with Susan as the possible betrayer of Roxana in the closing section. By an extraordinary coincidence Susan turns up as the '*Sister*' (i.e., close companion) of the wife of the captain of the ship in which Roxana and her husband have engaged to go to Holland. Roxana immediately recognizes the girl as her 'Cook-Maid in the *Pallmall*' though she is not sure whether the girl has recognized her. A few days later Roxana, dressed in 'a kind of *Dishabille* ... a loose Robe, like a Morning-Gown' (p 283), is visited by the captain's wife and her '*Sister*,' who are both 'taken up much about the Beauty of the Dress; the charming Damask; the noble Trimming, *and the like*.' Naturally Roxana's daughter is reminded of the Turkish dress which she had seen years before and tells the 'charming Story' of 'the Lady *Roxana*,' so that, *in a word*,' as Roxana remarks: 'I was oblig'd to sit and hear her tell all the Story of *Roxana, that is to say,* of myself, and not know at the same time, whether she was in earnest or in jest; whether she knew me or no; or, *in short,* whether I was to be expos'd, or not expos'd' (pp 284–5). Susan tells of the 'gaming and dancing' of the servants, particularly 'one Mrs. *Amy*,' 'the Lady's Favourite,' of the rumour that Roxana was the king's mistress, of the extraordinary beauty of her mistress, of the great masquerade party and the king's appearance there in disguise, and finally of her mistress's dance in the Turkish costume: 'Here she went on to Describe the Dress, as I have done already; but did it so exactly, that I was surpriz'd at the Manner of her telling it; there was not a Circumstance of it left out' (p 288). Susan's accurate description of the dress not only convinces Roxana that her daughter knows her, but also alerts the Quaker, who 'immediately perceiv'd it was the same Dress that she had seen me have on.' Forced to keep up conversation in order not to show her alarm by her silence, Roxana at last suggests to the girl that 'Roxana' was surely not her lady's real name. To which Susan makes the pointed reply: 'No, no Madam, *said she*, I know that; I know my Lady's Name and Family very well; *Roxana* was not her Name, that's true indeed' (p 289). Roxana is now virtually certain that Susan knows her identity: 'Here she run me a-ground again; for I durst not ask her what was *Roxana*'s real Name, lest she had really dealt with the Devil, and had boldly given my own Name in for Answer' (p 289). Like Moll and Jack, and at times Defoe himself, Roxana lives in fear of having her name discovered. She is now so frightened of her daughter that she adopts various disguises and pretences to avoid her, which makes the wretched girl the more desperate to bring Roxana to acknowledge her as her daughter. Near the end of the novel Roxana is reduced to calling her daughter, whom earlier to have kissed was 'a secret inconceivable Pleasure to me ... to know that I kiss'd my own Child; my own Flesh and Blood, born of my Body' (p 277), '*my Plague*,' and '*Tormentor*' (p 302), and she says that Susan 'hunted me, as if, *like a Hound*, she had had a hot Scent' (p 317) and that 'she haunted me like an Evil Spirit' (p 310). Eventually Amy, seeing her mistress almost mad with fear and frustration,[35] murders the girl.

The paramount significance of the dress, which provides Susan with convincing evidence of Roxana's identity, is that it is the masquerade costume of a courtesan, a dress that 'wou'd not look modest' in England. It serves within the structure of the novel as a device linking the public immorality of the masquerade party, Defoe's vivid example of the moral and social decay of his age, directly to the destruction of private individuals. Even when she has outwardly reformed, Roxana carries about with her, and sometimes puts on, the Turkish dress, the memento of her glamorous and shameful life, and this leads eventually both to the death of Susan and to the utter destruction of the happiness and prosperity of Roxana and Amy.

The dress is a disguise, one of Roxana's most successful changes of costume both at her masquerade in Pall Mall and later, in private, with her husband and the Quaker. It is associated with Roxana's most flagrant mode of life, the opposite extreme from her disguise as a Quaker which she takes up not long afterward. Roxana's adoption of Quaker dress reflects the importance given to all forms of dress in this novel, and calls attention not only to her need for disguise, but also to her ability at it: 'I had not only learn'd to dress like a QUAKER, but so us'd myself to THEE and THOU, that I talk'd like a QUAKER too, as readily and naturally as if I had been born among them ... and there was not a QUAKER in the Town look'd less like a Counterfeit than I did' (p 213). Roxana's Quaker costume, particularly since she never loses her fondness for her Turkish dress, is of course hypocritical, a fact that she recognizes: 'But all this was my particular Plot to be more compleatly conceal'd' (p 213). The introduction of the Quaker woman and the Quaker dress at this point in the story serves as a foil for Roxana's deception and hypocrisy. The Quaker who 'wou'd not Lye' drives home to Roxana, and to the reader, the fact that Roxana has become a living lie, a 'cursed Piece of Hypocrisie,' 'a Piece of meer Manage, and fram'd Conduct, to conceal a pass'd Life of Wickedness' (p 300). The Quaker's words to Susan that Roxana is 'a Person above any Disguises, so she cou'd not believe that she wou'd deny her being her Daughter, if she was really her Mother' (pp 306–7) are the supreme irony of the novel.

The Quaker's gratitude to Roxana springs from the fact that Roxana had assisted her when she and her four children were deserted by her husband. This 'Similitude of Cases' recalls Roxana's own situation near the beginning of the novel which had been the start of her decline into 'Wickedness':

Was it possible I cou'd think of a poor desolate Woman with four Children, and her Husband gone from her, and *perhaps good for little if he had stay'd*; *I say*, was I, that had tasted so deep of the Sorrows of such a kind of Widowhood, able to look on her, and think of her Circumstances, and not be touch'd in an uncommon Manner? No, No, I never look'd on her, and her Family, tho' she was not left so helpless and friendless as I had been, without remembring my own Condition; when *Amy* was sent out to pawn or sell my *Pair of Stays*, to buy a Breast of Mutton, and a Bunch of Turnips; nor cou'd I look on her poor Children, tho' not poor and perishing, like mine, without Tears; reflecting on the dreadful Condition that mine were reduc'd to, when poor *Amy* sent them all into their Aunt's in *Spittle-Fields*, and run away from them.   (Pp 252–3)

Through this parallel situation Defoe skilfully recalls, on the eve of the return of Susan to claim Roxana as her mother, Roxana's original crime in abandoning her children. Tragically Roxana has lived so long by disguise and deception that she is trapped by her own mode of existence. On the one hand she longs to reveal herself to her child; on the other hand she is desperately afraid of the consequences werc she to do so. All of Defoe's fiction is filled with disguises and deceptions which reflect his profound sense of the cheats and shams and snares and betrayals of the lives of most men and women. But in the earlier novels the emphasis is very largely on the power of the protagonist to survive in such a world. In *Roxana* Defoe turns for the first time to a problem of central concern for the English novel, that of human relationships. In it he explores, in a less sophisticated way than his greater successors such as Thackeray or George Eliot or Dickens, the ways in which normal human relationships – the love between a mother and child – are made impossible by the supremely human practice of deception, hypocrisy, disguise. It is not surprising that in his last novel Defoe's darkening vision of the human lot finds expression as tragedy.

6 Epilogue: Defoe's Artistry and the Tradition of the Novel

The achievement of Daniel Defoe in the history of the English novel is considerable not only because he drew fiction away from romance and moral allegory and turned it firmly towards realism, but because he focused upon a universal human problem, the clash between the force of personal needs and desires and the contending social forces which demand compromise and accommodation. After Defoe this inevitable and universal opposition of forces, usually worked out under the heightened stress of courtship, marriage, and family life, became central to English fiction. Moreover, later novelists took over and developed and refined artistic devices that Defoe, himself a borrower of techniques, had found appropriate for the rendering of his moral vision.

The common theme of Defoe's novels is the struggle of erring individuals against an indifferent, and often hostile, society. In *Robinson Crusoe* this theme is worked out in the highly structured and symbolic contrast between Crusoe's life alone on the island and the framing story of his life in the world of men. The opposition of good and evil which, in its starkest form, this theme implies is mirrored in the inner turmoil of Crusoe whose spiritual suffering and conversion are prerequisites for the inward calm and happiness that alone make possible the unimaginable horror of over twenty years of solitary confinement. But *Robinson Crusoe*, supreme though it is among Defoe's novels, is atypical of most later English fiction since it operates near the level of myth and, at times, of allegory. The family theme is there – Crusoe's original sin is running away from home in violation of his father's commands and his mother's entreaties – and Defoe's sense of the family as a microcosm of society is underlined by the little parodies of family life on the island. But for over half the novel Crusoe's difficulty lies not in his relations with his family or other people, but in his geographical distance from them. In *Moll Flanders* Defoe wrote the first of what may be called his social novels. Like Crusoe, though in a different sense, Moll is cut off from normal life, but her isolation is caused as much by an unjust social and economic order as by her own wilful wickedness. Defoe was a moral and social reformer (he would not have made as great a distinction between these two terms as we do), and in *Moll Flanders* and *Colonel Jack* and *Roxana* he gave to the novel a strong thrust in the direction of social didacticism. Moll Flanders, however, like Colonel Jack, makes her accommodation with society by remaining largely unentangled with other people. It is only in his final novel that Defoe began to develop both of the great twin themes of personal and social relations (and personal relations *through* and *in* social relationships) that will mark the fullest thematic development of English fiction. In *Roxana* the centre of interest is not merely the story of Roxana's marital, and extramarital, adventures and her relationships with her children, but rather it is *the problem* of her marital and maternal relationships. Roxana lives *in* society (in a way that the social outcast Moll never does), and the tension between social conventions (respectability) and personal emotion (which would destroy her precarious respectability) shapes the novel.

During the brief five-year span in which he wrote his novels Defoe took two steps that were to be of major importance in the history of the novel. To *Moll Flanders* he brought from *Robinson Crusoe* the protagonist's moral problem, the clash between his worldly ambition and his sense of wrong-doing, and gave it a social context. Moll's problems and her solutions to them reflect a society in which she must either exploit differences in class and sex or be exploited by them. Then in *Roxana* the social context is shown to have a direct bearing on the inner life of the heroine; personal relations are destroyed by the pressure of social demands. Fiction after Defoe was to explore and develop in ways more subtle and complex than his the complicated interrelationship of social and personal relations. In *Clarissa*, for example, the heroine is not only a suffering and desperately hoping individual; she is also a daughter and a sister and a lover (each of these relations is vitally important), and, further, the victim of an exploitative social system. After Richardson and Fielding the indissoluble interconnection between social and personal themes is a touchstone of major works of fiction. What is important about Defoe is that he stands within, not apart from, this tradition.

On the other hand Defoe's narrowly restricted focus did much to prevent his moving further in the direction he initiated. His auto-biographical narrative method restricted the development of secon-dary characters in the novels. Only in *Roxana*, and there only partially, is the protagonist's relationship with another character developed and sustained. This limited perspective was confirmed by Defoe's choice of protagonists who are either geographically isolated, like Crusoe, or who assume false positions in society that make them vulnerable to exposure. In varying degrees they are cut off from the normal expec-tations of family life and social intercourse. Finally, Defoe failed to employ his first-person narrative technique for the purpose that we would naturally associate with this fictional form, namely, to reveal the inner life of his protagonist. In *Roxana*, in ways that we have seen, Defoe took an important step in this direction, but the eighteenth-century 'psychological' novel waited until Richardson's magnificent achievement in *Clarissa*.

None the less, some of the most conspicuous features of much English fiction are first found in Defoe, and not as is sometimes imagined, merely in embryonic form. The complex tension between public respectability and private corruption and despair fascinated Richardson and Fielding, Dickens, George Eliot, and James, as it fasci-nated Defoe. To give narrative shape to his moral vision Defoe found themes and devised techniques which would reappear in later fiction. For example, we earlier noticed the significance attached to clothing, especially to changes of clothing, in Defoe: Robinson Crusoe's animal skins and later his return to European clothes, Moll's and Jack's various 'disguises,' Roxana's infamous masquerade costume and her Quaker's dress. Like Defoe, both Richardson and Fielding use clothing and changes of clothing to underscore shifting social status (which is fre-quently fraught with considerable emotional tension) and to suggest the ironic contrast of a shabby external appearance hiding a good heart, or a mean spirit hidden by gorgeous clothes. Pamela rightly views Mr B's gifts of clothing with suspicion and then with something more than suspicion when he begins his attempted seduction of her, and she is scrupulous about returning those gifts and assuming her own simple country clothes for her journey home. In Fielding clothing – or the lack of it, as in the case of Joseph Andrews discovered stripped, robbed, and beaten in a ditch – is used, often comically, to point out to us the way in which judgments about moral character are made solely on the basis of external appearance. Again, the reaction in the church-yard to Molly Seagrim's finery is a hilarious example of the importance of clothing as an indication of class in the eighteenth century, and the indignation that follows when such outward signs are violated. It is easy to forget, in an egalitarian age, the degree to which all classes of people in the eighteenth century wore what were virtually uniforms. The fact that it was possible to tell occupation, class, and social level within class simply by one's clothing helps to explain not only Defoe's strictures about servants dressing above their station, but also the importance given to clothing and disguise in eighteenth-century fiction in general. The novelists' interest in dress can scarcely be said to diminish in the nineteenth century, as readers of Emily Brontë, Thackeray, George Eliot, and Dickens know. Of course as social attitudes to clothing change, so do the uses that writers of fiction make of dress. Henry James makes a fine and subtle distinction between the self-confident innocence of Isabel and the cynical experience of Madame Merle in a revealing conversation about clothes and those other 'things' in which we read personality: 'one's house, one's furniture, one's garments, the books one reads, the company one keeps.' For Madam Merle 'these things are all expressive.' For Isabel 'nothing express me': 'Certainly the clothes which, as you say, I choose to wear, don't express me.' But Madame Merle has already supplied the answer: 'I know a large part of myself is in the clothes I choose to wear.'[1] Colonel Jack or Roxana might well have said the same thing.

The language of fiction, as David Lodge reminds us,[2] is one of the most persuasive means through which the world of the novel is created. In his novels Defoe's sense of the uncertainty and insecurity of all human endeavour, and the need for deviousness to survive the machinations of men and the devil, is conveyed by the language of equivocation and of hypocrisy. Richardson's vocabulary of theological references (Lovelace is associated with Don Juan and hell; the 'angelic' and 'divine' Clarissa with the Bride of Christ and heaven) defines the moral opposites of that novel and helps to account for its tragic ending. Jane Austen's use of financial words in *Pride and Prejudice*; Emily Brontë's natural vocabulary of storms, the moors, trees, and animals to describe characters and incidents; and Dickens's melting and dissolving images to suggest the morally and physically murky world of *Bleak House* – these are better known but perhaps no more effective than Defoe's own suggestive language. The names that writers give their fictional characters are concentrated examples of the force of the choice of words. Again, Defoe's rejection of unmistakable type names in favour of plausible, but discreetly appropriate, names inaugurated a practice that has been followed by many of his successors.

Perhaps the central technical problem of eighteenth-century fiction is that of narrative point of view, the relation in which the narrator stands to his story. Defoe's immediate successors, Richardson and Fielding, adopted such divergent solutions that they have become convenient historical examples of two extremes – the internal approach to character which emphasizes psychological development and the external approach which emphasizes plot. So well known was their quarrel that Sterne was able to exploit the problem and its solutions and to build his novel around an elaborate formal parody. And in a sense the English novel has been grappling with these two alternative narrative modes ever since. In *Pride and Prejudice*, for example, Jane Austen reconciles psychological insight with external evaluation of motive by locating the narrative centre of the novel close to, but just outside, Elizabeth Bennet. The novel proceeds with, but not from, the heroine. In *Bleak House* Dickens adopts the curious expedient of having two narrators, the external author and a highly subjective character. And in *A Portrait of a Lady* James so brilliantly manipulates point of view that our absorption into – then sudden removal from – the subjective consciousness of Isabel Archer reflects and dramatizes her intellectual and moral growth. But the brilliant technical mastery of James and others rests on two centuries of experimentation that began with Defoe.

Defoe's use of the narrative mode of the first-person testimony served the immediate end of authenticating the account, an essential requirement in early novels of realism which were meant to be indistinguishable from history. The additional importance of the method of fictitious autobiography is that it locates the point of view firmly in the narrator's consciousness, a point of disadvantage from which the material world is beheld. To that external world the protagonist must make his adjustment; in this process of adjustment, the response of ordinary people to extraordinary demands, Defoe found the moral clash that shaped his, and subsequent, fiction. However, the disadvantage of the autobiographical narrative mode is that the reader has little means of assessing the truth of the narrator's perceptions, the accuracy of his picture of the outside world. The protagonist-narrator's disadvantaged view remains uncorrected by a more objective author. In *Pamela* this situation is so extreme that the reader may suspect the perceptions and therefore the motives of the narrator – as Fielding scathingly demonstrates in *Shamela*.

One of the curiosities of Defoe is that, having selected the most subjective of narrative forms, he then largely avoids introspection and concentrates his focus on the world outside the narrator. It is this practice that gives Defoe, in Ian Watt's phrase, 'a very central position between the subjective and external orientation of the novelist.'[3] It remained to Richardson to explore the possibilities of subjective narrative. But Richardson, by reducing the gap between the time of action and the time of narration to a minimum, eliminated the long temporal perspective of the memoir that, in Defoe, still permitted a modicum of detachment and distance. One of the advances in narrative method that Richardson made between *Pamela* and *Clarissa* was the introduction of more than one pair of letter-writers, a device that increased the reader's capacity to assess the motives of characters. In a sense this was a return to Defoe's more balanced position. Fielding, in reacting to the self-deluding temporizing (as he saw it) of Pamela, abandoned the first-person narrative mode of Richardson – and of Defoe – altogether. The narrators of *Joseph Andrews* and of *Tom Jones* not only tell us a story; they also tell us what we should think about it. But while Fielding gave up the narrative mode that would seem to offer the greatest possibility for the introspective examination of the mind of the protagonist, his kind of narrative offered an enduring solution to the problem, conspicuous in both Defoe and Richardson, of the creation of a world of secondary characters that has a reality apart from the protagonist. (The complex epistolary method of *Clarissa* allowed for important secondary characters, but only at the price of inordinate length.) What Defoe's narrative method seems to have provided was an initial narrative form capable of being extended in either a subjective or an external direction. This suggests that the prominence of the literary war between Richardson and Fielding has probably obscured an important fact about Defoe, namely, that the various experiments in narrative method after Defoe may be seen as responses, or alternatives (at least in a negative sense), to his way of telling a story.

Daniel Defoe's art of fiction, no less than that of his successors, is to be sought in the means by which vision becomes form. In the four novels which have been the subject of this study Defoe found the themes – of human limitation, of endurance, of triumph, and of failure – that expressed his imaginative vision of the human condition. In working out these themes he devised structures, created images, and discovered the language that gave shape and meaning to his ideas. And much that he created was absorbed into later fiction. In his work, as in that of his followers, we can see the ways in which the moral vision of the lot of man was transmuted by the techniques of his narrative into the art of his novels.

Notes

There is as yet no modern scholarly edition of Defoe's works, though a
40-volume edition has been announced by the University of Southern
Illinois Press. For Defoe's fictional works I have used the Oxford English
Novels editions wherever possible. For the rest of his writings I have used
the two largest collections of his works, *The Novels and Miscellaneous Works of
Daniel De Foe* (Oxford/London 1840, 1841) and *Romances and Narratives by
Daniel Defoe*, ed George A. Aitken (London 1895), or original editions. *The
Letters of Daniel Defoe* are edited by George Harris Healey (Oxford 1955).
Defoe's sequels to *The Life and Strange Surprizing Adventures of Robinson
Crusoe* present a special case, since unfortunately they are not printed in the
Oxford English Novels series. The best modern edition of *The Farther
Adventures of Robinson Crusoe* is *The Shakespeare Head Edition of the Novels and
Selected Writings of Daniel Defoe* (Oxford: Basil Blackwell 1927, 1928), which
I have used. *The Farther Adventures* begins at vol II, p 109, in the three
volumes devoted to the two main parts of *Robinson Crusoe*. For *The Serious
Reflections During The Life and Surprising Adventures of Robinson Crusoe, With
His Vision Of The Angelick World* (not included in the Shakespeare Head
edition) I have used the appropriate volume of the *Romances and Narratives*.

NOTES TO PREFACE

1 Preface to *The Portrait of a Lady* (1881; rpt Harmondsworth: Penguin 1971),
p ix. The Preface was first published in 1908.
2 Ian Watt, *The Rise of the Novel* (London 1957; rpt Harmondsworth: Penguin
1963).

3 Ibid, p 33: 'Formal realism ... is the narrative embodiment of a premise ... that the novel is a full and authentic report of human experience.'

4 Ibid, p 15.

5 Arthur W. Secord, *Studies in the Narrative Method of Defoe* (1924; rpt New York: Russell and Russell 1963), p 232. Cf J. Paul Hunter, *The Reluctant Pilgrim* (Baltimore: Johns Hopkins University Press 1966), pp 12, 13 and nn.

6 James Sutherland, Introduction to his edition of *Moll Flanders* (Boston: Houghton Mifflin 1959), p ix.

7 Jonathan Bishop, 'Knowledge, Action, and Interpretation in Defoe's Novels,' *Journal of the History of Ideas*, 13 (1952), 13.

8 Mark Schorer, 'Technique as Discovery,' *Hudson Review*, 1 (1948); rpt in John W. Aldridge, ed, *Critiques and Essays on Modern Fiction 1920–1951* (New York: Ronald Press 1952), pp 69–70.

9 Maximillian E. Novak, *Economics and the Fiction of Daniel Defoe* (Berkeley: University of California Press 1962); and *Defoe and the Nature of Man* (London: Oxford University Press 1963).

10 E.g., Robert R. Columbus, 'Conscious Artistry in *Moll Flanders*,' *Studies in English Literature*, 3 (1963), 415–32; William H. Halewood, 'Religion and Invention in *Robinson Crusoe*,' *Essays in Criticism*, 14 (1964), 339–51; Howard L. Koonce, 'Moll's Muddle: Defoe's Use of Irony in *Mall Flanders*,' ELH, 30 (1963), 377–94.

11 G.A. Starr, *Defoe and Spiritual Autobiography* (Princeton: Princeton University Press 1965).

12 Hunter, *The Reluctant Pilgrim.*

13 John J. Richetti, *Defoe's Narratives: Situations and Structures* (Oxford: Clarendon Press 1975).

14 Everett Zimmerman, *Defoe and the Novel* (Berkeley and Los Angeles: University of California Press 1975).

15 Barbara Hardy, Introduction to her edition of George Eliot, *Daniel Deronda* (Harmondsworth: Penguin 1967), p 24. See also Angus Wilson, *The Wild Garden* (Berkeley: University of California Press 1963), pp 149–50.

NOTES TO CHAPTER ONE

1 There is a conspicuous similarity among the four major novels. Robinson Crusoe is imprisoned for twenty-seven or twenty-eight years on his island; Moll was 'Twelve Year a Whore' and 'Twelve Year a Thief'; Colonel Jack was 'Six and twenty Years a Thief'; and Roxana speaks of 'six and twenty Years of Wickedness.' The coincidence in time may reflect Defoe's sense of some similar period in his own life.

2 *Review*, 12 December 1704.

3 Daniel Finch, Second Earl of Nottingham, Secretary of State for the Southern Department. For an estimation of Nottingham's persecution of Defoe and for an account of the role of the judges at Defoe's trial see John Robert Moore, *Defoe in the Pillory and Other Studies* (Bloomington: Indiana University Press 1939).

4 *The Letters of Daniel Defoe*, ed G.H. Healey (Oxford: Clarendon Press 1955), p 6. Cf Colonel Jack's fear of being called a coward.

5 *Letters*, p 10. Cf Crusoe's miraculous deliverance from shipwreck.

6 *Letters*, p 19.

7 *Memoirs of the Life of Sir John Clerk of Penicuik* (Edinburgh 1892), p 64, quoted by Healey, *Letters*, p 158n.

8 *Letters*, pp 158–9. This frequently quoted letter is, as Maximillian Novak observes, 'unquestionably one of the best keys we have to Defoe's personality' (*Economics and the Fiction of Daniel Defoe* [Berkeley: University of California Press 1962], p 3). But, Novak cautions, 'it is suspiciously modelled to fit the personality of Harley, his audience, who was, if possible, even a more devious man than Defoe.'

9 *Letters*, p 10n.

10 For a discussion of contemporary opinion of Defoe as a trickster see above, pp 10–12. Cf Maximillian E. Novak, 'Defoe's *Shortest Way with the Dissenters*: Hoax, Parody, Paradox, Fiction, Irony, and Satire,' *Modern Language Quarterly*, 27 (1966), 402–17.

11 Harley, however, attended church, unlike Defoe.

12 Defoe's ability to survive changes of government has been ably put by James Sutherland in his biography of Defoe: 'Defoe, in fact, proceeded in his political life as if he were a permanent civil servant, and at the same time allowed himself the privilege of taking sides.' See his *Defoe* (London: Methuen 1937; rpt 1950), p 178.

13 See *An Appeal to Honour and Justice* (1715), in *Romances and Narratives by Daniel Defoe*, ed George A. Aitken (London 1895), VIII, 172, 196, 201, 207.

14 For Defoe's account of his activity see *Letters*, pp 450–3.

15 *The Family Instructor. In Two Parts* (1718), in *The Novels and Miscellaneous Works of Daniel De Foe* (Oxford/London 1840, 1841), XVI, 403.

16 *Conjugal Lewdness: Or, Matrimonial Whoredom* (London 1727), p 170. Subsequent references are given in the text.

17 Not, however, in the matter of divorce: 'I will not follow Mr. *Milton*, and carry it up to this, that it [marriage] may be dissolved again upon that single account' [i.e., that there was not a 'resolved settled affection, sincerely embraced before the matrimony was contracted'], *Conjugal Lewdness*, p 118.

18 *The Great Law of Subordination Consider'd* (London 1724), pp 14, 284. In *The*

Compleat English Gentleman (1725) Defoe warns shopkeepers not to allow their apprentices to be mistaken for them; see *The Novels and Miscellaneous Works*, XVII, ch 13, esp pp 99–102.

19 See *The Poor Man's Plea* (1698), and *The Weekly Journal* (5 April 1719). The latter is reprinted in William Lee, *Daniel Defoe: His Life and Recently Discovered Writings* (London 1869), II, 32.

20 *Review*, 26 December 1706.

21 *The Novels and Miscellaneous Works*, XVI, 190–1.

22 See *Serious Reflection During the Life and Surprising Adventures of Robinson Crusoe, With His Vision Of The Angelick World*, in *Romances and Narratives*, III, 275. Subsequent references are given in the text.

23 *The Political History of the Devil, as well ancient as modern, In two parts*, in *The Novels and Miscellaneous Works*, X, 157–8. Cf p 236, and *A System of Magick; or, a History of the black art*, in *The Novels and Miscellaneous Works*, XII, 141.

24 J. Paul Hunter, *The Reluctant Pilgrim* (Baltimore: Johns Hopkins University Press 1966), p 198.

25 *An Essay on the History and Reality of Apparitions*, in *The Novels and Miscellaneous Works*, XIII, 38. Cf *Serious Reflections*, pp 23 and 182.

26 *Robinson Crusoe*, ed J. Donald Crowley (London: Oxford University Press 1972), p 196.

27 *History and Reality of Apparitions*, p 179. The phrase, however, occurs commonly in Defoe's discussion of the 'invisible world' intermediate between God and man. The following works by Rodney M. Baine can be consulted: 'Daniel Defoe and *The History and Reality of Apparitions*,' *Proceedings of the American Philosophical Society*, 106 (1962), 335–47; *Daniel Defoe and the Supernatural* (Athens: University of Georgia Press 1968); 'Defoe and the Angels,' *Texas Studies in Literature and Language*, 9 (1967), 345–69.

28 A number of these can be found in *The General Catalogue of Printed Books in the British Museum* in the General Appendix to the section on Defoe, which gives a list of 'Contemporary Satires and Controversial Pamphlets on Defoe.' Cf Novak's list of attacks on Defoe in the Defoe section of *The New Cambridge Bibliography of English Literature* (Cambridge: Cambridge University Press 1971), II, 906–7.

29 *Reflections upon a Late Scandalous and Malicious Pamphlet entitul'd The Shortest Way with the Dissenters* (London 1703), p iii.

30 *The Dictionary of National Biography*, ed Leslie Stephen and Sidney Lee (London: Smith, Elder 1885–1901, and frequently reprinted by Oxford University Press).

31 John Robert Moore estimates that Defoe used 'eighty-seven different fictitious personalities – sometimes to conceal his authorship or to stimulate

sales, but more characteristically to establish a point of view' ('Defoe's Persona as Author: *The Quaker's Sermon,*' *Studies in English Literature,* 11 (1971), 507.

32 On the relation of Defoe's fiction to his fondness for mystification and his fear of exposure see Homer O. Brown, 'The Displaced Self in the Novels of Daniel Defoe,' ELH, 38 (1971), 562–90.

33 See Alan D. McKillop, *The Early Masters of English Fiction* (Lawrence: University of Kansas Press 1956), pp 5 and 6; Maximillian E. Novak, 'Defoe's Theory of Fiction,' *Studies in Philology,* 61 (1964), 650–68; and G.A. Starr's appendix on 'Fiction and Mendacity' in his *Defoe and Casuistry* (Princeton: Princeton University Press 1971). I am indebted in my discussion of Defoe's attitude to fiction to Novak's very full consideration of this topic, although I differ from Novak in the emphasis I give to Defoe's two kinds of lying. Novak does not discuss the changing tone of the prefaces to the novels.

34 The prefaces to many of Defoe's works (including *The Storm* and the novels) are printed throughout in italics and emphasis is indicated by roman type. When quoting from these prefaces I have reversed this arrangement.

35 *Letters,* p 42.

36 See Lee, *Daniel Defoe,* II, 35.

37 Now generally called *Roxana.* Rodney M. Baine ('The Evidence from Defoe's Title Pages,' *Studies in Bibliography,* 25 [1972], 185–91) has suggested that the title was not selected by Defoe. There is, however, no way of knowing whether Defoe would have known what the title was to be, or even if he approved of it. The original title was presumably adapted from Mrs Haywood's *Idalia; Or, The Unfortunate Mistress,* published in 1723, the year before *Roxana.*

38 *Colonel Jack,* ed Samuel Holt Monk (London: Oxford University Press 1965).

39 *Roxana,* ed Jane Jack (London: Oxford University Press 1964).

40 In *The Shakespeare Head Edition of the Novels and Selected Writings of Daniel Defoe* (Oxford: Basil Blackwell 1927).

41 *Moll Flanders,* ed G.A. Starr (London: Oxford University Press 1971). Subsequent references are given in the text.

42 Novak, 'Defoe's Theory of Fiction,' p 656.

43 Arthur W. Secord, 'The Origins of Defoe's *Memoirs of a Cavalier,*' in his *Robert Drury's Journal and Other Studies* (Urbana: University of Illinois Press 1961), p 72.

44 *The King of the Pirates,* in *Romances and Narratives,* XVI, 10. Subsequent references are given in the text.

45 Similarly, at the end of his story Captain Singleton and his companion

Quaker William, 'in long Vests of Silk,' pass for 'Persian Merchants' or as 'Two Armenian Merchants.' See Captain Singleton, ed Shiv K. Kumar (London: Oxford University Press 1969), pp 264 and 272.

46 Romance and Narratives, XVI, 110–11. Aitken identifies this work only as 'An Account of the Cartoucheans in France,' the head-title of the original edition.

47 The Life and Actions of Jonathan Wild, in Romances and Narratives, XVI, 260–1.

48 Lives of Six Notorious Street-Robbers, in Romances and Narratives, XVI, 348.

49 Applebee's Journal (25 September 1725); rpt in Lee, Daniel Defoe, III, 430.

50 Ibid.

51 Ian Watt, The Rise of the Novel (London 1957; rpt Harmondsworth: Penguin 1963), pp 19–20.

52 Ibid, p 20. In an earlier article on the same subject, however, Watt distinguished between the name of the hero of Robinson Crusoe and the names of the eponymous heroes of the other novels: 'Robinson Crusoe is the only one of Defoe's main characters who is given a full name and maintains it' ('The naming of characters in Defoe, Richardson, and Fielding,' Review of English Studies, 25 (1949), 322.

53 Though even the casual authenticity of Crusoe's name has been challenged by critics who remember that Crusoe is an englishing of Kreutznaer and see suggestions of Christian symbolism in the fact that the German for 'cross' is 'Kreutz': see Robert W. Ayers, 'Robinson Crusoe: "Allusive Allegorical History",' PMLA, 82 (1967), 399–407. However, 'Kreutz,' like 'cross,' bears another meaning that is equally, perhaps more, likely, that is, 'cross' as a verb, a meaning related to our word 'cruise,' which is what the anglicization of Kreutznaer to Crusoe might more readily suggest. In this connection it is interesting to remember also that Captain Woodes Rogers's A Cruising Voyage Round the World, which has often been taken as a source, or at least a source of inspiration, for Robinson Crusoe, appeared in 1712, only seven years before the novel. But I prefer to leave these speculations alone. If a pun is intended it is of minor importance in the novel. And that is not the case with Moll Flanders.

54 Colonel Jack, preface.

55 See Gary J. Scrimgeour, 'The Problem of Realism in Defoe's Captain Singleton,' Huntington Library Quarterly, 27 (1963), 21–37.

NOTES TO CHAPTER TWO

1 Daniel Defoe, Robinson Crusoe, ed J. Donald Crowley (London: Oxford University Press 1972). Subsequent references are to this edition and are given in the text. References to The Farther Adventures of Robinson Crusoe are

to *The Shakespeare Head Edition of the Novels and Selected Writings of Daniel Defoe* (Oxford: Basil Blackwell 1927, 1928).

2 For a discussion of Defoe's 'emblematic method' see J. Paul Hunter, *The Reluctant Pilgrim* (Baltimore: Johns Hopkins University Press 1966).

3 Edwin Benjamin, 'Symbolic Elements in *Robinson Crusoe*,' *Philological Quarterly*, 30 (1951), 205–11.

4 Maximillian Novak, 'Robinson Crusoe's "Original Sin",' *Studies in English Literature*, 1 (1961), 19–29, and *Economics and the Fiction of Daniel Defoe* (Berkeley: University of California Press 1962).

5 William Halewood, 'Religion and Invention in *Robinson Crusoe*,' *Essays in Criticism*, 14 (1964), 339–51.

6 G.A. Starr, *Defoe and Spiritual Autobiography* (Princeton: Princeton University Press 1965).

7 Hunter, *The Reluctant Pilgrim*.

8 Two recent studies deal with the spiritual dimension of the novel in strikingly different ways. Everett Zimmerman, in *Defoe and the Novel* (Berkeley and Los Angeles: University of California Press 1975), by treating all three parts of *Robinson Crusoe* together, concludes that the providential pattern is not sustained. The journey to the promised land (sighted emblematically at the end of *The Strange Surprizing Adventures*) becomes in *The Farther Adventures* a circular journey that takes Crusoe back to the point at which he began. In a synthesis of previous major interpretations John J. Richetti, *Defoe's Narratives: Situations and Structures* (Oxford: Clarendon Press 1975), sees Crusoe as an assertive self caught between two historical factors (dynamic capitalism and conservative religious ideology) which might have crushed him but over and through which he triumphs.

9 See Hunter, *The Reluctant Pilgrim*; Starr, *Defoe and Spiritual Autobiography*; and Novak, 'Robinson Crusoe's "Original Sin".'

10 Defoe often uses this word metaphorically; see e.g., *Robinson Crusoe*, p 113; *Moll Flanders*, ed G.A. Starr (London: Oxford University Press 1971), p 30.

11 For a further discussion of the island as a demi-paradise see Hunter, *The Reluctant Pilgrim*, pp 171–2, and Richetti, *Defoe's Narratives*, pp 46–7.

12 The notion that Defoe's novels end with a 'typical anticlimactic "adventure"' (William H. McBurney, '*Colonel Jacque*: Defoe's Definition of the Complete English Gentleman,' *Studies in English Literature*, 2 [1962], 321) is curiously persistent. It crops up once again in Richetti's study, p 61: 'Once Crusoe leaves the island ... the rest is rather tedious accounting of the wealth he richly deserves for his extraordinary feat of survival and mastery.'

13 E.g., Starr suggests in *Defoe and Spiritual Autobiography* that the vicissitudes of Crusoe's life after his conversion 'either fail to discompose him or else

agitate him only when he forgets he is under divine protection' (p 113). This statement is factually true, but the emphasis downplays Crusoe's tribulation.

14 For another interpretation of this much discussed passage see Zimmerman, *Defoe and the Novel*, pp 28 and 29. Zimmerman's note on p 29 usefully surveys previous discussions.

15 Barbara Hardy, *The Appropriate Form* (London: Athlone Press 1964), p 57.

16 See John Robert Moore, '*The Tempest* and *Robinson Crusoe*,' *Review of English Studies*, 21 (1945), 52–6, and his 'Defoe and Shakespeare,' *Shakespeare Quarterly*, 19 (1968), 71–80.

17 Or, as Richetti perceptively remarks in *Defoe's Narratives*, God 'catches Crusoe on the island and tames him the same way that Crusoe catches goats in a pit and tames them' (p 50).

18 In the *Farther Adventures of Robinson Crusoe* the paradox of the happy prisoner is further developed, creating an ironic parallel with Crusoe's happy imprisonment on the island and a contrast with his unhappy wanderings since. The Muscovite Prince speaks of being shut in by 'stronger Things than Bars and Bolts' (III, 205), and then goes on in these words to reject Crusoe's offer of a deliverance: 'Here I am free from the Temptation of returning to my former miserable Greatness; there I am not sure but that all the Seeds of Pride, Ambition, Avarice and Luxury, which I know remain in Nature, may revive and take Root, and in a Word, again overwhelm me, and then the happy Prisoner, who you see now Master of his Soul's Liberty, shall be the miserable Slave of his own Senses, in the Full of all personal Liberty: Dear Sir, let me remain in this blessed Confinement ... for I am but Flesh, a Man, a meer Man, have Passions and Affections as likely to possess and overthrow me as any Man: O be not my Friend and my Tempter both together!' (III, 208).

19 He is bothered, however, by 'Goats, and wild Creatures which I call'd Hares,' and by birds which eat his crops, but his own life is never in direct danger from the 'beasts' on the island.

20 Hunter, *The Reluctant Pilgrim*, p 198.

NOTES TO CHAPTER THREE

1 Daniel Defoe, *Moll Flanders*, ed G.A. Starr (London: Oxford University Press 1971), p 182. Subsequent references are to this edition and are given in the text.

2 For more information about the possible source of this name and the identity of Moll Flanders see Gerald Howson, 'Who was Moll Flanders?' *Times Literary Supplement*, 18 January 1968, pp 62–4; cf Starr, Introduction to his edition of *Moll Flanders*.

3 In this remark lies the pride of the professional thief which Defoe and Gay and Dickens are able to exploit for its humour and irony. One remembers the lament of Charlie Bates that the Artful Dodger is 'going abroad for a common two-penny halfpenny sneeze-box! I never thought he'd a done it under a gold watch, chain, and seals at the lowest' (*Oliver Twist*, ed Peter Fairclough [Harmondsworth: Penguin 1966], p 390).

4 Everett Zimmerman's perception that 'Newgate ... is another version of the Mint' (*Defoe and the Novel* [Berkeley and Los Angeles: University of California Press 1975], p 98) is borne out by Defoe's emphasis on the discovery of Moll's name, assumed in the Mint and then exposed in Newgate.

5 For a valuable discussion of the dual tendency in Defoe's protagonists towards self-concealment and self-exposure see Homer O. Brown, 'The Displaced Self in the Novels of Daniel Defoe,' ELH, 38 (1971), 562–90.

6 For a different interpretation of the sense of the inevitability of Moll's arrest that the novel conveys see John J. Richetti, *Defoe's Narratives: Situations and Structures* (Oxford: Clarendon Press 1975), pp 132–3.

7 For another interpretation of the incest and marriage pattern and its structural function see Douglas Brooks, '*Moll Flanders*: An Interpretation,' *Essays in Criticism*, 19 (1969), 46–59. Brooks postulates a structure for the novel built up from a 'series of echoes and repetitions,' of which the incest motif in several of Moll's 'marriages' is the most important. Much of Brooks's argument is useful, particularly what he has to say about the place in the structure of the novel of the two journeys to Virginia, but Brooks, to my mind, places too much significance upon verbal echoes (as Arthur Sherbo pointed out in a rejoinder in *Essays in Criticism*, 19 (1969), 351–4). I prefer to see such details as a part of Defoe's shaping vision of the nature of man and society.

8 The debate over the kind and degree of irony in *Moll Flanders* is extensive. Ian Watt, who began the controversy in his chapter on *Moll Flanders* in *The Rise of the Novel* (London 1957; rpt Harmondsworth: Penguin 1963), reviewed the question in his 'The Recent Critical Fortunes of *Moll Flanders*,' *Eighteenth-Century Studies*, 1 (1967), 109–26. The strongest defender of conscious irony in the novel has been Maximillian Novak and two of his papers must be mentioned here: 'Defoe's Use of Irony,' in *The Uses of Irony: Papers on Defoe and Swift Read at a Clark Library Seminar, April 2, 1966* (Los Angeles: University of California Press 1966), and 'Conscious Irony in *Moll Flanders*: Facts and Problems,' *College English*, 26 (1964), 198–204. Contributions to the debate since Watt's review article include Douglas Brooks, '*Moll Flanders*: An Interpretation'; Maximillian Novak, 'Defoe's "Indifferent Monitor": The Complexity of *Moll Flanders*,' *Eighteenth-Century Studies*, 3 (1970), 351–65; John Preston, *The Created Self: The Reader's Role in Eighteenth Century Fiction* (London: Heinemann 1970); William J. Krier, '"A

Courtesy Which Grants Integrity": A Literal Reading of *Moll Flanders*,' ELH, 38 (1971), 397–410.

9 One of the best discussions of the confusion of spiritual and mercenary values in Moll's (but *not* Defoe's) mind is Juliet McMaster's 'The Equation of Love and Money in *Moll Flanders*,' *Studies in the Novel*, 2 (1970), 131–44.

10 Hence the importance of the court. The monarch, like the head of the family, ought to set a good example. Defoe's concern about the behaviour of George I and the Prince of Wales and his comparison (implied, as we will see, in *Roxana*) with the court and times of Charles II goes very deep.

11 The real alternative – mistress or wife – which is what Moll is most concerned with here, is made clearer in the second edition which reads: 'a Woman should never be kept for a Mistress, that had the Money to make herself a Wife.' In *Roxana* the proposition is reversed. See above, pp 116–17.

12 *Religious Courtship*, in *The Novels and Miscellaneous Works of Daniel De Foe* (Oxford/London 1840, 1841), XIV, 204–5. Subsequent references are to this edition and are given in the text.

13 Watt, *The Rise of the Novel*, p 127.

14 Zimmerman's discussion of Defoe's view of marriage contracted without love is excellent. See his *Defoe and the Novel*, pp 81–5.

15 E.g., William Lee, *Daniel Defoe: His Life and Recently Discovered Writings* (London 1869), III, 96; *Colonel Jack*, ed Samuel Holt Monk (London: Oxford University Press 1965), p 153.

16 Cf Lee, *Daniel Defoe*, III, 179: How Happy ... is it for the greatest Part of Mankind, that Nature has made no Glass Beehives to the Heart; that it is not in Man to know what is in Man! What a Sink of Wickedness! What a Hell of Treachery and Falshood would be every Day the Subject of our Speculations! ... How happy are we, that we see no more than the Outsides of one another!'

17 This is the subtitle of Daniel Defoe, *The Great Law of Subordination Consider'd*.

18 See Daniel Defoe, *Conjugal Lewdness: Or, Matrimonial Whoredom* (London 1727).

19 In *An Essay on the History and Reality of Apparitions*, in *The Novels and Miscellaneous Works*, XIII, 208–9, Defoe recounts a very similar story which he claims to have had from 'the person's own lips,' a man who sounds strangely like what Defoe often was himself, in 'perplex'd circumstances, distress'd for want of money, a perishing family a craving necessity.' Starr notes both this and another analogue in *The Political History of the Devil* on p 194n of his edition of *Moll Flanders*.

20 *Conjugal Lewdness*, p 102.

21 Moll's closing phrase cannot dispel the impression that she still takes considerable pleasure in recounting her criminal achievements. Whatever

'sincere Penitence' means to a woman like Moll, she clearly believes that repentance and confession (of which the novel is the result) are the appropriate responses to her changed circumstances. For other considerations of the question of Moll's sincerity in her repentance see Richetti, *Defoe's Narratives*, p 136 ('The sincerity of Moll's repentance need not be debated; it is an effective means for restoring her consciousness, for underlining the gravity of her situation'); and Zimmerman (*Defoe and the Novel*, pp 94–5), who argues that Moll's repentance is her way of severing herself from the past and its fears.

22 There is a greater range of disagreement about the artistry of *Moll Flanders* than any of Defoe's other novels. Opinions vary from the disparagements of Mark Schorer in 'A Study in Defoe: Moral Vision and Structural Form,' *Thought*, 25 (1950), 275–87, for whom the novel reveals the impoverished mind not merely of Moll, but of Defoe, and the reservations of Ian Watt (*The Rise of the Novel*, pp 126–7), who is content to deny 'structural irony' to the novel, to various defences of the novel by the following: Dorothy Van Ghent, 'On *Moll Flanders*,' in her *The English Novel* (New York: Rinehart 1953); Terence Martin, 'The Unity of *Moll Flanders*,' *Modern Language Quarterly*, 22 (1961), 115–24; Robert Columbus, 'Conscious Artistry in Moll Flanders,' *Studies in English Literature*, 3 (1963), 415–32; Howard Koonce, 'Moll's Muddle: Defoe's Use of Irony in *Moll Flanders*,' ELH, 30 (1963), 377–94; Arnold Kettle, 'In Defence of "Moll Flanders",' in John Butt, ed, *Of Books and Humankind* (London: Routledge and Kegan Paul 1964); Maximillian Novak, 'Conscious Irony in *Moll Flanders*'; Douglas Brooks, '*Moll Flanders*: An Interpretation.'

23 Daniel Defoe, *The Family Instructor*, in *Novels and Miscellaneous Works*, XVI, ix.

24 Daniel Defoe, *The Compleat English Gentleman*, ed Karl D. Bülbring (London 1890), p 13–14.

25 For further considerations of these characteristic phrases see Richetti, *Defoe's Narratives*, p 108, and Starr's edition of *Moll Flanders*, pp 367–8.

NOTES TO CHAPTER FOUR

1 *Colonel Jack*, ed Samuel Holt Monk (London: Oxford University Press 1965). All references are to this edition and are given in the text.

2 But see Monk's Introduction to *Colonel Jack*, p xiv; and William McBurney, '*Colonel Jacque*: Defoe's Definition of the Complete English Gentleman,' *Studies in English Literature*, 2 (1962), 321–36.

3 Ernest Baker, *History of the English Novel* (1924–39; rpt New York: Barnes and Noble 1950), III, 206.

4 McBurney, '*Colonel Jacque*,' p 321.

5 Ibid, p 335.
6 Michael Shinagel, *Daniel Defoe and Middle-Class Gentility* (Cambridge, Mass.: Harvard University Press 1968). Shinagel's 'misuse of biographical conjecture' and his 'simple misreadings' have been succinctly exposed in a review by Maximillian E. Novak, *Philological Quarterly*, 48 (1969), 348–9.
7 Other studies are less willing to accept Colonel Jack as Defoe's *alter ego* and draw attention to the shading of irony and the narrative distance. James Walton, 'The Romance of Gentility,' *Literary Monographs* 4 (Madison: University of Wisconsin Press 1971), pp 89–135, sees the various steps in Jack's path to gentility as typical motifs of romance. These include the motif of beguilement by false goals: the fashionable London scenes and his military career betray Jack's addiction to false gentility. John J. Richetti, *Defoe's Narratives: Situations and Structures* (Oxford: Clarendon Press 1975), argues that Jack's belief in his gentle birth works as a powerful personal myth setting him apart from and giving him mastery over ordinary experience. This use of the theme of gentility 'is crucial to the mechanics of the narrative.' Everett Zimmerman, *Defoe and the Novel* (Berkeley and Los Angeles: University of California Press 1975), agrees with earlier commentators that 'incident after incident in *Colonel Jack* shows the central character's behaviour being guided by his notions of gentility,' but he argues that *The Compleat English Gentleman* exposes the falseness of Jack's notions and thus 'suggests the strong possibility of extensive irony in *Colonel Jack*.' Both Maximillian E. Novak, in *Economics and the Fiction of Daniel Defoe* (Berkeley: University of California Press 1962), and Monk in his Introduction to the novel recognize the upward social mobility in Jack's history but stress the importance of education in the process. Monk suggests that *Colonel Jack* is really a *Bildungsroman*. One study denies that there is any real progress in Jack's life. G.A. Starr (*Defoe and Casuistry* [Princeton: Princeton University Press 1971]), for whom 'a crucial question is whether Colonel Jack achieves moral growth,' finds that 'the hero's evolution fails to provide a thematic structure for the book as a whole.' In this view *Colonel Jack* is not an early but a faulty *Bildungsroman*.
8 This section of the chapter appeared in a rather different form as 'Jacobite and Gentleman: Defoe's Use of Jacobitism in *Colonel Jack*,' *English Studies in Canada*, 4 (1978), 15–24.
9 But see Rodney M. Baine, 'The Evidence from Defoe's Title Pages,' *Studies in Bibliography*, 25 (1972), 185–91.
10 The OED under this meaning cites Defoe's own use of Colonel Jack's contemptuous reference near the end of his history to 'Jack Spaniard.'
11 During his brief residency in France Jack had been called 'Monsieur *Jacque*, and Colonel *Jacques*, and so gradually Colonel *Jacque*' (p 185).

12 For the use of the sobriquet 'Jack' for a Jacobite see G. Holmes, *British Politics in the Age of Anne* (London: Macmillan 1967), p 18 and n; and for an example of Defoe's use of it outside his fiction see William Lee, *Daniel Defoe, His Life and Recently Discovered Writings* (London 1869), III, 46.

13 Most studies of *Colonel Jack* either do not deal with the Jacobite interlude or mention it only in passing, but there are some attempts to account for Jacobitism in the novel. McBurney, *'Colonel Jacque,'* mentions the Jacobite sequence but is puzzled by it; rather tentatively he suggests that in Jack's political repentance 'Defoe seems to have ... decided to purge Jacque of his one dishonorable trait – the political indifference and thoughtless toying with treason which had characterized his entire sporadic military career.' Monk in his Introduction to his edition of the novel observes that Jack 'becomes for unexplained reasons a Jacobite' and suggests that in doing so Jack is acting out of character. Walton, 'The Romance of Gentility,' sees Jack's 'atonement with his king and country' and subsequent political obligations as a motif of the 'distinctly romantic or aristocratic code of honor.' Recently two studies have pointed out a connection between the Jacobite element and Defoe's characterization of the hero. Richetti, in *Defoe's Narratives*, treats Jack's Jacobite career as part of his entanglement in actual historical events; Jack's role in history is as a free and distinct character (or 'self') who exploits historical circumstances. In *Defoe and the Novel* Zimmerman offers the most convincing explanation of the Jacobitism when he suggests that it appeals to Jack's 'social pretensions.'

14 *Review*, 14 May 1709.

15 Daniel Defoe, *A Dialogue between a Whig and a Jacobite* (London 1716), pp 8, 10, 11.

16 Daniel Defoe, *The History of the Jacobite Clubs* (London 1712), p 39.

17 Daniel Defoe, *Hannibal at the Gates. Or, The Progress of Jacobitism* (London 1712), p 4.

18 Daniel Defoe, *Bold Advice: Or, Proposals For the entire Rooting out of Jacobitism in Great Britain* (London 1715), p 35.

19 *The Memoirs of Majr. Alexander Ramkins* (London 1719), 158–9.

20 Such as those just cited. Prominent among Defoe's many other anti-Jacobite tracts are: *Reasons against The Succession of the House of Hanover* (London 1713); *And What if the Pretender Should Come?* (London 1713); *An Answer to a Question that No Body Thinks of, Viz. But what if the Queen should die?* (London 1713); and *An Address to the People of England: Shewing The Unworthiness of their Behaviour to King George* (London 1714).

21 As it certainly was; Ramkins appears in the DNB, but the account of his life is based solely on these *Memoirs*. Both John Robert Moore in his *Checklist of the Writings of Daniel Defoe* (Bloomington: Indiana University Press 1960) and

Novak in the section on Defoe in the *New Cambridge Bibliography of English Literature* (Cambridge University Press 1971) identify Defoe as the author of the *Memoirs*.

22 In *A General Pardon Consider'd* (London 1717) Defoe enforces the same arguments about the value of a general amnesty. The king should act as the 'Father of his Country' and be willing to show mercy to his rebellious subjects who will then rectify their mistakes and own 'the Regard they pay to the Duty of Gratitude.'

23 Daniel Defoe, *The Compleat English Gentleman*, ed Karl D. Bülbring (London 1890), p 30.

24 The ending of the book arises from this episode. After Jack flees from Virginia he takes up clandestine trading with Mexico and becomes immoderately wealthy. But, as Novak has demonstrated, Jack violates 'the rules of mercantile morality' and thus commits 'a far worse crime than any of the petty thefts he had committed as a hungry young pickpocket' (*Economics and the Fiction of Daniel Defoe*, p 125). Jack's gentility, in short, remains highly doubtful even at the end of the novel.

25 *The Family Instructor*, vol II, in *The Novels and Miscellaneous Works of Daniel De Foe* (Oxford/London 1840, 1841), XVI, 194.

26 For different treatment of this passage see Zimmerman, *Defoe and the Novel*, pp 135–6.

27 A major theme of seventeenth- and early eighteenth-century treatises on family order is that society should be organized on the basis of a system of mutual duties and obligations between pairs of related groups such as these. For example, see William Perkins, *Christian Oeconomie* (1609); William Gouge, *Of Domestical Duties* (1622; and frequently reprinted); William Fleetwood, *The Relative Duties of Parents and Children, Husbands and Wives, Masters and Servants* (1705); and Richard Baxter, *The Christian Directory*, vol I of his *Practical Works* (1707). Defoe's own *Family Instructors* as well as his *The Great Law of Subordination Consider'd* (1724) are in this tradition.

28 McBurney, '*Colonel Jacque*,' p 324.

29 See *Twenty-five Sermons Preached at the Anniversary Meetings of the Children Educated in the Charity Schools in and about the Cities of London and Westminster* (London 1729).

30 Dr Sherlock's sermon is given in the *Twenty-five Sermons*, but the table entitled 'The present State of Charity-Schools in and about London and Westminster' is not. It may be found, following other copies of Sherlock's sermon, in the British Library's collection of Sherlock's Sermons (Pressmark 694. g. 8) and in a collection of Charity Sermons (Pressmark 694. h. 12). The definitive work on the charity schools is M.G. Jones, *The Charity School Movement* (Cambridge: Cambridge University Press 1938; rpt London: F. Cass 1964).

31 Daniel Defoe, *Charity Still a Christian Virtue* (London 1719), p 2.
32 *The Compleat English Gentleman*, p 3.
33 My italics, except the word '*France.*'
34 Jack's feeling that as a gentleman he ought to be able to handle a sword is another example of his false criteria. Defoe was very much interested in French attempts to suppress duelling. He published a translation of Louis xiv's edict against duels as an appendix to the first volume of the collected issues of the *Review* (1705), and in 1713 he wrote a long pamphlet, *An Account of the Abolishing of Duels in France* (London 1713) which includes, along with other regulations and resolutions, a translation of Louis's edict.
35 This section includes the history of Jack's military career (another of the false means by which he tries to become a gentleman). See above, pp 97–8.
36 Cf the similar situation in *Roxana* where Roxana's own daughter is accidentally taken on as a servant in Roxana's house.
37 In his Introduction to *Colonel Jack*. Monk uses the examples of landscape and architecture but his remarks apply equally well to clothing.
38 See the verses printed on the title-page of Daniel Defoe, *The Friendly Daemon* (London 1726).

NOTES TO CHAPTER FIVE

1 *Roxana, The Fortunate Mistress*, ed Jane Jack (London: Oxford University Press 1964). Subsequent references are to this edition and are given in the text.
2 Cf Wallace Jackson, '*Roxana* and the Development of Defoe's Fiction,' *Studies in the Novel*, 7 (1975), 181–94.
3 *The Poor Man's Plea* (1698), in *The Shortest Way with the Dissenters and Other Pamphlets*, a volume in *The Shakespeare Head Edition of the Novels and Selected Writings of Daniel Defoe* (Oxford 1927), p 3.
4 *The Weekly Journal* (5 April 1719); rpt in William Lee, *Daniel Defoe: His Life and Recently Discovered Writings* (London 1869), II, 32.
5 Cf Defoe's tracts: *The Anatomy of Exchange-Alley* (London 1719); *The Gamester. A Benefit-Ticket for all that are concern'd in the Lotteries* (London 1719); *The Gamester. No. II* (London 1719).
6 See Thomas Wright, *England under the House of Hanover* (1848), I, 94.
7 Cf John J. Richetti, *Defoe's Narratives: Situations and Structures* (Oxford: Clarendon Press 1975), pp 192–4.
8 Works of this title by Mary de la Riviere Manley appeared in 1707 and by Captain Alexander Smith [Defoe?] in 1715.
9 *The Perplex'd Dutchess: or, Treachery Rewarded* (1727) is by Mrs Haywood.
10 This title, as Rodney M. Baine has cautioned, may not have been Defoe's but the booksellers.' See Baine's 'The Evidence from Defoe's Title

Pages,' *Studies in Bibliography*, 25 (1972), 185–91, and his 'Roxana's Georgian Setting,' *Studies in English Literature*, 15 (1975), 459–71. See above, pp 15 and 157, n 37.

11 *The Mary Carleton Narratives 1663–1673* (Cambridge, Mass.: Harvard University Press 1914), pp 79–84.

12 There is some reason for supposing that these women were not George's mistresses but his half-sister and his morganatic wife. See John M. Beattie, *The English Court in the Reign of George I* (Cambridge: Cambridge University Press 1967), p 240 and n. But the fact that they were popularly believed to be his mistresses and the fact that they were German would have made them natural targets for Defoe.

13 Maximillian Novak, 'Crime and Punishment in Defoe's *Roxana*,' *Journal of English and Germanic Philology*, 65 (1966), 460–1.

14 This section of the chapter appeared in a slightly different form as '*Roxana* and the Masquerades,' *Modern Language Review*, 65 (1970), 499–502.

15 See John Robert Moore's Foreword to his *A Checklist of the Writings of Daniel Defoe* (Bloomington: University of Indiana Press 1960).

16 Wright (*England under the House of Hanover*, I, 96), suggests that there 'was probably a satirical aim in a paragraph of the *London Journal* for 11 February 1724, which stated that: 'At the last *ridotto* or ball at the Opera House in the Haymarket, a daughter of his grace the Archbishop of Canterbury won the highest prize'.'

17 *The Weekly Journal, or Saturday Post*, 25 January 1724.

18 See *Catalogue of Prints and Drawings in the British Museum* (London 1870–1954), II, no. 1742.

19 See G.F.R. Barker's article on Heidegger in the DNB.

20 *Catalogue of Prints and Drawings*, no. 1742. 'Pasquin No. xcv' is a mistake, possible for no. ix. Cf nos. 1743–6 and 1719.

21 Ibid, no. 1747.

22 Edmund Gibson, *A Sermon Preached to the Societies for the Reformation of Manners* (London 1723/4).

23 The outcry against the masquerades did not end here. In 1728 Fielding wrote *The Masquerade*, which he ironically dedicated to Heidegger. And of course the first part of Richardson's *Sir Charles Grandison* is an extended attack on the masquerades, as are parts of Fielding's *Tom Jones* and *Amelia*.

24 See Daniel Defoe, *The Dumb Philosopher; or Great Britain's Wonder* (1719).

25 Daniel Defoe, *A System of Magick; Or, a History of The Black Art* (London 1727), p 336.

26 Once when her carriage was surrounded by a hostile mob which took her for her unpopular rival the Duchess of Portsmouth, Nell Gwyn, put her

head out of the window and said: 'Pray, good people, be civil; I am the protestant whore.'

27 I assume that 'above Fifty' is still less than fifty-one.

28 Defoe was evidently careful with his chronology. We can work out from Roxana's casual remarks that, of her 'six and twenty Years of Wickedness,' three were spent in England before she and her landlord left for France (see p 49), and that she had returned to England eight years before the time that she writes about her 'six and twenty Years of Wickedness.' This leaves fifteen years that she was on the Continent. On p 188 Roxana tells us that 'when I went from England, which was Fifteen Years before, I had left five little Children.'

29 Cf p 198 where Roxana reports that 'All this was acted in the first Years [i.e., 1715 and on] of my setting-up my new Figure here in Town, and while the Masks and Balls were in Agitation.'

30 Defoe's association with *Mist's Weekly Journal*, it is interesting to observe, did not end until October of this year.

31 Novak, 'Crime and Punishment in Defoe's *Roxana*,' p 446.

32 Robert Hume, 'The Conclusion of Defoe's *Roxana*,' *Eighteenth-Century Studies*, 3 (1970), 478.

33 G.A. Starr, *Defoe and Casuistry* (Princeton: Princeton University Press 1971).

34 *The Novels and Miscellaneous Works of Daniel De Foe* (Oxford/London 1840, 1841), x, 157.

35 This is how Roxana tells the story. Zimmerman, in *Defoe and the Novel* (Berkeley and Los Angeles: University of California Press 1975), rightly observes that Amy has a personal 'motive for the murder: Susan threatens to supplant her' (p 169).

NOTES TO CHAPTER SIX

1 Henry James, *The Portrait of a Lady* (Harmondsworth: Penguin 1971), pp 201–2.

2 David Lodge, *The Language of Fiction* (London: Routledge and Kegan Paul 1966).

3 Ian Watt, *The Rise of the Novel* (London 1957; rpt Harmondsworth; Penguin 1963), p 307.

Index

Aitken, George A. 158
Amy (Roxana's servant) 8, 26, 116, 118–21, 128–30, 132, 137–8, 140–5
animals, in *Robinson Crusoe* 37, 42, 47–8, 50–4
Applebee's Journal 158
Aubin, Penelope 122
Austen, Jane 133, 149–50
autobiography, spiritual 30–2, 41
Ayers, Robert W. 158

Baine, Rodney M. 156–7, 164, 167–8
Baker, Ernest 93–4, 163
Barker, G.F.R. 168
Baxter, Richard 166
Beattie, John M. 168
Behn, Aphra 14
Benjamin, Edwin 30, 159
Bernbaum, Ernest 122
biblical parallels, in *Robinson Crusoe* 29
Bishop, Jonathan x, 154
Bordoni, Faustina 125

Brontë, Emily 149
Brooks, Douglas 161, 163
Brown, Homer O. 157, 161

Captain Singleton 24–5, 157–8
Carleton, Mary 122–3, 168
charity schools 102–4, 166
children, treatment of 25, 60–4, 74, 78, 128, 139–41, 144. *See also* family relations; murder
Clayton, Sir Robert 126, 131
clothing: as metaphor for fiction 17–18; in *Robinson Crusoe* 43–4; in *Moll Flanders* 68–9, 72, 78–9, 90–2; in *Colonel Jack* 111–12; in *Roxana* 141–5; as a fictional technique 148–9. *See also* disguise
Colonel Jack 15, 17, 19, 21, 23–6, 90, **93–115**, 138–9, 147, 154, 163–7
Columbus, Robert R. 154
'Concurrence of Days' 29, 34, 46–7, 71
Conrad, Joseph 133
crime and punishment: in *Robinson Crusoe* 29; in *Colonel Jack* 102, 104,

In this index Defoe's novels are entered separately (by short titles). His non-fictional works and his letters are given under his name.

108; in *Roxana* 129, 140, 144–5.
See also Newgate; prisons; sin
Cuzzoni, Francesca 125

deception. *See* disguise and
Defoe, Daniel: dissenting
background and education 3–4;
bankruptcy 4; imprisonment 4;
political espionage 5–6; love of
role-playing 5, 12–13, 20–1,
156–7; contemporary reputation
of 5–6, 10–12, 156; political beliefs
(*see also* Jacobitism) 6
– *Letters* 5–6, 11–13, 155, 157
– non-fictional works: *An Account of
the Abolishing of Duels in France* 167;
An Address to the People of England
165; *The Anatomy of Exchange-Alley*
167; *And What if the Pretender Should
Come?* 165; *An Answer to the Question
that No Body Thinks of* 165; *An Appeal to Honour and Justice* 155; *Bold
Advice* 96, 165; *A Brief Historical
Account of the Lives of Six Notorious
Street-Robbers* 22, 76, 158; *Charity
Still a Christian Virtue* 103, 167; *The
Compleat English Gentleman* 87, 100,
105, 156, 163, 166–7; *Conjugal
Lewdness* 7–9, 76, 82, 155, 162; *A
Dialogue between a Whig and a Jacobite*
95, 165; *The Dumb Philosopher* 168;
*An Effectual Scheme for the Immediate
Preventing of Street-Robberies* 76; *An
Essay on the History and Reality of Ap-
paritions* 10, 156, 162; *The Family
Instructor* 6–8, 14–15, 24, 84,
100–1, 117, 155, 163, 166; *The Four
Years Voyages of Capt. George Roberts*
19; *The Friendly Dæmon* 113, 167;
The Gamester 167; *A General Pardon
Consider'd* 166; *The Great Law of
Subordination Consider'd* 7, 76,

117–18, 155, 162, 166; *Hannibal at
the Gates* 96, 165; *The History of the
Jacobite Clubs* 96, 165; *The King of
the Pirates* 18–20; *The Life of
Jonathan Wild* 21, 76, 158; *Memoirs
of John, Duke of Melfort* 18; *The
Memoirs of Majr. Alexander Ramkins*
18, 96–7, 165–6; *Narrative of all the
Robberies, Escapes, Etc., of John Sheppard* 76; *A Narrative of the Proceedings in France* 20; *A New Voyage
Round the World* 19; *The Political
History of the Devil* 9–10, 139, 156,
162; *The Poor Man's Plea* 121, 156,
167; *Reasons against The Succession of
the House of Hanover* 165; *Religious
Courtship* 7, 66–8, 162; *Review* 4,
8–9, 95, 156, 165, 167; *The Shortest
Way with the Dissenters* 4, 10–11, 68,
155; *The Storm* 12–13, 18; *A System
of Magic* 126, 168; *The True-born
Englishman* 87
deliverance: of Crusoe 28–37; by
Crusoe 31, 36–7, 49; spiritual
meaning of 33–8, 49–50
delusion 18, 95–100, 102, 108–13.
See also disguise
Dickens, Charles 133, 145, 148–50,
161
disguise and deception 10–14, 17; in
Defoe's own life 6, 11, 20, 26; in
Memoirs of a Cavalier 19; in *Robinson
Crusoe* 42; in *Moll Flanders* 55–64,
68–80, 83–92; in *Colonel Jack* 93–7,
106–15; in *Roxana* 133, 136–45.
See also delusion

Eliot, George 145, 148–9

family relations 6–8, 24–5, 146–7;
in *Robinson Crusoe* 30, 32, 46, 52;
in *Moll Flanders* 60–6, 74, 78; in

Roxana 117–18, 120. *See also* children; marriage; morality

Farther Adventures of Robinson Crusoe, The. See Robinson Crusoe

fiction, Defoe's theory of 12–23

Fielding, Henry 133, 147–51, 168

Finch, Daniel, Second Earl of Nottingham 5, 155

first-person technique 3, 148, 150–1

Fleetwood, William 166

Friday 46, 49, 90, 119

Gay, John 126, 161

gentility: in *Moll Flanders* 57, 62, 77, 87–92; in *Colonel Jack* 94–9, 104–15; of merchants 131

geography in the novels 25, 70. *See also* Virginia

Gibson, Edmund 125, 168

Gildon, Charles 11

Gouge, William 166

gratitude 98, 100–1, 104, 109, 130

Gwyn, Nell 126, 168–9

Halewood, William 30, 154, 159

Hamilton, Anthony 123

Hardy, Barbara xi, 154, 160

Hardy, Thomas 128, 133

Harley, Robert, First Earl of Oxford 4–6, 11–13, 18, 75, 155

Haywood, Eliza 14, 122, 157, 167

Healey, G.H. 6, 153, 155

Heidegger, J.J. 124–5, 168

Hendley, William 103–4

hints, secret. *See* warnings

Hogarth, William 125

Holmes, G. 165

Howson, Gerald 160

human condition, Defoe's vision of 3, 8, 10, 26–9, 31, 33–41, 50–1, 54, 70, 75, 83, 110, 113–15, 133, 137,

146–8. *See also* short-sightedness; reason

Hume, Robert D. 131, 169

Hunter, J. Paul x–xi, 10, 30, 154, 156, 159–60

incest 25, 60–4, 70–1, 75, 82–3

irony: in *Moll Flanders* 56, 60–4, 68, 70–5, 80–2; in *Colonel Jack* 94–5, 99–101, 108–10; in *Roxana* 131

Jackson, Wallace 167

Jacobitism 18, 95–104, 165–6

James, Henry ix, 133, 148–50, 153, 169

Jemy (Moll's Lancashire husband) 26, 58, 63, 68, 70–3, 81–3, 88, 90–2

Jones, M.G. 166

Journal of the Plague Year, A, 8, 123, 127

Judas discuver'd, and catch'd at last 11

Kettle, Arnold 163

Kielmannsegge, Sophie Charlotte von, Countess of Darlington 123

Koonce, Howard L. 154, 163

Krier, William J. 161–2

lace, importance of in *Moll Flanders* 56–60

language: in *Robinson Crusoe* 51–4; in *Moll Flanders* 57, 67–8, 83–92; in *Colonel Jack* 110–15; in *Roxana* 133–9; of fiction 149. *See also* naming of characters

Lodge. David 149, 169

McBurney, W.H. 94, 102, 159, 163, 165–6

McKillop, Alan D. 157

McMaster, Juliet 162

Mandeville, Bernard 103
Manley, Mary de la Rivière 14,122,167
marriage 7, 82, 132; the marriage
  debate 65–8, 116–17; Moll's marriage career 65–75; Jack's marriages 107–8. *See also* Defoe, *Conjugal Lewdness*
Martin, Terence 163
masquerades 117, 121, 124–7, 139,
  141–4, 168–9
Memoirs of a Cavalier 18–19
Milton, John 7, 155
Mist's Weekly-Journal 6, 11–12, 14–15,
  121, 124, 127, 156, 167–9
Moll Flanders 7–8, 16–17, 19, 21,
  23–6, **55–92**, 93, 102, 114, 116–19,
  127–8, 135, 138, 147, 154, 160–3
Moll's Governess 26, 60, 73–4,
  77–80, 119
Moll's mother 60–1, 64, 70–1, 74–5,
  78, 81–2, 88, 90
money: in *Robinson Crusoe* 44–6; in
  Moll Flanders 63, 68–71, 82; in *Colonel Jack* 112–13; in *Roxana* 135–6
Monk, Samuel Holt 163–4, 167
Moore, John Robert 123, 155–7, 160,
  165, 168
morality: decline in public 6–9, 24–6;
  in *Moll Flanders* 76–80; in *Roxana*
  117–18, 121–7, 130–3, 135–6, 140,
  143
murder, of children 60, 64, 74, 77,
  120, 143

naivety: of Moll Flanders 57, 61–3; of
  Colonel Jack 95–100, 102, 110–12
naming of characters, Defoe's prac-
  tice in 23–4; Moll Flanders 56–60;
  Colonel Jack 94–5, 104, 107, 109;
  Amy 119; Roxana 123, 140–1;
  Crusoe 158

Newgate 4, 58–65, 68–71, 75, 77–8,
  80–2, 87–8, 91–2, 115
Novak, Maximillian E. x–xi, 18, 30,
  123, 130, 154–9, 161–9
numerical symbolism. *See* 'Concurrence of Days'

Perkins, William 166
poses, Defoe's use of literary 3, 12,
  15–23, 156–7
Preston, John 161
prisons 47–50, 60–1. *See also* Newgate
providence 10, 28–9, 37, 39, 55. *See
  also* human condition; short-
  sightedness

Raleigh, Walter 122
Read's Journal 11
reason, insufficiency of 28, 37–42,
  51. *See also* short-sightedness
*Reflections upon a Late Scandalous and
  Malicious Pamphlet* 11, 156
Richardson, Samuel 7, 147–51, 168
Richetti, John J. xi, 154, 159–61,
  163–5, 167
Robinson Crusoe 6, 10, 14–17, 19,
  21–6, **28–54**, 71, 90, 135, 139,
  146–7; 154, 158–60; *The Farther
  Adventures of Robinson Crusoe* 16,
  160; *Serious Reflections of Robinson
  Crusoe* 14, 16, 156
Rogers, Captain Woodes 158
Roxana 6–8, 14–17, 21, 23–6, 90,
  116–45, 147, 154, 167–9
Roxana's daughter. *See* Susan

Schorer, Mark, x, 154, 163
Schulenburg, Ehrengard Melusine
  von der, Duchess of Munster and
  Duchess of Kendal 13

Scotland 5–6, 11, 20, 75
Scrimgeour, Gary J. 158
Secord, Arthur W. x, 18, 154, 157
Serious Reflections of Robinson Crusoe.
  See Robinson Crusoe
servants, role of 7–8, 100–1, 117–18,
  127, 140. *See also* Defoe, *The Great
  Law of Subordination*
Sheppard, Jack 18, 76
Sherbo, Arthur 161
Sherlock, Thomas 103, 166
Shinagel, Michael 94, 164
short-sightedness, human 10, 26–9,
  33–4, 39–40, 50, 55, 63, 110, 113,
  115. *See also* human condition; reason
sin 24; of Robinson Crusoe 30, 33–5,
  38–9, 55; of Moll Flanders 65, 76;
  of Roxana 119–21, 129–33,
  138–45. *See also* incest; morality;
  murder
slavery 32–4
Smith, Captain Alexander [Defoe?]
  167
snares: in *Robinson Crusoe* 48; in *Moll
  Flanders* 69, 83–92; in *Colonel Jack*
  114–15; in *Roxana* 133, 137–8

spirits. *See* warnings
spiritual autobiography. *See*
  autobiography
Starr, G.A. x–xi, 30, 137, 154, 157,
  159–60, 164, 169
Stephen, Leslie 11, 156
Sterne, Laurence 150
Susan (Roxana's daughter) 25, 118,
  120, 127, 140–5
Sutherland, James x, 154–5

Thackeray, W.M. 145, 149

Van Ghent, Dorothy 163
Virginia 70–3, 81–2, 89–92, 98–109

Walton, James 164–5
warnings, spiritual 10, 29, 34, 40, 156
Watt, Ian ix–xi, 23, 29–30, 151, 153,
  158, 161–3, 169
Wild, Jonathan 18, 20–1
Wilson, Angus 154
Wright, Thomas 167–8

Zimmerman, Everett xi, 154,
  159–66, 169

This book

was designed by

ANTJE LINGNER

and was printed by

University of

Toronto

Press